# TACKLING INEQUALITIES

## Where are we now and what can be done?

Edited by Christina Pantazis and David Gordon

The POLICY PRESS

FIRST UNITED NATIONS DECADE FOR THI
*eradication of pover*
(1997-2006)

First published in Great Britain in 2000 by
The Policy Press
34 Tyndall's Park Road
Bristol BS8 1PY
UK

Tel no +44 (0)117 954 6800
Fax no +44 (0)117 973 7308
E-mail tpp@bristol.ac.uk
http://www.bristol.ac.uk/Publications/TPP

ISBN 1 86134 146 6

**Christina Pantazis** is a Research Associate at the School for Policy Studies and **David Gordon** is the Director of the Townsend Centre for International Poverty Research at the University of Bristol. David is also Head of the Centre for the Study of Social Exclusion and Social Justice, School for Policy Studies, University of Bristol.

Cover design by Qube Design Associates, Bristol
Photograph kindly supplied by Jean François Talivez, Arena Images
Printed in Great Britain by Hobbs the Printers Ltd, Southampton

# Contents

# List of tables and figures

## Tables

## Figures

# Preface

The idea for this book arose out of the Radical Statistics' annual conference which was held in Bristol in February 1998. The conference, on tackling inequalities, attracted a record audience and, disappointingly, numbers were such that people were turned away. For this reason we decided to publish the contributions plus other contributions on the theme.

## Radical Statistics

Radical Statistics is a group of statisticians and others who share a common concern about the political assumptions implicit in the process of compiling and using statistics and an awareness of the actual and potential misuse of statistics and its techniques. In particular, we are concerned about the:

- mystifying use of technical language used to disguise social problems as technical problems;
- lack of control by the community over the aims of statistical investigations, the way these are conducted and the use of the information produced;
- power structures within which statistical workers are employed and which control their work and the uses to which it is put;
- fragmentation of statistical questions into separate specialist fields in ways that can obscure common problems.

## Our history

Radical Statistics was formed in January 1975 and is proud to have been a part of the radical science movement. This movement dates back to before the Second World War. Its most influential expression was in J.D. Bernal's book, *The social function of science* (1939). This argued that science was the motor of human progress and history. The bombing of Hiroshima and Nagasaki and other events led to the disillusionment and eventual collapse of this pre-war movement. Some years later, in 1969, involvement in the anti-Vietnam war campaigns led a new generation of young radical scientists to found the British Society for Social Responsibility in Science (BSSRS).

The idea that statistics can be used as a tool for social change has a much longer history and lay behind statistical developments in the mid-19th century. Some of these ideas surfaced anew in the 1970s in the form of a heightened interest in social statistics in general and social indicators in particular. Radical Statistics rejected the idea that statistics were solely for measuring the 'economic' well-being of the State. We felt that statistics should and could be used for 'radical' and 'progressive' purposes. Statistics should be used to identify 'social' needs and to underpin rational planning to eliminate these needs. Many of these ideas were expressed in a book *Demystifying social statistics*, published in 1979 (Irvine et al).

These movements grew together through the 1970s. At its height, BSSRS had more than 1,200 members and a number of affiliated organisations including the Politics of Health Group, Radical Statistics Group, Radical Statistics Health Group and the Radical Science Journal Collective. Sadly, only Radical Statistics has managed to retain an active membership and survive the numerous political defeats of the 18 years of Conservative Party rule from 1979 to 1997. BSSRS finally collapsed in the early 1990s, leaving only its charitable arm, the Science and Society Trust. Since the demise of BSSRS, Radical Statistics has not been affiliated to any other organisation.

## Our activities

Apart from our annual conference and occasional conferences on single issues, most of our activities are focused on producing publications, which are often used by campaigning groups, journalists, politicians and others. These have included books, pamphlets, broadsheets and articles in political and topical journals and our newsletter, *Radical Statistics*, which appears three times a year. In 1999 we published *Statistics in society: The arithmetic of politics* (Dorling and Simpson, 1999) to celebrate our 25th Anniversary. Its 47 chapters include some of our most influential work.

Often, our work has reached a wider audience anonymously. For example, an influential Channel 4 documentary, 'Cooking the books', which set in train much needed changes in government statistics, showed 10 examples of misleading use of statistics by the Conservative government. Most of these examples came from the Radical Statistics Health Group's book *Facing the figures: What really is happening to the*

*National Health Service*, published in 1987, or from other material produced by Radical Statistics.

Many of our activities are still based around subject-based working groups. Some, notably those on health and education, have had a long existence. Others, such as groups on Nicaragua, nuclear disarmament, surveys for pressure groups and the Poll Tax, have been formed to respond to issues which were topical at the time. Regional and local sub-groups have also campaigned on issues as diverse as food safety, community planning, economic statistics and women's rights. More recently, the Radical Statistics Health Group has produced *Official health statistics: An unofficial guide* (Kerrison and Macfarlane, 2000). This is a new and expanded edition of its *Unofficial guide to official health statistics* (Radical Statistics Health Group, 1980).

## What is radical about statistics?

The members of Radical Statistics believe that statistics can be used as part of radical campaigns for progressive social change. We have always seen our role as belonging to a spectrum of campaigning organisations rather than as an academic or professional organisation. Working with Radical Statistics is unlikely to help anyone build their career.

Although we have no 'party line', most of us share the view that the needs of the community can never be met fully by competition. The pursuit of profit alone will not eliminate the problems of poverty, inequality and discrimination. Only rational, democratic and progressive planning can tackle the manifest injustices of our present society and help the least 'powerful' groups to realise their full potential. Meaningful statistics are needed for this process. To paraphrase the old Marxist adage, the purpose of statistics in general and Radical Statistics in particular is not only to describe the world but also to change it.

If you wish to join us, please write to Radical Statistics,
c/o 10 Ruskin Avenue, Heaton, Bradford, BD9 6EB.

*Dave Gordon and Alison Macfarlane*

# References

Bernal, J.D. (1939) *The social function of science*, London: Routledge.

Dorling, D. and Simpson, S. (eds) (1999) *Statistics in society: The arithmetic of politics*, London: Arnold.

Irvine, J., Miles, I. and Evans, J. (eds) (1979) *Demystifying social statistics*, London: Pluto Press.

Kerrison, S. and Macfarlane, A. (2000) *Official health statistics: An unofficial guide*, London: Arnold.

Radical Statistics Health Group (1980) *The unofficial guide to official health statistics*, London: Radical Statistics.

Radical Statistics Health Group (1987) *Facing the figures: What really is happening to the National Health Service*, London: Radical Statistics.

# Acknowledgements

We would like to thank all those helped make the 1998 Radical Statistics annual conference on 'Inequalities: where are we now and what can be done?' such a successful event. We would particularly like to thank Katherine Green and Frances Byrne for their help and support. Troika members Danny Dorling and Ray Thomas also assisted with the conference and gave their encouragement to this book. We would also like to thank Dawn Pudney of The Policy Press for her support and patience in editing this book. Finally, special thanks to Helen Anderson who read through the manuscript and made helpful suggestions.

# List of acronyms

| | |
|---|---|
| ABS | Australian Bureau of Statistics |
| APA | Additional Personal Allowance |
| BCS | British Crime Survey |
| BSE | Bovine Spongiform Encephalopathy |
| BSSRS | British Society for Social Responsibility in Science |
| CDP | Community Development Project |
| CJD | Creutzfeldt-Jakob disease |
| COT | Committee on Toxicity of Food |
| CPAG | Child Poverty Action Group |
| CSO | Central Statistics Office |
| DETR | Department of the Environment, Transport and the Regions |
| DfEE | Department for Education and Employment |
| DfID | Department for International Development |
| DHSS | Department for Health and Social Security |
| DoE | Department of the Environment |
| DoH | Department of Health |
| DSS | Department of Social Security |
| DTI | Department of Trade and Industry |
| EAZ | Education Action Zone |
| EC | European Community |
| ECHP | European Community Household Panel Survey |
| EHCS | English House Condition Survey |
| EMU | European Monetary Union |
| EPA | Education Priority Area |
| ESRC | Economic and Social Research Council |
| EU | European Union |

| | |
|---|---|
| FES | Family Expenditure Survey |
| FSM | free school meals |
| GATT | General Agreement on Tariffs and Trade |
| GDP | gross domestic product |
| GHS | General Household Survey |
| GNP | gross national product |
| HAZ | Health Action Zone |
| HBAI | Households Below Average Income |
| ILO | International Labour Organisation |
| IMF | International Monetary Fund |
| IS | Income Support |
| JRF | Joseph Rowntree Foundation |
| LEA | local education authority |
| LFS | Labour Force Survey |
| LIF | Low Income Families |
| LMA | labour market account |
| LS | Longitudinal Study |
| LSE | London School of Economics |
| LSMS | Living Standards Measurement Study |
| MAFF | Ministry of Agriculture, Fisheries and Food |
| MAI | Multinational Agreement on Investment |
| MCA | Married Couple's Allowance |
| MP | Member of Parliament |
| MRC | Medical Research Council |
| MS | multiple sclerosis |
| MUD | moral underclass discourse |
| NCDS | National Child Development Study |
| NGO | non-governmental organisation |
| NHS | National Health Service |
| NYPD | New York Police Department |
| OECD | Organisation for Economic Cooperation and Development |

| | |
|---|---|
| OFSTED | Office for Standards in Education |
| ONS | Office for National Statistics |
| OP | organo phosphate |
| OPCS | Office of Population Censuses and Surveys |
| PA | pyrrolizidine alkoloids |
| PEP | Priority Estates Project |
| PMT | pre-menstrual tension |
| QCA | Qualifications and Curriculum Authority |
| RCDIW | Royal Commission on the Distribution of Income and Wealth |
| RCT | randomised controlled trial |
| RDA | Rural Development Area |
| RDA | Regional Development Agency |
| RED | redistributionist discourse |
| RPI | Retail Price Index |
| RSL | Registered Social Landlord |
| SB | Supplementary Benefit |
| SCAA | School Curriculum and Assessment Authority |
| SID | social integrationist discourse |
| SMR | standardised mortality ratio |
| SNP | Scottish National Party |
| SPI | Survey of Personal Income |
| WFTC | Working Families Tax Credit |
| UCAS | Universities and Colleges Admissions Service |
| UNDP | United Nations Development Programme |
| UN | United Nations |
| VAT | Value Added Tax |
| WHO | World Health Organisation |
| WTO | Warsaw Treaty Organisation |
| ZEP | Zones d'Education Prioritaire |

# Notes on contributors

**Walter Barker** is Director of the Early Childhood Development Centre in Bristol. He has developed semi-structured programmes of parent support and empowerment, based on either professional health visitors or experienced parents selected from the community. These programmes operate nationally and internationally. He has also helped develop statistical instruments for monitoring health visiting outcomes.

**Colin Chalmers** has part-time lectureships at both the London School of Economics and the University of Westminster. He is statistical consultant on a number of projects. Currently the major one involves design, analysis and advice on the execution of experiments for measuring inhaleable dust. He also has links with organisations concerned with child, mental and drug health needs.

**George Davey Smith** is Professor of Clinical Epidemiology in the Department of Social Medicine at the University of Bristol. His research interests are in socioeconomic differentials in health; life-course influences on chronic diseases in adulthood; and AIDS/HIV prevention in India. Recent publications include *The widening gap* (with David Gordon, Mary Shaw and Danny Dorling).

**Danny Dorling** is a Reader in the School of Geographical Sciences at the University of Bristol. His research tries to show how far understanding the patterns of people's lives can be enhanced using statistics about the population. Part of this research involves developing new technology to analyse and popularise quantitative information about human geography, in particular, introducing the use of novel cartographic techniques into geographical research. The substantive side of this concern is with how the fortunes of people living in Britain are distributed and are changing.

**David Gordon** is the Head of the Centre for the Study of Social Exclusion and Social Justice and also the Director of the Townsend Centre for International Poverty Research. He combined his background in biology and geology with anti-poverty policy, while helping to find safe public water supplies in the South Pacific. He has researched and published in the fields of the scientific measurement of poverty, crime and poverty, childhood disability, area-based anti-poverty measures, the causal effects of poverty on ill-health, housing policy and rural poverty.

**Alan Murie** is Professor of Urban and Regional Studies and Director of the Centre for Urban and Regional Studies at the University of Birmingham. His research interests relate to housing and housing policy and especially the importance of housing in processes of inequality and social exclusion.

**Christina Pantazis** is a member of the Centre for the Study of Social Exclusion and Social Justice. Her research interests lie in the areas of crime and poverty, and poverty more generally. She is particularly interested in the study of social harm. She has co-edited (with David Gordon) *Breadline Britain in the 1990s* and is co-editor of *Radical Statistics*, journal of the Radical Statistics Group.

**Ian Plewis'** research interests are in educational and social statistics, evaluation and primary education. He has particular interests in the design and analysis of longitudinal studies and multilevel modelling and is the author of *Statistics in education*, an intermediate level textbook.

**Peter Townsend** is Emeritus Professor of Social Policy in the School for Policy Studies at the University of Bristol. His research interests include current developments in international social policy; social planning, with special reference to welfare reform and pensions; and inequalities in health and the development of the rights of people with disabilities. He has writen extensively on poverty, health, social policy and old age. Publications include *Poverty in the United Kingdom* and *The international analysis of poverty*.

**Ivan Turok** is Professor of Urban Economic Development at the University of Glasgow. His research interests cover urban and regional development, local labour markets and area regeneration. He is currently leading a four-year ESRC integrated case study of economic competitiveness, social cohesion and urban governance in Scottish cities. His publications include *The jobs gap in Britain's cities* (with N. Edge), *The coherence of EU regional policy* (with J. Bachtler), and *Targeting urban employment initiatives* (with U. Wannop).

# ONE

# Introduction

*Christina Pantazis*

The growing divide between the poor and the rich is probably the most significant social change to have occurred under 18 years of Conservative government. The New Labour government inherited a country more unequal than at any other time since the Second World War (Barclay, 1995; Hills, 1995; 1998a; see also Chapter Two). There are now wider gaps in income inequality between different family types, different economic status groups, different housing tenures, and between different regions (Goodman et al, 1997; Hills, 1998a). People on benefits such as the unemployed, lone parents, and pensioners, are over-represented in the bottom income distribution, as are children because of their disproportionate representation in households where there are fewer earners. Compared with other European countries, the United Kingdom (UK) now has the highest proportion of children living in households where income is below half that of the average (Eurostat, 1997) – or what is generally considered as the best proxy for an official poverty line.

Despite the overall growth in incomes under the previous Conservative governments, rates of growth were not shared equally throughout the population. The Households Below Average Income (HBAI) statistics demonstrate that whereas the income of the richest 10% of the population grew from 60% to 68% between 1979 and 1994/95, the income of the poorest group grew by only 10% (before housing costs) or fell by 8% if calculated after housing costs (Hills, 1998a). Some groups – including children – have become worse off in absolute terms (Bradshaw, 1999; see also Chapter Two). These differing fortunes have resulted in a significant change in the overall share of total income. Throughout the 1960s, 1970s and early 1980s, the poorer half of the population had roughly one third of total income (after housing costs), while the richest 10% had about one fifth. By 1996 the richest 10% controlled 28% of the total income, while the whole of the poorer half of the population had only one quarter of total income (see Chapter Two).

This book brings together a collection of contributions on the pressing issue of tackling inequalities in society. Many of the chapters chart the extent of social inequalities inherited by the New Labour government, and offer a critique of the government's policies aimed at tackling those inequalities. Options for reducing inequalities are examined across key areas of social policy: income, wealth and standard of living, as well as employment, education, housing, crime and health. Nearly all the contributions are based on papers presented at the 1998 annual conference of the Radical Statistics Group, 'Inequalities: where are we now and what can be done?', hosted at the University of Bristol. The main purpose of the conference was to contribute to the emerging policy debate about the urgent need to tackle inequalities.

## Inequality, poverty and politics

Until New Labour's election victory in 1997 the negative effects of the growth in inequality had little impact on political debate, and this was more so under Margaret Thatcher than John Major. The evidence of growing inequality in income and wealth and their deleterious effects (for example, see Walker and Walker, 1987; Barclay, 1995; Hills, 1995) may have led to John Major's public acknowledgement that inequality might not be such a good thing, when he declared that he aimed to achieve a 'classless society' and 'a nation at ease with itself'. He even went as far as to declare that he saw his job as seeking to reduce inequality (see Young, 1995), and there were policy changes introduced by his government (eg the abolition of the Poll Tax) which may have contributed to the fall in income inequality from the mid-1990s onwards (Hills, 1998a). In contrast, one of the first acts of his predecessor Margaret Thatcher, when she came to power in 1979, was to abolish the Royal Commission on the Distribution of Income and Wealth (set up by the previous Labour government) – which would have provided information on earnings, distribution of household income and personal wealth. Indeed Thatcher's governments were marked by their unashamed confidence in the economic utility of inequality.

Rather than seeing inequality as something negative that should be reduced, the Thatcher governments deliberately pursued a strategy of inequality in the belief that efficiencies in the economy would result (Walker and Walker, 1987). The (ir)rationale for this strategy was supplied by trickle-down theory which is premised on the notion that by providing incentives to the rich, for example, through lower taxation, the rich will be spurred into entrepreneurial activity, boosting growth and creating jobs. Providing incentives to the poor to make them work harder, for example, by making welfare less attractive, could also boost economic growth. Reg Prentice, a former Minister for Social Security, indicated this in the following way: "If you believe economic salvation can only be achieved by rewarding success and the national income is not increasing, then you have no alternative but to make the unsuccessful poorer" (quoted in Loney, 1987, p 8).

Social security and taxation policies provided the most direct means for the Thatcher governments to reward the rich while making the poor poorer. Under Thatcher there were substantial reductions in income tax for people living on higher incomes, particularly in the 1980 and 1988 Budgets. Nigel Lawson's 1988 'give away' budget, which reduced the top rate of income tax from 60 to 40%, resulted in £2 billion in tax cuts going to the richest 5% of the population (Cook, 1997). During this period the tax burden shifted from the very rich to the middle and poorer groups as existing regressive taxes were raised (eg VAT) and new taxes introduced (eg the Poll Tax). At the same time social security benefits were for various lengths of time frozen (eg Child Benefit), pegged with prices rather than earnings (eg the state pension), cut (eg Unemployment Benefit, Income Support for 18- to 24-year-olds), or withdrawn (eg Income Support for the vast majority of 16- to 17-year-olds) (Oppenheim and Harker, 1996). The Conservatives managed successfully to squeeze benefits but overall spending on benefits increased as the welfare state ended up picking up the costs of social and economic policies and changes – most notably unemployment. The deliberate strategy of inequality, based on changes to tax levels and social security benefits, failed to bring the expected economic rewards.

The reality is that trickle-down has not been associated with higher productivity or investment. In Britain, growth rates were lower in the 1980s than in the more egalitarian 1970s, and have been lower still in the 1990s. As a measure of the nation's income, gross domestic product (GDP) actually fell in the early 1980s and early 1990s (CSO, 1995). The outcome of a deliberate strategy of inequality served not to increase economic growth but, instead, helped to replenish a dying breed of poorly skilled and badly paid group of workers – consisting predominantly of 'domestic servants' – who mainly benefit the more well-off so that they can gain extra time for leisure.

While Thatcher's governments actively encouraged inequality, the existence of poverty was disputed. According to her governments, the success of capitalism had put an end to poverty. This was most spectacularly explained in 1989 by John Moore, the then Secretary of State for Social Security: "It is capitalism that has wiped out the stark want of Dickensian Britain" and "it is capitalism that has caused the steady improvements in the living standards this century" (Moore, 1989, p 14). He added that critics of the government's policies were:

> ... not concerned with the actual living standards of real people but with pursuing the political goal of equality.... We reject their claims about poverty in the UK, and we do so knowing that their motive is not compassion for the less well-off.... Their purpose in calling 'poverty' what is in reality simply inequality, is so they can call western capitalism a failure. (Moore, 1989, p 14)

In 1996, the then Social Security Minister Peter Lilley revived the idea that poverty had been abolished by claiming that government policies had continued to increase the prosperity of the whole population – including the most vulnerable groups (Lilley, cited in Brindle, 1996). In a rebuttal of the Joseph Rowntree Foundation's (JRF's) claim that inequality had reached near-record levels, Lilley argued, "to define poverty purely as a fraction of average income is to distort the meaning of the word" (Lilley, cited in White, 1995). The apparent mass ownership of consumer durables such as telephones and videos was evidence for the lack of poverty in Britain, and this, in Lilley's opinion, justified his government's inaction regarding the introduction of a national poverty eradication plan as agreed by countries, including Britain, at the 1995 United Nation's Summit on Social Development (see UNDP, 1997). According to Lilley and other Conservative politicians, the UN recommendations principally related to the needs of developing countries (where people lack a minimum standard of living based on a person's biological needs for food, water, clothing and shelter). They believed that, if pockets of poverty in Britain exist, then this is either temporary (see Norman Fowler's letter to *The Guardian*, 1996) or the result of the feckless behaviour of some people – absolving government of any responsibility for their predicament. In stark contrast to these views, the British public perceives absolute poverty as a large-scale problem. In 1997, as many as 20% of the British population felt that they had less income than the level they identified as being enough to keep a household like theirs out of absolute poverty (Townsend et al, 1997).

Lilley's suggestion that even the less well-off had improved living standards under the Conservatives is untrue, and fails to link their living standards to the standard of living of other groups. In other words, it fails to acknowledge the widely supported theory of relative poverty, defined by Townsend as:

> Individuals, families and groups in the population can be said to be in poverty when they lack the resources to obtain the types of diet, participate in the activities and have the living conditions and amenities which are customary, or at least widely encouraged, or at least encouraged or approved, in the societies to which they belong. They are, in effect, excluded from ordinary patterns, customs and activities. (Townsend, 1979, p 31)

Throughout the 1980s and 1990s the proportion of people unable to consume and participate in the types of activity that others were taking for granted because of a shortage of money grew substantially from 14 to 20%, affecting 11 million people (Gordon and Pantazis, 1997). The growth in income inequality during this period resulted in a situation where increasing numbers of people were foregoing many of the things that the rest of society was taking for granted. However, there is also evidence that some groups became worse off in absolute terms during this period (Hills, 1998a; see also Chapter Three). For example, the HBAI statistics show that 3% of children were worse off in absolute terms between 1979 and 1995/96. According to Bradshaw: "three percent does not sound very much but it is an absolutely extraordinary finding that by 1995/96 300,000 more children were living in households with incomes below the 1979 real terms threshold" (Bradshaw, 1999, p 2). The active encouragement of inequality under the Conservatives saw increases in levels of poverty – even when defined on their terms.

## New Labour, equality and redistribution

Labour entered the May 1997 Election as a remarkably different Party from previous elections. At the end of an 18-year period of exile, Labour had transformed itself into a Party that could appeal, without apparent contradiction, to the whole of the nation – to the middle classes as well as the working classes, and to businesses as well as trade unions (for accounts of the Labour Party's transformation, see, for example, Jones, 1996; Driver and Martell, 1998). In marked contrast with previous election pledges, there were no promises in New Labour's manifesto to redistribute wealth and income (Labour Party, 1997). Instead, it promised that a Labour government would be committed to the Conservative spending plans set out in Kenneth Clarke's last budget, and that income taxes would not increase during its first parliamentary term. Labour's plans for the welfare state would not involve any additional money (from higher income taxes), except from the 'windfall tax' on the privatised utilities, which would pay for the Welfare to Work programme. Extra funding for health and education would come from efficiency savings and from the phasing out of Conservative programmes (such as the Assisted Places Scheme) or from the benefits of economic growth.

Despite the lack of a radical election agenda, there were hopes that New Labour's electoral victory would herald a new era of progressive political change. New Labour may have shied away from redistribution, but it had acknowledged and was committed to dealing with the legacy of poverty and inequality inherited from the Conservatives. For example, in a pre-election interview Blair claimed: "I believe in a more equal society.... I want a just society, by which I mean extending opportunity, tackling poverty and injustice" (cited in Hutton et al, 1997). However, within three months of New Labour being elected to office, former deputy leader of the Labour Party Roy Hattersley published an article in *The Guardian* accusing New Labour of no longer being "a force for a more equal society" (Hattersley, 1997). Hattersley, who has always been to the right of the Party and who along with Neil Kinnock began modernising the Labour Party in the 1980s in the belief that only change would make it electable, claims that he cannot support Blair's modernisation programme.

According to Hattersley the form of Blair's modernisation of the Labour Party has junked socialism and equality for centre-ground politics. As part of this process of modernisation Hattersley is not against the removal of Clause IV, for example (because bizarrely "old ideological battles were always between advocates of extended public ownership and proponents of equality" [Hattersley, 1997]). His central criticism is directed at New Labour's belief that the defence of the poor through redistribution is no longer a viable option and he takes issue with David Blunkett, the Secretary of State for Education and Employment, who he quotes as saying: "The truth is that any government entering the 21st century cannot hope to create a more equal or egalitarian society simply by taking from one set of people and redistributing it to others, as envisaged when the rich were very rich and the poor made up the rest" (Hattersley, 1997). Not only does this suggest that the very rich are no longer very rich (which is clearly not true: see Chapter Two), but Hattersley also argues that it implies, in the context of a global economy, that higher taxation is not a realistic policy option (which is also not true when you consider that the top rate of taxation is higher in most other industrialised countries).

Blunkett responded with a letter in the same newspaper three days later accusing Hattersley of simply "preaching socialism" and "philosophising about overcoming inequality" when the difference is that New Labour is "determined to transform our society" (Blunkett, 1997). He accused Hattersley of misrepresenting his remarks; what he actually indicated was that cash transfers to the poor do not remove poverty and had been shown to be "ineffective and unsustainable". Creating opportunities "in education and employment, and developing greater equality in circumstances through improved health and housing" is preferable to simply raising benefits: "You can give the poor some money for a period of time but they still remain poor." However, there is no reason why a reliance on benefits (and for most people this tends to be temporary) should result in poverty (see Paul Spicker's letter to *The Guardian*, 1997). The reason why people on benefits remain poor is because benefits are fixed at inadequate levels. In the words of Ruth Lister: New Labour has succeeded in subtly shifting "from arguing that poverty cannot simply be about extra benefits for those on benefit ... to a position that is not about better benefits, period" (Lister, cited in Adonis, 1997).

Neither the Prime Minister, Tony Blair, nor Chancellor Gordon Brown were able to hold back from this public debate about the extent to which New Labour is committed to equality. However, in contrast to Blair (Blair, 1997), Brown provided a more measured response by putting forward the case "why Labour is still loyal to the poor" (Brown, 1997). In doing so he draws on the distinction between equality of outcome, which is "neither desirable or feasible," (favoured by Hattersley) and equality of opportunity (favoured by New Labour). Invoking the 'third way' approach, Brown is against a narrow view of equality of opportunity (which is favoured by the Conservatives) and against equality of outcome with its necessary extreme government intervention and its failure to take into account "work, effort or contribution" which is "people's nightmare of socialism "(Brown, 1997).

The starting point for Brown is that people are provided with the opportunities to fulfil their potential: "... if every person is to be regarded as of equal worth, all deserve to be given an equal chance in life to fulfil the potential with which they are born". In addition to these ethical considerations, "prosperity for a company or country can only be delivered if we get the best out of people". Equality of opportunity is "recurrent, life-long and comprehensive: employment, educational and economic opportunities for all, as well as political and cultural opportunities too, with an obligation on government to pursue them relentlessly". Thus New Labour's Welfare to Work programme is designed to improve employability by expanding education, training and employment opportunities. Because in "our information-age economy, the most important resource of a firm or a country is ... the skills of the whole workforce" (Brown, 1997). With the emphasis on getting people into work, Brown claims that "the first principle of our modernisation of the welfare state is to take action to open up work opportunities to those denied them". Reducing inequality of opportunity, rather than inequality of outcome, is the key issue for New Labour.

However, equality of opportunity and equality of outcome are not only different concepts, but there is also the possibility that equality of opportunity on its own will lead to inequality of outcome. But New Labour does not appear to have a problem with inequalities of outcome if they are the result of hard work (Levitas, 1998). This is why it proposes to link top directors' pay to corporate performance but will fail to introduce a ceiling on top executives' pay. However, for a variety of reasons, including position of power in the labour market, people will be rewarded differently despite equal effort. There are huge disparities in rewards for the top and bottom, but also who gets what rewards is only tenuously linked to their contribution to the economy (Grieve Smith, 1997). A recent survey revealed that top directors in Britain's biggest companies received pay rises of more than 26% last year – which was five times the growth in average earnings (Buckingham and Finch, 1999). The average remuneration enjoyed by Britain's best paid executives was just less than £1 million; it would take almost 50 years for one of their employees to earn that amount.

There are particular dangers inherent in the approach taken by New Labour that emphasises rewards on the basis of a labour market attachment. For example, how are the economically inactive, such as the young, the old, the incapacitated and the ill, to be rewarded? According to Brown, New Labour "will protect and defend – and not forget – the sick and the elderly" (Brown, 1997). The government promises to provide security to those who cannot work. However, at the same time it claims that simply raising benefits is not enough. So how are those who are dependent on benefits to share in greater opportunities and higher living standards? The reality is that New Labour has failed to restore the link between pensions and national earnings and has made cuts to single-parent benefit (that led to the backbench revolt in December 1997). Further still, it plans to go ahead with cuts in benefits to the disabled. New Labour's Welfare to Work – with its element of compulsion – may result in opportunities for coercion and decreased living standards.

Ensuring similar outcomes for all is obviously a more costly exercise than providing opportunities to people to be rewarded for equal talent and effort. Nevertheless, pursuing equality of opportunity still requires resources. New Labour's manifesto commitment to keeping to the previous government's spending targets for two years and its pledge not to raise standard or top rates of income taxation for the whole parliamentary term may have limited the extent to which it has been able to reverse the unequal access to opportunity thus far. Piachaud (1997) asks whether New Labour is properly resourcing the Welfare to Work programme to put the young unemployed, long-term unemployed and lone parents into work. If unemployment is seen as the biggest cause of limited opportunities by New Labour then Piachaud may be correct in saying that the amount of resources targeted by the government at its Welfare to Work programme suggests that equality of opportunity is not getting much of a priority over equality of outcome.

New Labour's shift in commitment from equality of outcome to equality of opportunity (even in its extended version) may have buried a central tenet of the Labour movement. That shift was further reinforced by the declaration by the Trade and Industry Secretary, Stephen Byers, that wealth creation is now more important than the redistribution of wealth. In his first speech as Trade and Industry Secretary at the Mansion House in the City of London he pledged not to hinder the work of entrepreneurs and promised that there would be no "drip drip" of employment laws:

> The reality is that wealth creation is now more important than wealth distribution. Governments should not hinder (entrepreneurs) but work to ensure the market functions properly and contributes to creating a strong, just and fair society. (cited in Watt et al, 1999)

He added that more wealth and opportunities, rather than redistribution, could reduce inequality: "I firmly believe that the best way to address inequality and social exclusion is to create a more affluent, more successful Britain with opportunities for everyone to fulfil their potential".

## New Labour, the third way and modern welfare

New Labour has committed itself to making society more equal, not by redistributing wealth and income, but through extending opportunities.

The central means by which New Labour aims to achieve a more equal society is through a popular and modernised welfare state based on the 'third way' – a supposedly new approach that differs from both the Old Left and the New Right (see Driver and Martell, 1998; Powell, 1999). According to Blair, the:

> 'Third Way' is ... the best label for the new politics which the progressive centre-left is forging in Britain and beyond. The Third Way stands for a modernised social democracy, passionate in its commitment to social justice and the goals of the centre-left, but flexible, innovative and forward-looking.... It is founded on values which have guided progressive politics for more than a century – democracy, liberty, justice, mutual obligation and internationalism. But it is a *third way* because it decisively moves beyond an Old Left preoccupied by state control, high taxation and producer interests; and a New Right treating public investment, and often the very notions of 'society' and collective endeavour, as evils to be undone. (Blair, 1998, p 1; italics in original)

While it may be a little premature to say whether New Labour has successfully restructured the modern welfare state based on a 'third way' (Powell, 1999), Blair reaffirmed his government's commitment to welfare in his Beveridge Lecture in March 1999: "The third way in welfare is clear: not to dismantle it; or to protect it unchanged; but to reform it radically" (Blair, 1999; Walker, 1999). In possibly Blair's clearest indication thus far of how he envisages the welfare state as we approach the end of the 20th century, he pledged his government to restore Britain's post-war welfare state as a politically popular vehicle. He also stated his government's clear commitment to a 20-year programme to eradicate child poverty – which was in marked contrast to his pre-election declaration that unless the next Labour government raised the living standards of the poorest it would have failed.

In his lecture, Blair invoked many of the themes of the third way to describe what a "modern popular welfare state" should look like. According to Blair a modern welfare state should be rooted in social justice, which incorporates: decency so that people are able to "meet their needs for income, housing, health and education"; merit which "demands that life chances should depend on talent and reward, not the chance of birth; and that talent and effort should be handsomely rewarded"; mutual responsibility so that people accept that they have duties as well as rights; fairness where "power, wealth and opportunity will be in the hands of the many not the few"; and values which change with time (Blair, 1999). The characteristics of a modern welfare state will: tackle social exclusion, child poverty and community decay in an active way, through tackling the fundamental causes such as unemployment, poor education, poor housing, the crime and drugs culture; be a hand-up not hand-out; provide security by focusing on those who need it most; end fraud and abuse; encompass public/private partnership; re-emphasise active welfare, schools and health, not just benefits. Again by invoking a third way approach, Blair says that the welfare state will be supportive of both social justice and economic efficiency. Accordingly, the welfare state will be connected to an "economic vision" which will encompass "stability" and the "knowledge economy" (Blair, 1999), as well as a strong notion of social justice.

However, there is an obvious danger that Blair's vision of creating a more popular welfare state will be seriously undermined unless social justice is enmeshed with strong notions of distributive justice and a clear commitment to ending income inequalities. In an effort to abandon income and wealth redistribution for the nebulous fairness, New Labour may be jeopardising the success of the welfare state. The welfare state can only remain popular so long as everyone uses it (Hutton, 1997; Johnson, 1997). Eighteen years of increasing income inequalities has resulted in people who have been able to afford more than just a basic pension, health and education opting in favour of the private sector. For example, the proportion of policy holders of private medical insurance has doubled from 3 to 6% between 1982 and 1995 (ONS, 1997). A squeeze on public spending inevitably provides a lower quality service, which is subsequently taken up by fewer people. Thus the divergence in income between the rich and the poor leads to a growing difference in the quality of services they use. Once this process starts it can become much more difficult to persuade voters that it should be reversed. The lesson is that if New Labour's vision of a modern and popular welfare state is to materialise, it must provide decent funding for the welfare state, combined with policies to tackle inequality and poverty.

Despite the up-turn in the economy, New Labour faces continued criticism for the lack of resources which it has directed to the welfare state, although it has introduced a number of schemes and reforms which aim to meet its objectives of reducing inequality of opportunity and poverty. The Social Exclusion Unit, set up by the Prime Minister in December 1997, has a remit to help improve government action to reduce social exclusion by producing 'joined up solutions to joined up problems' (http://www.cabinet-office.gov.uk/seu/index/faqs.html; see

Chapters Five and Six). Social Security Secretary Alistair Darling announced that the government would produce a poverty audit by the end of 1999 (DSS, 1999a). As a result we will know the scale of poverty and social exclusion, and the degree to which it has been solved and will have a benchmark on which to judge the government's progress (DSS, 1999b; for a critique see Levitas, 2000).

New Labour has introduced various national measures to reduce poverty and inequality of opportunity, including the minimum wage, a guaranteed income for pensioners on Income Support and the New Deal for the young, the over-50s, lone parents and disabled people although it has already been suggested that this initiative carries with it the danger of increased coercion and depressed living standards. Furthermore, the success of the New Deal may depend on the extent of employment opportunities, rather than the skills people have (see Chapter Three). Most significantly, using the language of fairness New Labour has introduced policies which aim to increase income to the poorest households, particularly those with children. Based on the belief that "children are 20% of our people but 100% of our future" and that poor children means poor adults, Chancellor Gordon Brown made the provision of greater financial help for families with children the centrepiece of the March 1999 Budget (Brown, 1999). The Children's Tax Credit, the increase by 20% in Child Benefit and the new Working Families Tax Credit (WFTC), replacing Family Credit (introduced in the March 1998 Budget), are the central planks that will contribute towards the government's pledge to end child poverty.

Research has shown that the Chancellor has made a start at reversing the unfairness that existed under the previous governments since the effect of his three budgets on household incomes has been progressive (the lower the income, the higher the average proportional gain in household income) although some households are worse off (Immervoll et al, 1999). However, the effects of these budgets have not been redistributionist in the Old Labour sense. For example, many of the improvements in the last Budget were achieved by redirecting money from companies rather than from very wealthy individuals. The three budgets did not seek to tackle the vast inequality among individuals – an aspect that many Old Labour supporters may have wished for (see Chapter Two, for further detail on the effect of the budgets).

There have also been numerous policy continuities with the Conservatives and these may seriously jeopardise the extent to which inequality of opportunity and poverty are reduced under New Labour. The commitment to low income tax and public sector spending, the government's unwillingness to raise benefit levels for most people and the reduction in single-parent and disability benefits are the main policy continuities with the previous government. There are some examples where New Labour has gone beyond the Conservatives in cutting back the welfare state (for example, ending student grants and introducing student tuition fees) (Powell, 1999).

Unlike the Conservatives, however, area-based policies form a key strategy in this government's programme for the alleviation of poverty and inequality. They include Health, Employment, Education Action Zones (see Chapters Three, Four and Seven), Sure Start, and New Deal for Communities (see Chapters Five and Six) and involve more than 100 Local Authority Areas. According to the recent Treasury document *Tackling poverty and extending opportunity*: "People living in the most deprived areas are more likely than average to have no qualifications. This makes them much less likely to be able to take advantage of work opportunities" (HM Treasury, 1999, p 15). A concentration of people with few educational skills and qualifications, who are therefore less employable, threatens to undermine the government's strategy towards a more inclusive society. There are also characteristics of deprived areas themselves that mean people who live there have fewer opportunities than those in better-off areas: "Physical isolation can mean that there are few work or training opportunities locally, and transport links may be poor. High levels of worklessness in the area mean that people are less likely to have contacts in work, so a frequent source of information about jobs is denied to them" (HM Treasury, 1999, p 13). However, area-based policies do not appear to have had much success in the past, so there is a danger that New Labour may have learned little from these previous failures. These issues are taken up in Chapters Two, Four, Five, Six and Seven.

## Inequality, social cohesion and economic efficiency

Contemporary debates about the need to reduce inequality have become entwined with arguments about social cohesion and economic efficiency, and have clearly been present in New Labour's thinking (Borrie, 1994; Barclay, 1995; Hills, 1998a). Notwithstanding the contested meaning of social cohesion (see Kearns and Forrest, 1998) there is some evidence that an increasing lack of social cohesion is dependent on the extent of income differentials (Wilkinson, 1996). Wilkinson suggests that an important characteristic of egalitarian societies is their social cohesion, which is crucial to the smooth running of society:

> They have a strong community life. Instead of social life stopping outside the front door, public space remains a social space. The individualism and the values of the market are restrained by a social morality. People are more likely to be involved in social and voluntary activities outside the home. These societies have more of what has been called 'social capital' which lubricates the workings of the whole society and economy. There are fewer signs of anti-social aggressiveness, and society appears more caring. In short, the social fabric is in better condition. (Wilkinson, 1996, p 4)

Narrower income differences and increased social cohesion have a crucial role in increasing life expectancy. Death resulting from violent crime and also death rates from some of the most important diseases are reduced when income differentials are lowered (Wilkinson, 1996). Wilkinson's argument is that despite rising living standards in the UK, health inequalities persist (see Chapters Seven, Eight and Nine). He makes the controversial claim that it is relative income levels not absolute income levels that are crucial to understanding current health inequalities. He shows that among the industrialised countries, it is those with the most egalitarian systems, rather than the most wealth, that have the best health. Similarly, higher crime rates, including homicide and violence, are associated with wider income differences and are indicative of a socially disintegrative society (see Chapter Six). This is true of both Western industrialised countries (see Oliver, 1997) and developing nations (Fajnzylber et al, 1998). New Labour's support for policies aimed at reducing inequalities (at least in terms of opportunity) appear to be, in part, based on this argument. According to Blair, "comfortable Britain ... knows the price it pays for economic and social breakdown in the poorest parts of Britain" (Blair, cited in Elliot, 1997).

Arguments about economic efficiency have also surfaced in debates about the need to tackle inequalities. While New Right governments throughout the world have deliberately followed policies of inequality in the belief that economic growth will follow, these strategies do not appear to be grounded in empirical evidence. Indeed from the evidence it appears that the threat to economic performance provides another imperative for governments to tackle inequalities. The evidence is that narrower income differences are associated with faster – not slower – economic growth (Glyn and Miliband, 1994; Wilkinson, 1996; Oxfam, 1997). A study based on an analysis of 56 countries suggested that in less equal societies concerns about social and political conflict are more likely to lead to government policies that hinder growth (Persson and Tabellini,

1994). Glyn and Miliband (1994) found that societies with wider inequality have more ill-health, social stress and crime which cramp economic growth. The evidence from the UK is clear: growth rates were lower in the 1980s and the 1990s than in the more egalitarian 1970s. This argument appears to be acknowledged by the current government. Thus, Tony Blair claims that social cohesion appears to characterise a society which is not only more fair, but also more economically efficient: "Social cohesion – a society in which there is no gross inequality nor the absence of opportunity for significant numbers of citizens – is an indisputable part of an efficient economy" (Blair, cited in Ellison, 1998, p 39).

On the other hand, contemporary debates about the need to reduce inequality have generally excluded moral arguments (Levitas, 1998). It seems that arguments based on morality are no longer sufficient. The Joseph Rowntree *Inquiry into Income and Wealth*, for example, declared that:

> ... our prime concern is not with morality.... We are concerned with the overall social effects which impact on the whole community; with the accumulation of problems as those being left behind are concentrated in particular areas; and with the long-term costs of what has happened. (Barclay, 1995, p 32)

And

> ... regardless of any moral arguments or feelings of altruism everyone shares in an interest in the cohesiveness of society. As the gaps between the rich and poor grow, the problems of the marginalized groups which are being left behind rebound on the more comfortable majority. (Barclay, 1995, p 34)

However, morality does have a crucial place in discussions about reductions in inequality. Without a moral stance it is quite logical to follow the claim made by the Inquiry "that it might be possible to justify inequality – a widening gap between incomes of rich and poor – on the grounds that the beneficial effects on growth would raise living standards of the poorest" (Barclay, 1995, p 32).

## Organisation of the book

Most of the chapters in this book examine the increased level of inequality inherited by the New Labour government, and offer a critique of the policies adopted by the government to deal with them. Options for reducing inequalities are examined across key areas of social policy: income, wealth and standard of living: health, employment, education, housing and crime. The book is based around two central themes. Firstly, the New Labour government has responded to the increasing spatial concentrations of poverty and inequality by introducing a plethora of area-based policies to deal with the lack of opportunities in deprived areas. Many of the chapters focus on New Labour's area-based policies and draw attention to the ecological fallacy and how it may be an unsound basis on which to build social policy (Chapters Two, Four, Five, Six and Seven).

The second theme of the book is the use and interpretation of official statistics. All of the contributions rely on and utilise official statistics, but in doing so demonstrate a critical awareness of social inequalities, showing how statistics can be used to obscure or distort data relating to inequality. Statistics relating to income in particular are likely to be misused (see Chapter Two). Since the 1970s there have been a number of important books which tried to 'demystify' the use of social statistics (see Irvine et al, 1979; Levitas and Guy, 1996; Dorling and Simpson, 1999). The contributions in this book follow in a similar vein. Some chapters are based on analysis of government and other statistical and survey data (Chapters Two, Three, Six, Seven, Nine), some discuss published statistics (Two, Four, Five, Six, Eight), and Chapter Ten offers a perspective on world poverty statistics.

David Gordon in Chapter Two considers the most glaring inequalities in society – namely those relating to income, wealth and standard of living. After consideration of the problems and common confusions surrounding definitional issues, and using a range of statistical sources, Gordon demonstrates just how unequal British society had become when New Labour took office. He argues that a redistribution of income and wealth from the poor to the rich took place under the previous Conservative governments – reversing the trend from the 15th century onwards towards greater equality. Gordon proposes that in addition to the minimum wage, New Labour should introduce the maximum wage and wealth taxes as effective measures to reverse the rising trend of inequality.

Work is at the heart of the government's drive for social inclusion with strategies aimed at increasing demand at the bottom of the labour market and increasing supply through the New Deal and other policies. However, if Blair is right – that the biggest cause of inequality is unemployment and that the best guarantee of a decent wage is the ability to earn and one's employability – then his government will have to take more notice of labour market inequalities. Ivan Turok in Chapter Three examines urban economic change during the last two decades and the impact on local people. Turok considers some of the key dimensions of labour market inequality and discusses how these inequalities relate to issues of gender and socioeconomic occupation. He argues that current labour market disparities threaten to undermine Labour's New Deal policies aimed at getting people back into work: a shortage of employment opportunities, not poor skills or motivation, is the reason for the high levels of unemployment in many cities.

While work is considered as the central route to improved living standards, New Labour sees education and training as the means of enhancing employability. The role of government is to make "Britain the best educated and skilled country in the world; a nation, not of few talents, but of all the talents" (Blair, cited in Elliot 1997b). Crucially it sees the failure to secure a good education in the early years as key to determining life chances in adulthood. Thus, in a recent Treasury document, it was stated that: "the seed of inequality in adulthood is denial of opportunity in childhood. Education is the most important transmission mechanism – people with few skills and qualifications are much less likely to succeed in the labour market" (HM Treasury, 1999, p 7). In Chapter Four Ian Plewis considers inequalities in education and focuses on the likely impact of the Education Action Zones (EAZs) which New Labour regards as key in tackling educational inequalities. Plewis argues that the government's emphasis on raising standards through EAZs, league tables and targets may fail to reduce inequality and raise standards. The outcome of these policies is that they may even exacerbate educational inequalities.

In Chapter Five Alan Murie discusses how inequalities can be ended in the area of housing. While housing is not at the top of New Labour's policy agenda it has been identified with affecting outcomes in health (see Marsh et al, 1999) and education, as well as having an important role in improving employability. Murie examines how housing is a product and contributory factor in determining inequality, and focuses on how housing issues, such as poor housing conditions, homelessness and the residualised social housing sector, are linked to the wider processes of social exclusion. He offers a critical analysis of New Labour's focus on the worst estates and suggests that the focus of social exclusion in terms of the social housing sector is being made at the expense of housing problems elsewhere.

Christina Pantazis considers New Labour's policies on crime, in particular the New Deal for Communities, its initiative to reduce crime and disorder on Britain's most deprived estates. She offers an alternative approach to the government's proposals by suggesting that inequalities in crime and fear of crime should be seen in the context of other inequalities that are suffered disproportionately by people living in poverty. Her analysis of the 1994 British Crime Survey indicates that the relationship between poverty and crime is more complex than is currently recognised by the government and academics alike.

Chapters Seven, Eight and Nine examine various aspects and issues relating to inequalities in health. The impact of inequalities and ill-health has been recently revived with the publication of the report of the *Independent inquiry into inequalities in health* (Acheson, 1998; see also Gordon et al, 1999; Shaw et al, 1999). In Chapter Seven George Davey Smith and David Gordon examine socio-economic inequalities and health differences over the life-course. They consider the independent affects of childhood and adult social circumstances and their impact on health, and suggest that the effects of poverty in childhood have far-reaching consequences in both childhood and adult life. They suggest that widening inequality, and especially growing poverty among children, does not bode well for the future health trends. Offering a critical appraisal of the ability of the government's flagship policy of Health Action Zones to arrest the growth in socioeconomic inequalities in health, they recommend a range of fiscal measures aimed at improving the situation of people – especially children. With health inequality at its worst for at least 50 years, there is little that can be done about it without also tackling poverty.

Chapter Eight concerns the extent to which all governments pay little attention to or ignore research findings. Walter Barker and Colin Chalmers discuss examples, from the field of health, where evidence has been ignored. They suggest that there are a number of important points arising from this broad finding, particularly those that affect women's health. Crucially, they argue that it is probably the main reason why current inequalities in health provision are likely to continue: if inequalities in health are to be reduced governments of all political persuasions must stop ignoring research findings.

Chapter Nine raises the question of whether there should be a league table for ministers? In answering this question Danny Dorling examines the extent to which there is a close distribution between voting patterns and premature mortality. He shows how spatial inequalities in mortality are reflected in the spatial distribution of Members of Parliament (MPs) and suggests that given the unequal life chances of their own constituents, reducing health inequalities should be a priority for New Labour.

Dorling argues that despite New Labour's talk of opportunities, policies and programmes that are likely to have a significant impact on reducing health inequalities they have so far failed to materialise.

The final chapter considers how world poverty might be abolished as we enter the new millennium. Rapid technological change and globalisation have transformed the world economy at an unprecedented pace, but the benefits are being enjoyed by the rich and strong rather than the weak and poor. The process of global 'trickle-down' has failed to close the gap between wealthy and poor countries, while inequalities within countries also continue to widen. Peter Townsend discusses issues relating to the meaning and measurement of poverty and shows how the 1995 World Summit on Social Development, which incorporates overall and absolute definitions of poverty as a way to bridge the 'First' and 'Third' Worlds, has been a significant breakthrough in this context. Townsend argues that there is an urgent need for international social policies, involving investment in jobs and the reorganisation of the public and private sectors, to counter the problems of globalisation.

## References

Acheson, D. (chair) (1998) *Independent Inquiry into Inequalities in Health report*, London: The Stationery Office.

Adonis, A. (1997) 'Comment: New Labour's "wets" get hung out and dry', *The Guardian*, 26 October.

Barclay, P. (chair) (1995) *Income and wealth, Volume 1: Report of the Inquiry Group*, York: Joseph Rowntree Foundation.

Blair, T. (1997) *The Sun*, 29 July.

Blair, T. (1998) *The third way: New politics for the new century*, London: The Fabian Society.

Blair, T. (1999) *Beveridge Lecture*, Toynbee Hall, London, 18 March.

Blunkett, D. (1997) 'Letter: New Labour hits back', *The Guardian*, 29 July.

Borrie, G. (chair) (1994) *Social justice: Strategies for national renewal*, Report of the Commission on Social Justice, London: Vintage.

Bradshaw, J. (1999) 'Child poverty in comparative perspective: developing poverty measures' (Unpublished paper), Presented at the 'Developing poverty measures: research in Europe' Conference to launch the Townsend Centre for International Poverty Research, University of Bristol, 1-2 July.

Brindle, D. (1996) "Poverty, what poverty?" says Lilley', *The Guardian*, 17 April, p 1.

Brown, G. (1997) 'Why Labour is still loyal to the poor', *The Guardian*, 2 August, p 19.

Brown, G. (1999) 'Check against poverty: Chancellor of Exchequer's Budget Statement', 9 March.

Buckingham, L. and Finch, J. (1999) 'Top pay rises by 26 per cent', *The Guardian*, 19 July.

Cook, D. (1997) *Poverty, crime and punishment*, London: CPAG Limited.

CSO (Central Statistical Office) (1995) *Social Trends 25*, London: HMSO.

Dorling, D. and Simpson, S. (eds) (1998a) *Statistics in society: The arithmetic of politics*, London: Arnold.

Driver, S. and Martell, L. (1998) *New Labour*, Cambridge: Polity Press.

DSS (Department for Social Security) (1999) 'Fight against poverty returns to the centre stage of British politics', Press Release, 18 February.

DSS (1999b) *New ambitions for our country: A new contract for welfare*, Cm 3805, London: The Stationery Office.

Elliot, L. (1997a) 'Proof if trickle pudding is not in the eating', *The Guardian*, 15 September, p 19.

Elliot, L. (1997b) 'Time to make Britain work again', *The Guardian*, 4 October, p 82.

Ellison, N. (1998) 'The changing politics of social policy', in N. Ellison and C. Pierson (eds) *Developments in British social policy*, London: Macmillan.

Eurostat (1997) 'Income distribution and poverty in the EU12', *in Statistics in Focus: Population and Social Conditions*, vol 6.

Fajnzylber, P., Lederman, D. and Loayza, N. (1998) *Determinants of crime rates in Latin America and the world*, Washington, DC: World Bank.

Fowler, N. (1996) 'Letter: A poor show', *The Guardian*, 23 April, p 12.

Glyn, A. and Miliband, D. (1994) *Paying for inequality*, London: IPPR/ Rivers Oram Press.

Goodman, A., Johnson, P. and Webb, S. (1997) *Inequality in the UK*, Oxford: Oxford University Press.

Gordon, D. and Pantazis, C. (1997) *Breadline Britain in the 1990s*, Aldershot: Ashgate.

Gordon, D., Shaw, M., Dorling, D. and Davey Smith, G. (eds) (1999) *Inequalities in health: The evidence presented to the Independent Inquiry into Inequalities in Health*, Bristol: The Policy Press.

Grieve Smith, J. (1997) 'Still one law for the rich', *The Guardian*, 1 December, p 15.

Hattersley, R. (1997) 'Why I am no longer loyal to Labour', *The Guardian*, 26 July, p 21.

Hills, J. (1995) *Income and wealth, Volume 2: A summary of the evidence*, York: Joseph Rowntree Foundation.

Hills, J. (1998a) *Income and wealth: The latest evidence*, York: Joseph Rowntree Foundation.

Hills, J. (1998b) *Thatcherism, New Labour and the welfare state*, CASE Paper 13, London: Centre for Analysis of Social Exclusion, London School of Economics.

HM Treasury (1999) *Tackling poverty and extending opportunity*, London: The Treasury.

Hutton, W. (1997) 'Labour must stop ducking the issue of inequality', *The Guardian*, 3 August, p 22.

Hutton, W., Wintour, P and Adonis, A. (1997) 'Election 97: I am going to be a lot more radical in government than many people think', *The Guardian*, 27 April, p 3.

Immervoll, H., Mitton, L., Donoghue, C. and Sutherland, H. (1999) *Budgeting for fairness? The distributional effects of three Labour budgets*, Microsimulation Unit Research Note No 32, Cambridge: University of Cambridge.

Irvine, J., Miles, I. and Evans, J. (eds) (1979) *Demystifying social statistics*, London: Pluto Press.

Johnson, P. (1997) 'Why are we stuck with a two-tier society?', *The Guardian*, 28 July.

Jones, T. (1996) *Remaking the Labour Party*, London: Routledge.

Kearns, A. and Forrest, R. (1998) 'Social cohesion, neighbourhoods and cities', Paper for the 31st Social Policy Association Conference, University of Lincolnshire and Humberside, 14-16 July.

Labour Party (1997) *New Labour because Britain deserves better*, London: Labour Party.

Levitas, R. (1998) *The inclusive society*, London: Macmillan.

Levitas, R. (2000) 'What is social exclusion?', *Radical Statistics*, issue 73.

Levitas, R. and Guy, W. (eds) (1996) *Interpreting official statistics*, London: Routledge.

Loney, M. (1987) 'A war on poverty or on the poor?', in A. Walker and C. Walker (eds) *The growing divide*, London: CPAG Limited, pp 8-19.

Marsh, A., Gordon, D., Pantazis, C., Heslop, P. and Forrest, R. (1999) *Home Sweet Home?: The impact of poor housing on health*, Bristol: The Policy Press.

Moore, J. (1989) *The end of the line for poverty*, London: Conservative Political Centre.

Oliver, J. (1997) *Juvenile violence in a winner–loser culture*, London: Free Association Books.

ONS (Office for National Statistics) (1997) *Living in Britain: Results from the 1995 General Household Survey*, London: The Stationery Office.

Oppenheim, C. and Harker, L. (1996) *Poverty: The facts* (3rd edn), London: CPAG Limited.

Oxfam (1997) *Growth with equity*, Oxford: Oxford University Press.

Persson, T. and Tabellini, G. (1994) 'Is inequality harmful to growth?', *American Economic Review*, vol 84, pp 600-21.

Powell, M. (ed) (1999) *New Labour, new welfare state?: The third way in British social policy*, Bristol: The Policy Press.

Piachaud, D. (1997) 'Equality: poor war of words', *The Guardian*, 13 August.

Shaw, M., Dorling, D., Gordon, D. and Davey Smith, G. (1999) *The widening gap: Health inequalities and policy in Britain*, Bristol: The Policy Press.

Spicker, P. (1997) 'Equality is the central issue', *The Guardian*, 30 August.

Townsend, P. (1979) *Poverty in the United Kingdom*, London: Penguin.

Townsend, P., Gordon, D., Bradshaw, J. and Gosschalk, B. (1997) *Absolute and overall poverty in Britain in 1997: What the population themselves say: Bristol Poverty Line Survey*, Report of the Second MORI Survey, Bristol: Bristol Statistical Monitoring Unit.

UNDP (United Nations Development Programme) (1997) *Human Development Report 1997*, Oxford: Oxford University Press.

Walker, A. and Walker, C. (1987) *The growing divide: A social account 1979-1987*, London: CPAG Limited.

Walker, R. (ed) (1999) *Ending child poverty: Popular welfare for the 21st century?*, Bristol: The Policy Press.

Watt, N., Hencke, D. and Gow, D. (1999) 'Wealth creation is the priority, insists minister', *The Guardian*, 3 February.

White, M. (1995) 'Ministers launch drive to rebut Rowntree claim of growing inequality', *The Guardian*, 15 February.

White, M., Ahmed, K. and Brindle, D. (1997) 'The Election: Blair's pledge to heal society', *The Guardian*, 16 April, p 11.

Wilkinson, R. (1996) *Unhealthy societies: The afflictions of inequality*, London: Routledge.

Young, H. (1995) 'Inequalities which have made us far too complacent', *The Guardian*, 14 February, p 18.

# TWO

# Inequalities in income, wealth and standard of living in Britain

*David Gordon*

## Introduction

During the past 100 years, literally thousands of scientific papers have been published that discuss some aspect of inequalities in income, wealth or standard of living in the UK. However, a large number of these papers fail to define these terms adequately and often confuse inequality (and particularly income inequality) measures with poverty. Yet, these two concepts are distinct (Gordon and Spicker, 1999).

Given the high level of academic interest in inequality in Britain, there have been surprisingly few comprehensive analyses. During the 1970s, Tony Atkinson produced and edited a number of excellent studies on inequality (Atkinson, 1972, 1973, 1975) cumulating in his comprehensive book *The economics of inequality,* the second edition of which was published in 1983. The Joseph Rowntree Foundation's *Inquiry into income and wealth* updated some of Atkinson's work (Barclay 1995; Hills, 1998), but the only recent book on inequality in the UK, by the Institute of Fiscal Studies (Goodman et al, 1997), has a very different character. Atkinson's studies examined inequality in income and wealth, the distribution of earnings and the causes of the growing divide. He produced proposals for wide-ranging changes to the tax and social security system to reduce inequality. By contrast, the Goodman et al (1997) book deals almost exclusively with changes in income and expenditure, contains numerous factual errors in its brief discussion of poverty and, extraordinarily, makes no policy suggestions. The study of inequality is seen as a subject of dispassionate academic interest, devoid of concern for the victims of the growth in inequality. The authors display no desire to reduce inequality, merely to study it. What is of particular concern is that one of the authors, Stephen Webb, is now the Liberal Democrat Spokesperson on Social Security.

## Defining income

Income is an extremely difficult concept to define and measure. The term is sometimes used loosely to refer only to the main component of monetary income for most households – wages and salaries or business income. Others use the term widely to include all receipts including lump sum receipts and receipts that draw on the household's capital.

Classically, income has been defined as the sum of consumption and change in net worth (wealth) in a period. This is known as the 'Haig-Simons approach' (see Simons, 1938 in Atkinson and Stiglitz, 1980, p 260). Unfortunately, this approach fails to distinguish between the day-to-day 'living well' and the broader 'getting rich' aspects of individual or household finances. In technical terms, it fails to distinguish between current and capital receipts.

There are a number of international organisations that have provided guidelines on defining and measuring income. The United Nations (UN) provides two frameworks: the 1993 System of National Accounts (UN, 1992) and guidelines on collecting micro-level data on the economic resources of households (UN, 1977, 1989). The International Labour Organisation (ILO) has also produced guidelines on the collection of data on income of households, with particular emphasis on income from employment (ILO, 1971, 1992, 1993). Recently, the Australian Bureau of Statistics (ABS) tried to get an international agreement on definitions of income, consumption, saving and wealth via the informal 'Canberra Group' of statisticians[1]. The ABS has proposed the following definition:

> Income comprises those receipts accruing (in cash and in kind) that are of a regular and recurring nature, and are received by the household or its members at annual or more frequent intervals. It includes regular receipts from employment, own business and from the lending of assets. It also includes transfer income from government, private institutions and other households. Income also includes the value of services provided from within the household via the use of an owner-occupied dwelling, other consumer durables owned by the household and unpaid household work. Income excludes capital receipts that are considered to be an addition to stocks, and receipts derived from the running down of assets or from

the incurrence of a liability. It also excludes intra-household transfers. (ABS, 1995, p 33)

Townsend (1979, 1993) has argued that broad definitions of income (resources) should be used, particularly if international comparisons are to be made. When comparing individual or household incomes of people in different countries, it is crucial that account is taken of the value of government services in, for example, the fields of health, education and transport (Evandrou et al, 1992). Unfortunately, many studies of income inequality use relatively narrow definitions of income such as wages and salaries or business income. International comparisons based on narrow definitions of this type can be misleading and of only limited use (Gordon and Spicker, 1999).

## Defining wealth

Producing an adequate operational definition of the concept of wealth is even more fraught with problems than defining income. The Oxford English Dictionary (2nd edn) argues that the most widely-accepted economic definition of wealth is that attributed to Mill in 1848:

> Money, being the instrument of an important public and private purpose, is rightly regarded as wealth; but everything else which serves any human purpose, and which nature does not afford gratuitously, is wealth also.... To an individual, anything is wealth, which, though useless in itself, enables him to claim from others a part of their stock of things useful or pleasant. Take for instance, a mortgage of a thousand pounds on a landed estate. This is wealth to the person to whom it brings in a revenue. But it is not wealth to the country; if the engagement were annulled, the country would be neither poorer nor richer.... Wealth, then, may be defined, as all useful or agreeable things which possess exchangeable value; or in other words, all useful or agreeable things except those which can be obtained, in the quantity desired, without labour or sacrifice. (OUP, 1989)

However, statisticians usually use the much more limited concept of 'net worth' as a proxy for wealth. The ABS has defined net worth as the difference between the household's stock of assets and its stock of liabilities at a particular point in time. The concept of assets covers both financial and non-financial assets, including all consumer durables owned by the household. The concept of liabilities covers all debts owed by the household whether they be to other households, private institutions or government (ABS, 1995).

This definition of net worth/wealth excludes the value of human capital held by the household such as the education and skills of its members. Assets include financial assets such as cash, deposits in financial institutions, securities (shares, stocks and bonds) and equity in pensions and life insurance. Non-financial assets include owner-occupied dwellings, land and other buildings, household consumer durables, plant, machinery and stocks (of unincorporated enterprises), valuables (precious metals and stones, antiques, art objects and so on) and intangible non-produced assets (patents, goodwill and so on). Liabilities include all mortgages, loans and debts (ABS, 1995).

## Relationship between income, standard of living, poverty and wealth

Townsend (1979) defined poverty scientifically in terms of relative deprivation, as follows:

> People are relatively deprived if they cannot obtain, at all or sufficiently, the conditions of life – that is, the diets, amenities, standards and services – which allow them to play the roles, participate in the relationships and follow the customary behaviour which is expected of them by virtue of their membership of society. If they lack or are denied the incomes, or more exactly the resources, including income and assets or goods or services in kind, to obtain access to these conditions of life they can be defined to be in poverty.

> People may be deprived in any or all of the major spheres of life – at work, where the means largely determining position in other spheres are earned, at home, in neighbourhood and family; in travel; in a range of social and individual activities outside work and home or neighbourhood in performing a variety of roles in fulfilment of social obligations. (Townsend, 1993, p 36, and also see Townsend, 1979, p 31)

The 'relative deprivation' standard is built on the idea that, in all societies, there is a threshold of low income or resources marking a change in the capacity of human beings to meet their needs, material and social, enjoined by that society. Some such idea is the only one logically available to distinguish poverty from inequality – whether subjectively or objectively. In descending a scale of income (or income combined with the value of other types of resources), instances of deprivation steadily increase. However, below a certain level of income, the forms and instances of deprivation are hypothesised to multiply disproportionately to the fall of income – this level is the 'poverty line' (Townsend, 1979; Gordon and Townsend, 1990; Townsend, 1993).

In scientific terms, a person or household in Britain is 'poor' when they have both a low standard of living and a low income. They are 'not poor' if they have a low income and a reasonable standard of living or if they have a low standard of living but a high income. Both low income and low standard of living can only be accurately measured relative to the norms of the person's or household's society.

A low standard of living is often measured by using a deprivation index (high deprivation equals a low standard of living) or by consumption expenditure (low consumption expenditure equals a low standard of living). Of these two methods, deprivation indices are more accurate since consumption expenditure is often only measured over a brief period and is not independent of available income. Deprivation indices are broader measures because they reflect different aspects of living standards, including personal, physical and mental conditions, local and environmental facilities, social activities and customs (Gordon and Townsend, 1998). Figure 2.1 below illustrates these concepts.

**Figure 2.1: Definition of poverty in terms of income and standard of living**

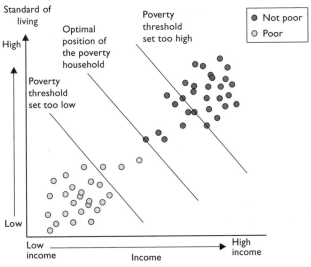

The 'optimal' poverty line/threshold is shown in Figure 2.1. It can be defined as the point that maximises the differences between the two groups ('poor' and 'not poor') and minimises the differences within the two groups ('poor' and 'not poor'). For scientific purposes, broad measures of both income and standard of living are desirable. Standard of living includes both the material and social conditions in which people live and their participation in the economic, social, cultural and political life of the country (Gordon and Townsend, 1998).

In contrast to the extensive debates and research on poverty, income and standard of living, the scientific study of wealth is in its infancy. Approaches to the measurement of wealth have tended to be purely statistical in character, with arbitrary cut-offs and thresholds used to define the wealth line such as the top 1%, 5% or 10% (Scott, 1993). However, the pioneering work of John Scott (1993, 1994) has attempted to introduce more rational and scientific definitions of the wealthy. The wealthy can be defined as those who have such large resources that they are privileged compared with the rest of the population. They are able to establish 'private' life-styles and modes of consumption from which the majority are excluded (Scott, 1993). The 'wealth line' can be defined as the "point in the distribution of resources at which the possibility of enjoying special benefits and advantages of a private sort escalates disproportionately to any increase in resources" (Scott, 1994, p 52). The poor are excluded from the norms of society because they do not have enough money to participate whereas the wealthy have so much money that they exclude themselves from the norms of society and retreat into a privileged (private) life-style. They use private medicine, their children go to private schools, they live in exclusive residential areas and so on. Poverty and wealth are not simply the 'bottom' and 'top' of the income distribution, they are polarised social conditions (Scott, 1994). They are both divisive and exclusionary and harmful to society as a whole.

## Low income statistics

During the last 20 years, there has been no official national survey of poverty in Britain. Those concerned with poverty and inequality at a national level have had to rely almost exclusively on the *Low Income Families* (LIF) series and its successor, the *Households Below Average Income* (HBAI) series, produced by the Department of Social Security (DSS) and the Social Services Select Committee. These have generated data on the size and characteristics of the population living on a low income over time and have proved useful in revealing the extent of and growth of financial inequality. Without them, we would not be able to say very much about trends in inequality since the early 1970s. However, they are limited because they are based exclusively on the Family Expenditure Survey (and now the Family Resources Survey) and have been restricted to a threshold of relatively low income – such as the lowest decile and half average household income. There has been no sustained comparative analysis of high and low income households.

## Low Income Families

The LIF series produced statistics on the number of benefit units and individuals with incomes below various thresholds of the Supplementary Benefit/Income Support standard for a family of their type. LIF statistics were published by the Department of Health and Social Security (DHSS)/DSS for the years 1972 to 1985 and by the Social Services Select Committee for the years 1979 to 1992. The LIF statistics were replaced by the HBAI statistics at the end of the 1980s so, for reasons of space, this analysis of income inequality will be confined to the more up-to-date HBAI statistics.

However, the last set of LIF data for 1992 demonstrated that 13,600,000 people were living in families with incomes at or less than the Income Support standard. Of this group 4,700,000 people (more than one third) were not receiving any Income Support since they had either not claimed it or were not entitled to claim it (Social Security Committee, 1995). So, Income Support was only being received by less than two thirds of those on the lowest incomes.

## Households Below Average Income

The HBAI (and their predecessor LIF) statistics have been published by the DSS for 1979 to 1996/97 based on analysis of annual Family Expenditure Survey (FES) data. The DSS estimates are based on amalgamating two years of FES data to increase the available sample size and this procedure results in their being of limited use for studying the rapid effects of policy changes. However, individual year HBAI estimates from the FES back to 1961 have been produced by the Institute of Fiscal Studies (Goodman and Webb, 1994). Recently, the DSS has also produced single year HBAI estimates for 1994, 1995 and 1996 based on the larger Family Resources Survey (DSS, 1998). The percentage of the population living in households with less than half the UK's average income between 1961 and 1996 is shown in Figure 2.2.

*Figure 2.2:* **Percentage of the population below half average incomes (after housing costs) (1961–96)**

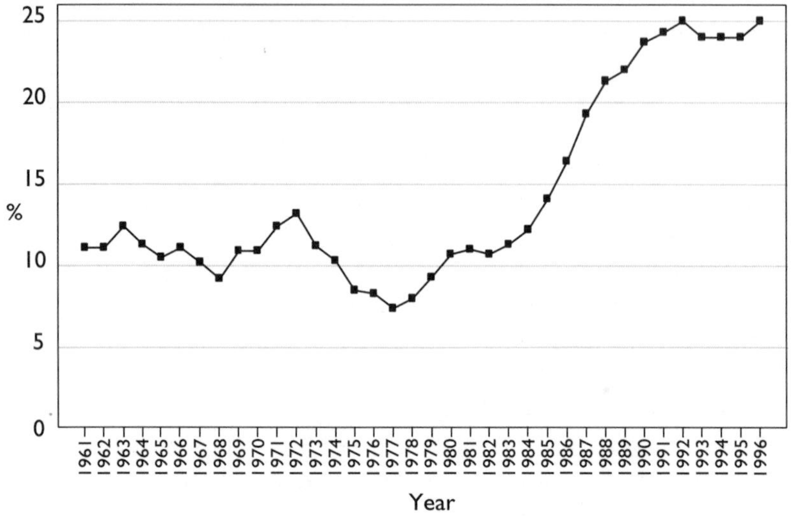

*Source:* Goodman and Webb (1994); updated by author using HBAI data

Figure 2.2 shows that, during the 1960s, the amount of income inequality in Britain remained fairly constant with around 11% of the population living on incomes below half of the average. The recession and 'stagflation' of the early 1970s, caused by the OPEC oil price increases, caused the numbers living on less than half average incomes to rise to a peak of just more than 13%. The relatively progressive government social and economic policies of the mid-1970s resulted in poverty and inequality falling rapidly to a low of less than 8% of the population in 1977/78. The 1979 election victory of the Conservative Party under Margaret Thatcher's leadership brought a reverse in social and economic policies designed to promote equity and caused a rapid growth in poverty and inequality which increased throughout the 1980s and early 1990s. The marginally more progressive social policies of the 1992 Conservative government (under John Major) resulted in a less rapid increase in inequality during the mid-1990s. However, by 1996, the latest available figures, one quarter (25%) of the British population was living on incomes that were so low that they were below half the average income. Eighteen years of Conservative rule resulted in the proportion of the British population living on low incomes more than trebling, from 8% to 25%.

By 1996, 14,100,000 people in Britain were living in households with incomes below half the average (after the deduction of housing costs).

Table 2.1 shows the change in the share of total income (after deducting housing costs) between 1979 and 1996 that was received by individuals by deciles of the income distribution.

**Table 2.1: Share of the total income received by income decile (after housing costs) (1979-96) (%)**

| Income decile | 1979 | 1996 | Change |
|---|---|---|---|
| Bottom 10% | 4.1 | 2 | -2.1 |
| 10-20% | 5.7 | 4 | -1.7 |
| 20-30% | 6.2 | 5 | -1.2 |
| 30-40% | 8 | 6 | -2.0 |
| 40-50% | 9 | 8 | -1.0 |
| 50-60% | 9 | 9 | 0 |
| 60-70% | 11 | 10 | -1.0 |
| 70-80% | 12 | 13 | +1.0 |
| 80-90% | 15 | 15 | 0 |
| Top 10% | 20 | 28 | +8.0 |
| Total | 100 | 100 | 0 |

*Source:* Calculated from HBAI (DSS, 1998)

The results shown in Table 2.1 are unambiguous. Between 1979 and 1996, the share of the total income in Britain of those in the top 10% increased from 20% to 28%. The richest 10% of the population received one fifth of the total income in 1979 and more than one quarter of the total income in 1996. The rich are now much richer than they were in 1979. The share of total income received by all those in the bottom half of society decreased, with the greatest losses occurring in the bottom 10%. These people saw their share of the total income fall by more than half (from 4.1% in 1979 to 2% in 1996).

Analysis of the latest HBAI data shows that the poorest 10% were not only 'relatively' poorer in 1996 than in 1979 but also 'absolutely' poorer. Table 2.2 shows the change in real median incomes (after allowing for inflation using the Retail Price Index [RPI]) by decile group between 1979 and 1996 (at April 1998 prices).

Between 1979 and 1996, the income of the British population rose on average by 43%, from £9,620 per year (£185 per week) to £13,728 per year (£264 per week), at April 1998 prices. However, this increase in income was not shared equally. The median incomes of those in the bottom 10% of the income distribution fell between 1979 to 1996, from £4,212 per year (£81 per week) to £3,692 per year (£71 per week), whereas the median incomes of those in the richest 10% increased from £18,044 per year (£347 per week) to £30,264 per year (£582 per week). During the 18 years of Conservative government, the poorest became £520 per year poorer, whereas the richest saw their median incomes increase by more than 50%, a gain of £12,220 per year.

*Table 2.2:* **Change in real median weekly incomes by decile group at April 1998 prices (after housing costs) (1979-96)**

| Income decile | 1979 (£) | 1996 (£) | Change (%) |
|---|---|---|---|
| Bottom 10% | 81 | 71 | −12 |
| 10-20% | 104 | 106 | +2 |
| 20-30% | 121 | 132 | +9 |
| 30-40% | 139 | 164 | +18 |
| 40-50% | 157 | 200 | +27 |
| 50-60% | 177 | 236 | +33 |
| 60-70% | 199 | 277 | +39 |
| 70-80% | 227 | 327 | +44 |
| 80-90% | 263 | 402 | +53 |
| Top 10% | 347 | 582 | +68 |
| Total population (mean) | 185 | 264 | +43 |

*Source:* Calculated from HBAI (DSS, 1998)

To understand how breathtakingly regressive and reactionary these increases in inequality were it is necessary to view them from an historical perspective. Rubinstein (1986) has shown that, from the end of the 17th century, which is the earliest period from which there is reliable evidence, income has become progressively more equally distributed in Britain. The rather sparse evidence available from earlier periods indicates that there has been a trend of a slow but progressive increase in income equality since the 15th century (Wedgwood, 1929; Saltow, 1968). From this historical perspective, what the Thatcher governments attempted to do was reverse a 500-year trend of increasing income equality. It is no surprise that their most obvious inequitable policy – the 'Poll Tax' – resulted in the largest social protest movement[2] and acts of civil disobedience in British history (Burns, 1993).

## International comparisons

The Organisation for Economic Co-operation and Development (OECD) was the first to use the 50% of average income line as a proxy indicator for poverty during the late 1970s, since this was the approximate average level of social assistance rates in their member countries in the mid-1970s. If the OECD was to undertake a similar survey today, then it would achieve a different result and presumably use a different threshold level (Forster, 1995). The methodology currently used by the OECD also differs from that used in the 1970s, in particular in its use of equivalence scales (OECD modified scale), and this affects the composition of the poor. However, when establishing the HBAI statistics in Britain, the DSS did not attempt to follow international standards and used a series of statistical procedures which have been adopted by no other country in the world. So, although there are below half average income statistics available for most industrialised countries, they are not directly comparable with the British HBAI statistics.

However, comparable below 50% of average income statistics have been produced by Eurostat (1998) from the 1994 wave of the European Community Household Panel (ECHP) Survey[3]. Table 2.3 shows the estimated number and percentage of people living on incomes of less than half the average (but based on different statistical procedures from those used in the HBAI series).

*Table 2.3:* **Number and percentage of the population living on incomes below half of the average in 14 European countries (1994)**

| Country | Number of people below 50% of average income | Population below 50% of average income (%) |
|---|---|---|
| United Kingdom | 11,426,766 | 20 |
| Germany | 11,327,673 | 14 |
| Italy | 9,321,853 | 17 |
| France | 7,949,907 | 14 |
| Spain | 7,196,406 | 19 |
| Portugal | 2,424,533 | 25 |
| Greece | 2,041,923 | 20 |
| Belgium | 1,474,158 | 15 |
| Netherlands | 1,275,048 | 8 |
| Austria | 1,108,082 | 14 |
| Ireland | 837,490 | 23 |
| Denmark | 386,015 | 7 |
| Finland | 192,153 | 4 |
| Luxembourg | 56,734 | 14 |

*Source:* Eurostat, unpublished analysis of the ECHP

Table 2.3 shows that one area where the previous Tory government was able to demonstrate leadership in Europe was in low income. Its policies resulted in the UK having more people living on less than half average incomes than in any other country in the European Community.

A similar comparative analysis for children has recently been published by HM Treasury based on the first (1993) wave of the ECHP data (HM Treasury, 1999). Figure 2.3 shows the percentage of children in 11 European Union countries who are living in households with incomes below half the median.

**Figure 2.3: Percentage of children living in households with income below half the median (1993)**

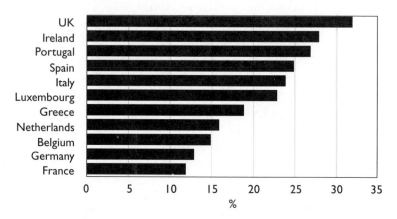

The results shown in Figure 2.3 are clear. There are both a greater number and a greater proportion of children living in low income households in the UK than in any other European Union country. Almost one third (32%) of all children in the UK were growing up in low income households in 1993. Income inequality is a greater problem in the UK than in any other European Union country.

## Problems with the HBAI statistics

Discussions on the statistical procedures followed by the HBAI have involved arcane debates about the appropriateness of the equivalence scales used to adjust income to need, the problems of measuring the incomes of the self-employed, whether income should be assessed before or after housing costs, what is the most appropriate income threshold, whether it should be related to mean or median incomes and whether poverty numbers, poverty gaps or some combination of both should be measured (see Townsend and Gordon, 1989, 1992; Townsend, 1996, for discussion). These dilemmas or choices have made a significant difference to the estimate derived of the size and structure of the poor population. For example, despite using a common equivalence scale, the HBAI 1994/95 estimates of the proportion of the population (individuals) living in households in poverty varies from 6% to 32% depending on whether 40, 50 or 60% of average income is used as the threshold, whether the self-employed are included or excluded and whether income is measured before or after housing costs. The definition of low income has determined not just the size but the composition of the poor population. This has an impact on the appropriateness of the policy response to poverty (Bradshaw et al, 1998).

Politicians have been able to take refuge from the clear evidence of rapidly increasing rates of inequality and poverty behind this debate about definitions. For example, one year when commenting on the publication of the HBAI figures, Peter Lilley claimed that the income poverty figures were an overestimate because the expenditure poverty figures produced lower estimates. The next year he claimed that the poverty estimates were exaggerated on the grounds that analysis of income poverty over time showed that there was a good deal of turnover of the poor population and this was a reason not to be concerned about the overall level of poverty (Hills, 1998). In fact, he misinterpreted and exaggerated limited data but this episode illustrates how the authority of the HBAI statistics have become undermined (Bradshaw et al, 1998).

A number of statistical procedures followed by the HBAI series are clearly designed to mislead the unwary – to lie with statistics. For example, only changes in the median incomes of the poorest 10% and richest 10% of society are reported and not the changes in the average (mean) incomes of these groups. Since both the top and bottom of the income distribution are skewed, the median will always yield a higher income for the bottom 10% and a lower income for the top 10% than would the mean, resulting in the impression that there is less income inequality (see Townsend and Gordon, 1992 for discussion).

Jean Corston, the MP for Bristol East, made repeated attempts to discover the changes in average incomes of the poorest and richest groups in Britain by asking a series of parliamentary questions during the late 1980s and early 1990s. The DSS simply refused to provide this information, claiming that it could not calculate the mean of the bottom and top 10% of the income distribution. I witnessed an extremely embarrassing meeting during which two senior statisticians from the DSS tried to explain in front of the head of the Government Statistical

Service why they would not calculate the average incomes of the poorest 10%. The reasons were clearly political and not statistical. I have been told (off the record) by an ex-senior statistician at the DSS that Peter Lilley (the then Minister for Social Security) circulated a memo saying that he only wanted to hear 'good news'.

Sir Ian Gilmour, who was a minister in both the Heath and Thatcher governments, explained the situation clearly:

> Measuring poverty in the Thatcher era is difficult because of the inadequate, and sometimes deliberately misleading obfuscation, of government statistics. That in itself is revealing. Just as a government will only find it necessary to fiddle the unemployment figures when unemployment is rising fast, it will only fudge and conceal the figures on poverty when it knows that poverty is spreading; when a government is reducing poverty it will make the statistics as transparent as possible and loudly proclaim them. Thus the Thatcher government abandoned the publication of statistics of low-income families and started a series on 'Households Below Average Income', usefully (from its point of view) breaking continuity and making exact assessments and comparisons difficult. (Gilmour, 1992)

## Wealth statistics

The statistical information on the distribution of wealth in Britain is almost entirely inadequate. Virtually nothing is known and the available statistics are extremely partial and sparse. Although the idea of a survey to gather data on personal wealth is by no means new, the measurement of total asset holdings by type, on a national sample, has not been attempted in Britain. The University of Oxford undertook a series of savings surveys in the 1950s and early 1960s that covered some asset holdings but their coverage was not nearly comprehensive enough to define net worth (Erritt and Nicholson, 1958; Knight, 1980).

In 1974, the Royal Commission on the Distribution of Income and Wealth (RCDIW) was established with the responsibility for conducting a "thorough and comprehensive enquiry into the existing distribution of income and wealth". It reviewed the existing sources of information on wealth holdings which were, principally, the wealth statistics which arise from the administration of Estates Duty and Capital Transfer Tax. This data relates to wealth holdings at the moment of death and may not be the best picture of the wealth of the living. These statistics relate only to individuals (rather than family or income units). They do not cover all wealth and are particularly deficient at the lower end of the wealth distribution. Data linking wealth and income did not exist and there is no source which directly gave information on inheritance.

The Royal Commission drew attention to "the lack of any reliable basis for linking wealth with income, for linking the wealth of husbands and wives, and for distinguishing between inheritances and gifts and life-cycle savings". It concluded that "a sample survey of wealth appears to be the only possible way of filling these gaps" (RCDIW, 1975). The Office of Population Censuses and Surveys (OPCS) undertook two feasibility studies on behalf of the Royal Commission to examine the possibility of a nationally representative wealth survey. However, Margaret Thatcher abolished the Royal Commission in 1979 before a third feasibility study had been completed (Knight, 1980). There has never been a wealth survey in Britain to this day. Recent analyses of wealth distribution have attempted to use commercial surveys, such as the NOP Financial Research Survey, but the quality of the data is poor (Banks et al, 1994).

The Inland Revenue and the Office for National Statistics (ONS) both produce some limited statistics on the distribution of marketable wealth[4] (such as assets that could in theory be sold or cashed in) by combining estimates of total personal wealth with estimates on the distribution of wealth using the estates multiplier method. This assumes that those who die in a year (after stratification by age, sex, marital status, tenure and country) are an adequate sample of the estates of the living (Good, 1990). This methodology is essentially the same as that invented by Chiozza-Money (1905) and Wedgwood (1929), and there has been little progress in the methodology of wealth measurement in Britain since the Edwardian era[5]. Figure 2.4 shows the change in the percentage of marketable wealth owned by the 'richest' 10% of the population in the UK between 1976 and 1994[6].

The wealthiest 10% owned just more than 50% of the marketable wealth in the UK in 1994 and this has not changed since the mid-1970s. However, if the value of dwellings is excluded from this calculation, then the wealth of the top 10% has increased from 57% in 1976 to 65% in 1994. The wealthiest increased the proportion of cash, stocks and shares and other financial assets that they owned during the 1980s and 1990s. However, their share of the overall distribution of marketable wealth did not change due to the rise in owner-occupation that also occurred during this period. Nevertheless, the richest 10% of people in Britain in the mid-1990s owned approximately one quarter of the total income and half the country's wealth. The poorest 10% of the population owned approximately 2% of the income and even less of the country's wealth.

**Figure 2.4: Percentage of marketable wealth owned by the most wealthy 10% (1976-94)**

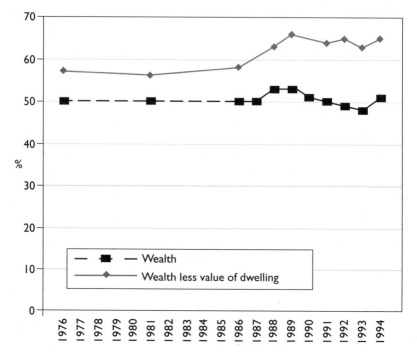

*Source:* Calculated from *Social Trends* (1995, 1998)

## The very wealthy

There are no official statistics on the very wealthiest or the very poorest people in the UK. The FES (which is used to construct the HBAI) is known to be unrepresentative of the very richest and the poorest households in Britain (DSS, 1991). It excludes the homeless and fails to measure accurately the number of pensioners and people with disabilities. Consequently, the FES overestimates the incomes of the bottom decile. Data on both the very poorest and the richest people in the HBAI is either excluded in the case of those with large negative incomes or substituted in the case of those with the highest incomes.

The Inland Revenue's Survey of Personal Income (SPI) data is used to substitute all those non-pensioners with net incomes greater than £100,000 and all pensioners with gross incomes greater than £100,000. This adjustment simply substitutes one set of problems for another and is unlikely to make the adjusted results more reliable (Townsend and Gordon, 1992). The deficiencies of the SPI, especially at the top end of incomes, have been known, from the time of Richard Titmuss (1962) through to the years of deliberation by the Royal Commission on the Distribution of Income and Wealth (1975-79), and to the present day. There are problems of converting tax units into households; adjusting for housing costs; measuring local taxes; converting financial years into calendar years; and locating those who really do have high incomes.

However, a limited amount of information on the wealth of the 'super-rich' has been published annually since 1989 by journalists on *The Sunday Times*, first as a book (Beresford, 1990) and now as a magazine supplement[7]. *The Sunday Times* Rich List attempts to produce a minimum estimate of the marketable wealth of the most wealthy people or families who either live or have extensive business interests in the UK[8]. However, what can be achieved by even the best investigative journalist methods is somewhat limited as they had no access to bank accounts or shareholdings in private equity portfolios.

Figure 2.5 shows the estimated identifiable wealth of the richest 1,000 people and families in the UK compared to the estimated marketable wealth of the least wealthy half of the population (eg the least wealthy 28 to 29 million people).

The data shown in Figure 2.5 are not strictly comparable since they are based on different definitions of wealth and use different methods. However, they do provide a reasonable 'ball-park' estimate of the gross disparities in wealth that exist in the UK at the end of the millennium. The richest 1,000 people and families own almost two thirds as much wealth as the least wealthy half of the population. The richest 1,000 had on average 15,000 times more wealth than the least wealthy 28 million. This size of disparity has profound democratic implications particularly when both Conservative and Labour governments during the 1990s have argued that cuts must be made in social spending as 'we cannot afford the welfare state'. No government in the 20th century has received the votes of 50% of the population at an election. However, throughout the 1980s and 1990s, governments of all political persuasions have progressively given less weight to the claims of the 'poorest' for a fair share of the national wealth. Senior Labour politicians are well aware of the consequences that these vast disparities in wealth have on society.

For example, Gordon Brown concluded his introduction to *Scotland the real divide* with these stirring words:

> This would mean restoring to the centre of the tax system two basic principles: the first, that those who cannot afford to pay tax should not have to pay it; and the second, that taxation should rise progressively with income. Programmes that merely redistribute poverty from families to single persons, from the old to the young, from the sick to the healthy, are not a solution. What is needed, is a programme of reform that ends the current situation where the top 10% own 80% of our wealth and 30% of income, even after tax. As Tawney remarked, 'What some people call the problem of poverty, others call the problem of riches'. (Brown and Cook, 1983, p 22)

**Figure 2.5: Estimated wealth of the richest 1,000 people in the UK compared with the wealth of the least wealthy half of the population (1989-99)**

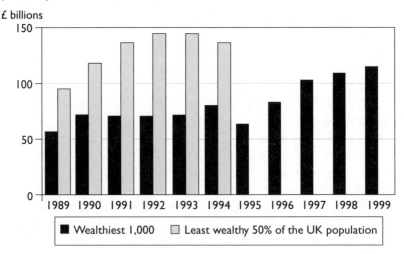

*Source:* Calculations by the author from *The Sunday Times* Rich List and *Social Trends*

Unfortunately, New Labour has completely abandoned the concept of the 'problem of riches' despite the fact that this problem continues to grow like a cancer of society.

## Inequalities in standard of living

There have been no official surveys in Britain specifically designed to comprehensively measure poverty, deprivation and standard of living in the general population[9]. The limited information we do have comes from unofficial sources such as the *Poverty in the UK* survey (Townsend, 1979) and the *Breadline Britain* surveys (Mack and Lansley, 1985; Gordon and Pantazis, 1997). However, the Poverty and Social Exclusion Survey of Britain funded by the JRF will be carried out by ONS as a follow-up to the General Household Survey in Autumn 1999 (Bradshaw et al, 1998). Surveys of this type are essential to help understand the effects that the huge disparities in income and wealth documented above have had on the poorest and most vulnerable sections of society.

The two *Breadline Britain* surveys, in 1983 and 1990, pioneered the 'consensual' or 'perceived deprivation' approach to measuring poverty. This sets out to determine whether there are some people whose standard of living is below the minimum acceptable to society. It defines 'poverty' from the viewpoint of the public's perception of minimum need:

> This study tackles the questions 'how poor is too poor?' by identifying the minimum acceptable way of life for Britain in the 1980s. Those who have no choice but to fall below this minimum level can be said to be 'in poverty'. This concept is developed in terms of those who have an enforced lack of *socially perceived* necessities. This means that the 'necessities' of life are identified by public opinion and not by, on the other hand, the views of experts or, on the other hand, the norms of behaviour per se. (Mack and Lansley, 1985, p 45)

In order to determine the population's standard of living, a representative sample of respondents was asked if they had a range of possessions and activities that people might consider important (Gordon and Pantazis, 1997).

The *Breadline Britain* surveys found that between 1983 and 1990 the number of people who could objectively be described as living in poverty increased by almost 50%. In 1983, 14% of households (approximately 7.5 million people) were living in poverty and, by 1990, 20% of households (approximately 11 million people) were living in poverty. The human costs and consequences of income and wealth inequalities were devastating:

- roughly 10 million people in Britain in 1990 could not afford adequate housing: for example, their home was unheated, damp or the older children had to share bedrooms;
- about 7 million went without essential clothing, such as a warm waterproof coat, because of lack of money;
- there were approximately 2.5 million children who were forced to go without at least one of the things they needed, like three meals a day, toys or out-of-school activities;
- around 5 million people were not properly fed by today's standards; as for example, they did not have enough fresh fruit and vegetables, or two meals a day;
- about 6.5 million people could not afford one or more essential household goods, like a fridge, a telephone or carpets for living areas;
- the poorest 20% of the population were approximately five times more likely to feel isolated and depressed due to lack of money, twice as likely to live in fear of crime and one-and-a-half times more likely to suffer from a serious illness.

A similar survey in Wales in 1995 (*Poor Wales*) found the same depressing picture:
- more than one in four people in Wales (more than 750,000 people) could not afford one or more of the necessities of life;
- roughly 150,000 Welsh people could not afford adequate housing, for example, their home is unheated, damp or in disrepair;
- about 170,000 went without adequate clothing – such as a warm waterproof coat or two pairs of waterproof shoes – because of lack of money;
- one in five households lived without adequate financial security, they could not afford household insurance or to save £10 for retirement or emergencies;
- around 100,000 did not have an adequate diet due to financial hardship, for example, they could not afford two meals a day or fresh fruit;
- more than 300,000 people in Wales could not afford one or more essential household goods, like a fridge, a telephone or a washing machine;
- more than one in ten Welsh families could not afford to buy their children toys or leisure equipment.

While one fifth of the British population have miserable, depressing lives due to lack of money and other resources, the wealth of the richest is quite literally unimaginable. For example Bill Gates (the richest man on the planet) is, at the time of writing, estimated to have the equivalent of £60 billion of wealth[10]. This is so much money that if a person was to earn £1 million every year after taxes and all expenditure, it would still take them 60,000 years to save up as much wealth as Bill Gates has now.

Similarly, the United Nations Development Programme (UNDP, 1999) estimates that "the assets of the 200 richest people are more than the combined income of 41% of the world's poorest people". The richest three people have more than the gross national product (GNP) of all 43 least developed countries.

## New Labour's policy response

Before the 1997 General Election, Tony Blair clearly stated Labour's commitment to reducing inequality:

> I believe in greater equality. If the next Labour Government has not raised the living standards of the poorest by the end of its time in office it will have failed. (Tony Blair, 1996, quoted in Howarth et al, 1998, p 9)

In his Beveridge Lecture on 18 March 1999, Tony Blair also committed the government to "lifting 700,000 children out of poverty by the end of the Parliament" and "to end child poverty for ever" over the next 20 years (Blair, 1999; and see also Walker, 1999).

These clear commitments, combined with New Labour's nervousness about alienating 'Middle England' by increasing direct taxes, has led many commentators to believe that Gordon Brown has attempted to redistribute income by stealth, using indirect taxation and other budgetary measures to take money from the 'rich' and give it to the 'poor'. The 1999 Labour Budget was hailed by many as a brilliant *tour de force* by the Chancellor that redistributed income in a relatively painless manner and would help to alleviate the scourge of child poverty. It was the first Labour Budget that was not constrained by the self-imposed requirement to maintain the spending limits laid down by the previous Conservative administration. A number of dramatic measures were introduced designed to help families with children. These included the:

• introduction of the 10p income tax band;
• abolition of the Married Couple's Allowance (MCA) and the Additional Personal Allowance (APA);

• introduction of the Children's Tax Credit.

Both the Microsimulation Unit in the Department of Applied Economics at the University of Cambridge and the Institute of Fiscal Studies have modelled the redistributional effects of these changes and have come to similar conclusions. Table 2.4 shows the combined impact of these Budget measures on the distribution of family incomes. The proportions of families gaining or losing are shown in each of 10, equal-sized income groups – or 'deciles' (Sutherland, 1999).

***Table 2.4:*** **Percentage of gainers and losers by income decile: 1999 Finance Bill changes**

| Income decile group | All families | |
| --- | --- | --- |
| | **Gainers** | **Losers** |
| Poorest | 1 | 1 |
| 2 | 7 | 3 |
| 3 | 21 | 4 |
| 4 | 39 | 6 |
| 5 | 63 | 10 |
| 6 | 73 | 13 |
| 7 | 73 | 19 |
| 8 | 71 | 25 |
| 9 | 66 | 32 |
| Richest | 57 | 41 |
| All | 47 | 16 |

The results in Table 2.4 are clear – overall, 47% of families gained on average about £1 per week from the budgetary changes and 16% of families were made worse off. However, among the poorest 10% of families in the bottom decile of the income distribution, 1% of families gained and 1% were made worse off, leaving 98% of the poorest families unaffected by these budgetary changes. On average, most people gained from the Budget, particularly families with children. However, among the families with the lowest incomes, a few families with children gained at the expense of poor families without children.

During the 1980s, Gordon Brown (Brown and Cook, 1983, p 22) argued that "programmes that merely redistribute poverty from families to single persons, from the old to the young, from the sick to the healthy, are not a solution." (p 22). Unfortunately, this was precisely the effect of the main changes of the 1999 Finance Bill.

However, there have now been three Labour Budgets since the Party's landslide election victory in May 1997 which together have introduced a large number of taxation, government spending and welfare benefit changes. The keyword used by Chancellor Gordon Brown in relation to all these three Budgets has been 'fairness'. Figure 2.6 shows the percentage of gainers and losers following all the changes made in the past three Labour Budgets (Immervoll et al, 1999).

*Figure 2.6:* **Percentage of gainers and losers following three New Labour Budgets**

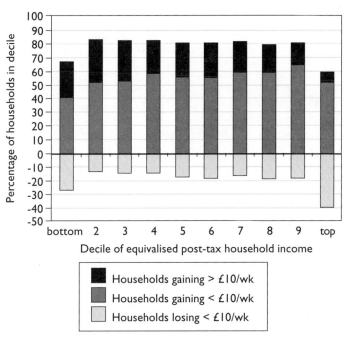

*Source:* POLIMOD

Again, the results are clear: the overwhelming majority of households are better off as a result of the changes made in the past three Labour Budgets. On average, households in every income decile have shared in the growing wealth of the country. However, there have been losers as well as gainers, as Figure 2.6 shows. Overall, 80% of households are better off and 20% are worse off but the largest proportion of losers are among the poorest (28.1%) and the richest (39.2%). More than one quarter of households in the lowest income group are poorer as the result of three Labour Budgets. It is questionable if this would be considered to be a 'fair' result by the average voter. Income has been redistributed by Labour but not all the poor have gained; many middle-income households have done better out of the Budget changes than have poor households, particularly low-income households dependent on welfare benefits.

However, to put this somewhat depressing picture into perspective, the Labour Budgets have been vastly more progressive than the previous Conservative Budgets. The last Tory Budget, in 1996, redistributed money from the poor to the rich as previous Conservative Budgets had done (Chadwick et al, 1997).

The past three Labour Budgets have introduced a number of welcome and progressive changes but, in total, they have done relatively little to reduce the huge inequalities in income and wealth that exist in Britain today.

## Area-based policies

One of the government's main strategies for alleviating poverty and reducing inequality is through a range of area-based policies. Since the report by the Social Exclusion Unit (1998) on *Bringing Britain together: A national strategy for neighbourhood renewal*, the number of area-based policies being pursued has exploded to include more than 110 Local Authority Areas. Major area-based inequality initiatives now include Health, Employment and Education Action Zones, New Start, Sure Start, Local Government Association New Commitment to Regeneration, Single Regeneration Budget, New Deal for Communities and Better Government for Older People. A new Cabinet Committee may have to be established in order to coordinate and maintain an overview of all these initiatives (Smith, 1999).

However, area-based inequality and anti-poverty policies have a long history of only limited successes or even outright failure. The lessons from the original 12 area-based anti-poverty neighbourhood projects, the Community Development Projects (CDPs), need to be remembered. These were set up by James Callaghan in 1969 (when he was Home Secretary) and ran for more than five years. The CDP workers became so disillusioned that they concluded in their final report that "in the final analysis the 'deprivation initiatives' were not about eradicating poverty at all, but about managing poor people" (CDP, 1977).

The government seems to have learned little from previous failures and ignored "the strongly held view of those working in regeneration and anti-poverty, that resources should be allocated overwhelmingly according to need and not by competition" (Alcock et al, 1998). Yet, much of the money for these new area-based initiatives has been allocated on the basis of competitive tender rather than purely on the basis of greatest need (Smith, 1999).

An area-based rather than people-based approach to attacking inequality, poverty and deprivation can only ever provide help for a relatively small minority of people since most 'poor areas' only contain a minority of 'poor' households and a majority of 'non-poor' households (Lee et al, 1995). For example, there are 1.1 million people in the Tyne and Wear Health Action Zone (HAZ) and the overwhelming majority of them are not poor nor do they have bad health. These problems have been understood for a long time. In 1975, the Education Priority Area (EPA) schools programme was criticised since "for every two disadvantaged children who are in EPA schools five are outside them" (Barnes and Lucas, 1975). Similarly, in 1979, Peter Townsend argued in *Poverty in the UK* that:

> An area strategy can never be the cardinal means of dealing with poverty or 'under privilege'.... However we care to define economically or socially deprived areas, unless we include over half the areas in the country, there will be more poor persons or poor children living outside them. (Townsend, 1979)

Similarly, Robson et al (1994), in their massive review of the effectiveness of urban area-based polices designed to reduce inequality and deprivation, argued that:

> The consensus was that places had been the typical mode of targeting in the past. However, many argued that, in future, programmes would need to focus as much upon target population groups as on deprived areas. The view that targeting areas automatically benefited the people living within them was clearly challenged. (Robson et al, 1994)

The problem of the relative lack of effectiveness of area-based policies has been known and well documented for more than 25 years (Barnes and Lucas, 1975; Townsend, 1979; Robson et al, 1994; Glennerster et al, 1999). Inequality is a national problem that requires national solutions.

## Maximum wage and wealth taxes

One idea 'New Labour' has not imported from the United States is that of the maximum wage, a topic that has been seriously debated in North America since the 18th century (Pizzigati, 1992). During the depression in the 1930s millions of Americans supported the Share-Our-Wealth movement, which was led by Huey Long until his assassination in 1936 (Long, 1935). The popularity of the idea of a maximum wage led President Franklin Roosevelt to propose in April 1942 that "no American citizen ought to have a net income, after he has paid his taxes, of more than $25,000". However, there was insufficient support in Congress to implement this proposal (Paul, 1954).

There has also been a long history of philosophical debate on the size the maximum wage ought to be to ensure both a just and fair society and to maintain sufficient incentive for individuals to succeed. Plato in *The Laws* argued that the ideal ratio between the wealth of the richest and the wealth of the poorest was 4 to 1, whereas Aristotle thought the appropriate ratio was 5 to 1. However, modern American debates have tended to favour a ratio of 10 to 1 (Pizzigati, 1992). If this idea were accepted in Britain it would imply a maximum wage set at about £75,000 per annum, with a 100% tax above this amount.

Throughout the 1960s, 1970s and early 1980s the Labour Party was committed to the idea of a wealth tax as an effective measure for reducing inequality. However, none of the Labour governments of the 1960s and 1970s seriously attempted to implement such a tax even though it was a commitment in every Labour manifesto between 1972 and 1982. Even during the height of 'Thatcherism' significant public support for a wealth tax was evident. A Gallup poll in February 1986 for London Weekend Television's *Fortune* programme found that 42% supported a wealth tax, 45% opposed the idea and 13% were undecided (Rentoul, 1989). The political problems Fine Gael encountered when introducing a wealth tax in Ireland in the 1970s led some commentators to suggest that the British Labour Party did not have enough advisors with sufficient experience of accountancy and business to produce an effective wealth tax (Sandford and Morrissey, 1985). However, Argentina, Denmark, Egypt, France, Germany, India, the Netherlands, Norway, Pakistan, Spain and Switzerland all currently have successful wealth taxes (Spicer & Oppenheim, 1989).

# Conclusions

As we enter the 21st century, Britain is a society with greater disparities in absolute wealth than at any time in history. During the 1980s and early 1990s, successive Conservative governments actively pursued a range of policies which effectively took money from the poor and gave it to the rich. The long-term trend towards greater equality in income and wealth, which has been evident since the 15th century, was reversed, at least temporarily. The human costs of this increase in inequality have been immense and millions have unnecessarily had to lead lives blighted by the spectre of poverty and want. Britain is becoming a more divided society, a trend that affects all our lives.

The Labour government has paid lip service to reducing the amount of inequality. However, to date, their polices have so far had little impact compared with the scale of the problem.

In 1899, William Smart (Adam Smith Professor of political economy at the University of Glasgow), who was not a radical even by Victorian standards, concluded his book on *The distribution of income* as follows:

> A distribution which gives very large incomes to a comparatively small number of persons is deeply to be deplored.... The worst evil of these large incomes is, perhaps, least noticed. It is that they bind up the labour and the wages of the many with the demand of the few – keep the many putting forth the whole of their energies in producing wealth that does not even ennoble the lives of the few. (Smart, 1899, p 336)

This statement is as true today as it was a hundred years ago. Let us hope that there will be no need to repeat these words in another hundred years time. One of the prime purposes of social policy is to create a more integrated and less divided society. Greater prosperity and less inequality of income and wealth are measures of the level of progress and civilisation in any society. Yet, Conservative government policies during the 1980s and 1990s led to a more divided and less civilised society. There are also elements in the new Labour government who seem to be ambiguous about social progress. For example, Stephen Byers in his first speech as Trade and Industry Secretary argued that "the reality is that wealth creation is now more important than wealth distribution".

As we enter the new millennium, there are both more millionaires and more children and young adults forced to beg on the streets of every major city than at any time since the Second World War. The problem of homelessness was even noted by George Young (then Housing Minister) when he stated that homeless beggars in London were: "the sort of people you step on when you came out of the Opera" (*The Guardian*, 29 June 1991, p 2). If the price of providing people with enough money so that they were no longer forced to beg was fewer millionaires, then it would be a price worth paying.

**Notes**

[1] Further details of the Canberra Group's (the Expert Group on Household Income Statistics) meetings and discussions can be found at http://lissy.ceps.lu/canberra.htm

[2] In terms of the number of people involved.

[3] The 1994 ECHP data was the latest available at the time of writing.

[4] It must be noted that the ONS and Inland Revenue definitions of marketable wealth differ considerably. ONS statistics include pension and tenancy rights but exclude consumer durables, whereas the Inland Revenue definition includes consumer durables but excludes pensions and tenancy rights. It is therefore unsurprising that the ONS and Inland Revenue statistics differ.

[5] The limitations of the estate multiplier method were discussed in detail in the initial report of the RCDIW (1975). The Inland Revenue revised its methodology for estimating personal wealth in 1978 (Dunn and Hoffman, 1978a, 1978b) and 1985 (Good, 1990). However, significant problems remain. For example, more than 600 multipliers are needed to estimate the wealth of the 'richest' 35% of the population and the wealth data for the 'poorest' 65% of the adult population has to be imputed (guessed) (Good, 1990).

[6] This data is taken from various years of *Social Trends*. Due to methodological changes in the way wealth is estimated consistent data is only available back to 1976 (Atkinson et al, 1989; Good, 1990).

[7] See http://www.sunday-times.co.uk for the 1999 Rich List.

[8] However, the wealth of Rupert Murdoch (the proprietor of *The Sunday Times*) is not examined.

[9] Somewhat surprisingly, the OPCS did attempt to measure deprivation and standard of living among disabled adults and children in the Disability Surveys.

[10] Details of Bill Gates' current wealth can be found at http://www.webho.com/WealthClock.

# References

ABS (Australian Bureau of Statistics) (1995) *A provisional framework for household income, consumption, saving and wealth*, Canberra, Australia: Australian Government Publishing Service.

Alcock, P., Craig, C., Lawless, P., Pearson, S. and Robinson, D. (1998) *Inclusive regeneration: Local authorities' corporate strategies for tackling disadvantage*, Sheffield: CRESR, Sheffield Hallam University.

Atkinson, A.B. (1972) *Unequal shares*, Harmondsworth: Allen Lane.

Atkinson, A.B. (ed) (1973) *Wealth, income and inequality*, Harmondsworth: Penguin.

Atkinson, A.B. (1975) (2nd edn, 1983) *The economics of inequality*, Oxford: Clarendon Press.

Atkinson, A.B. and Stiglitz, J.E. (1980) *Lectures on public economics*, London: McGraw-Hill.

Atkinson, A.B., Gordon, J.P.F. and Harrison, A. (1989) 'Trends in the shares of top wealth holders in Britain 1923–1981', *Oxford Bulletin of Economics and Statistics*, vol 51, no 3.

Banks, J., Dilnot, A. and Low, H. (1994) *The distribution of wealth in the UK*, IFS Commentary No 45, London: Institute of Fiscal Studies.

Barclay, P. (chair) (1995) *Income and wealth, Volume 1: Report of the Inquiry Group*, York: Joseph Rowntree Foundation.

Barnes, J. and Lucas, H. (1975) *Educational priority*, London: HMSO.

Beresford, P. (ed) (1990) *The Sunday Times book of the rich*, London: Weidenfeld and Nicolson.

Beresford, P. and Boyd, S. (1999) *The Sunday Times rich list 1999: Britain's richest 1,000*, published with *The Sunday Times*, 11 April 1999 (also at http://www.sunday-times.co.uk).

Blair, T. (1999) *Beveridge Lecture*, Toynbee Hall, London, 18 March.

Bradshaw, J., Gordon, D., Levitas, R., Middleton, S., Pantazis, C., Payne, S. and Townsend, P. (1998) *Perceptions of poverty and social exclusion*, Report to the Joseph Rowntree Foundation, Bristol: Townsend Centre for International Poverty Research, University of Bristol.

Brown, G. and Cook, R. (1983) *Scotland the real divide: Poverty and deprivation in Scotland*, Edinburgh: Mainstream Publishing.

Burns, D. (1993) *Poll Tax rebellion*, Stirling: AK Press.

CDP (Community Development Project) (1977) *Gilding the ghetto: The state and the poverty experiments*, Nottingham: CDP/The Russell Press Limited.

Chadwick, M., O'Donoghue, C., Redmond, G. and Sutherland, H. (1997) *Neither Santa Claus nor Scrooge?*, Microsimulation Research Unit Note, Cambridge: DAE, University of Cambridge.

Chiozza-Money, L.G. (1905) *Riches and poverty*, London: Methuen.

DSS (Department of Social Security) (1991) *Households Below Average Income: Stocktaking Report of a Working Group*, London: Government Statistical Service.

DSS (1998) *Households Below Average Income: 1979-1996/97*, London: Government Statistical Service.

Dunn, A.T. and Hoffman, P.D.R.B. (1978a) 'The distribution of personal wealth', *Economic Trends*, no 301.

Dunn, A.T. and Hoffman, P.D.R.B. (1978b) *Current developments in Inland Revenue estimates of personal wealth*, Studies in Official Statistics 35, London: HMSO.

Erritt, M.J. and Nicholson, J.L. (1958) 'The 1955 Savings Survey', *Bulletin of the Oxford University Institute of Statistics*, vol 20, no 2, p 115.

Eurostat (1998) Unpublished analysis of the 1994 wave of the European Community Household Panel Survey.

Evandrou, M., Falkingham, J., Hills, J. and Le Grand, J. (1992) *The distribution of welfare benefits in kind*, Welfare State Programme Discussion Paper WSP/68, London: London School of Economics.

Forster, M. (1995) *Income distribution in OECD countries*, Paris: OECD.

Gilmour, I. (1992) *Dancing with dogma: Britain under Thatcherism*, London: Simon and Schuster.

Glennerster, H., Lupton, R., Noden, P. and Power, A. (1999) *Poverty, social exclusion and neighbourhood: Studying the area bases of social exclusion*, CASE Paper 22, London: London School of Economics.

Good, F.J. (1990) 'Estimates of the distribution of personable wealth: marketable wealth of individuals 1976 to 1988', *Economic Trends*, no 444, pp 137-57.

Goodman, A.J. and Webb, S. (1994) *For richer, for poorer: The changing distribution of income in the United Kingdom, 1961-1991*, London: Institute of Fiscal Studies.

Goodman, A., Johnson, P. and Webb, S. (1997) *Inequality in the UK*, Oxford: Oxford University Press.

Gordon, D. and Pantazis, C. (eds) (1997) *Breadline Britain in the 1990s*, Aldershot: Ashgate.

Gordon, D. and Spicker, P. (eds) (1999) *The international glossary on poverty*, New York, NY, and London: Zed Books.

Gordon, D. and Townsend, P. (1990) 'Measuring the poverty line', *Radical Statistics*, no 47, pp 5-12.

Gordon, D. and Townsend, P. (1998) 'Success measures: response to the government Green Paper on welfare reform', *Radical Statistics*, no 70, pp 58-69.

Hills, J. (1995) *Inquiry into income and wealth*, 2 vols, York: Joseph Rowntree Foundation.

Hills, J. (1998) *Income and wealth: The latest evidence*, York: Joseph Rowntree Foundation.

HM Treasury (1999) *The modernisation of Britain's tax and benefit system number four: Tackling poverty and extending opportunity*, London: HM Treasury.

Howarth, C., Kenway, P., Palmer, G. and Street, C. (1998) *Monitoring poverty and social exclusion*, York: Joseph Rowntree Foundation.

ILO (International Labour Organisation) (1971) *Scope, methods and users of Family Expenditure Surveys, Report III: Twelfth International Conference of Labour Statisticians*, Geneva: ILO.

ILO (1992) *Report 1: General Report: Fifteenth International Conference of Labour Statisticians*, Geneva: ILO.

ILO (1993) *Report of the Conference: Fifteenth International Conference of Labour Statisticians*, Geneva: ILO.

Immervoll, H., Mitton, L., O'Donoghue, C. and Sutherland, H. (1999) *Budgeting for fairness? The distributional efffects of three Labour budgets*, Microsimulation Research Unit Note MU/RN/32, Cambridge: DAE, University of Cambridge (http://www.econ.cam.ac.uk/dae/mu/budget.htm).

Knight, I. (1980) *The feasibility of conducting a national wealth survey in Great Britain*, New Methodology Series NM6, London: OPCS.

Lee, P., Murie, A. and Gordon, D. (1995) *Area measures of deprivation*, Birmingham: CURS, University of Birmingham.

Long, H.P. (1935) *Share our wealth: Every man a king*, Washington, DC: National Books.

Mack, J. and Lansley, S. (1985) *Poor Britain*, London: Allen and Unwin.

OUP (Oxford University Press) (1989) (2nd edn) *Oxford English Dictionary*, Oxford: Oxford University Press.

Paul, R.E. (1954) *Taxation in the United States*, Boston, MA: Little Brown and Company.

Pizzigati, S. (1992) *The maximum wage: A common-sense prescription for revitalizing America – by taxing the very rich*, New York, NY: The Apex Press.

RCDIW (Royal Commission on the Distribution of Income and Wealth) (1975) *Report 1: Initial report on the Standing Reference*, London: HMSO.

RCDIW (The Diamond Commission) (1978) *Report No 6: Lower Incomes*, Cm 7175, London: HMSO.

Rentoul, J. (1989) *The rich get richer: The growth of inequality in Britain in the 1980s*, London: Unwin.

Reynolds, M. (1992) *Uncollectable: The story of the Poll Tax revolt*, Manchester: Greater Manchester Anti-Poll Tax Federation.

Robson, B., Bradford, M., Deas, I., Hall, E., Harrison, E., Parkinson, M., Evans, R., Garside, P., Harding, A. and Robinson, F. (1994) *Assessing the impact of urban policy*, London: HMSO.

Rubinstein, W.D. (1986) *Wealth and inequality in Britain*, London: Faber and Faber.

Saltow, L. (1968) 'Long run changes in British income inequality', *Economic History Review*, 2nd Series, no 21.

Sandford, C. and Morrissey, O. (1985) *The Irish wealth tax*, Dublin: ESRI.

Scott, J. (1993) 'Wealth and privilege', in A. Sinfield (ed) *Poverty, inequality and justice*, New Waverley Papers, Social Policy Series No 6, Edinburgh: University of Edinburgh, pp 19-28.

Scott, J. (1994) *Poverty and wealth: Citizenship, deprivation and privilege*, Harlow: Longman.

SEU (Social Exclusion Unit) (1998) *Bringing Britain together: A national strategy for neighbourhood renewal*, Cm 4045, London: The Stationery Office.

Smart, W. (1912) (2nd edn) *The distribution of income*, London: Macmillan.

Smith, G.R. (1999) *Area-based initiatives: The rationale for and options for area targeting*, CASE Paper 25, London: London School of Economics.

Social Security Committee (1995) *Low income statistics: Low income families 1989-92*, London: HMSO.

Social Trends (1995) *Social Trends 1970–1995*, CD-ROM, London: Central Statistical Office.

Social Trends (1999) *Social Trends 29*, London: The Stationery Office.

Spicer & Oppenheim (1989) (3rd edn) *The Spicer & Oppenheim guide to personal taxes around the world*, London: Spicer & Oppenheim International.

Sutherland, H. (1999) *The impact of the 1999 Finance Bill on children*, London: Save the Children.

Titmuss R.M. (1962) *Income distribution and social change*, London: Allen and Unwin.

Townsend, P. (1979) *Poverty in the United Kingdom*, London: Penguin Books.

Townsend, P. (1993) *The international analysis of poverty*, Milton Keynes: Harvester Wheatsheaf.

Townsend, P. (1996) 'The struggle for independent statistics on poverty', in R. Levitas and W. Guy (eds) *Interpreting official statistics*, London and New York, NY: Routledge, pp 26-44.

Townsend, P. and Gordon, D. (1989) *Low income households, Memorandum of Evidence to the House of Commons Social Services Committee*, 579, pp 45-73. Also published as Townsend, P. and Gordon, D. (1991) 'What is enough? New evidence on poverty allowing the definition of a minimum benefit', in M. Alder, C. Bell, J. Clasen, and A. Sinfield (eds) *The sociology of social security*, Edinburgh: Edinburgh University Press, pp 35-69.

Townsend, P. and Gordon, D. (1992) *Unfinished statistical business on low income?: A review of new proposals by the Department of Social Security for the production of public information on poverty*, Statistical Monitoring Unit Report No 3, Bristol: University of Bristol.

UN (United Nations) (1977) *Provisional guidelines on statistics of the distribution of income, consumption and accumulation of households, studies in methods*, Series M No 61, New York, NY: UN.

UN (1989) *National Household Survey Capability Program: Household Income and Expenditure Surveys: A technical study*, New York, NY: UN.

UN (1992) *Revised system of national accounts (provisional)*, August 1992 (to be presented to and adopted at the 27th session of the Statistical Commission, February–March 1993).

UNDP (United Nations Development Programme) (1999) *Human Development Report 1999*, Oxford: Oxford University Press.

Walker, R. (ed) (1999) *Ending child poverty: Popular welfare for the 21st century?*, Bristol: The Policy Press.

Wedgwood, J. (1929) *The economics of inheritance*, Harmondsworth: Penguin.

# THREE

# Inequalities in employment: problems of spatial divergence

*Ivan Turok*

## Introduction

Access to employment is crucial to people's ability to participate in many of the economic and social opportunities of society. Inequality in access to jobs contributes substantially to poverty and social exclusion, with debilitating effects on the morale, health, family status and even social networks of individuals and communities. Access to employment is also important for the efficient functioning of the economy. Spatial variations may create imbalances between the supply and demand for labour in different places and constrain the rate at which firms and the economy can grow. Labour shortages may be created in some places and surpluses in others.

This chapter considers some of the key dimensions of labour market inequality in Britain. It focuses on the geography of employment and unemployment and examines their incidence in relation to the issues of gender and socioeconomic status or occupation. Contradictory views exist about the current scale and distribution of unemployment. The Bank of England believes that the labour market is tight and that spatial disparities are insignificant. In contrast, the Unemployment Unit's broad measure of labour market slack is 4.7 million unemployed with wide regional variations (Bivand, 1999a). There are tentative signs of a shift in government thinking on the subject since Labour was elected. Its 1998 Budget Report observed that: "Around 11.75 per cent, or almost 4.25m, of working age people in the UK are still without work and wanting a job ... the number of inactive people who say they want a job as a proportion of the adult population is higher in the UK than in any other EU country" (HM Treasury, 1998a, p 86).

This chapter will argue that unemployment is not only high but, more importantly, is unevenly distributed across the country and is particularly high in Britain's major cities. This reflects the severe decline in employment over several decades, particularly of manual jobs in manufacturing, and the lack of suitable alternative opportunities accessible to the affected communities. Current labour market disparities are important for economic and social reasons and threaten to undermine some of Labour's flagship policies, such as the New Deal. Many of the previous government's policies disregarded such disparities. There was a tendency to believe that market mechanisms would remove them through out-migration, outward commuting and upward occupational mobility. This chapter examines the extent to which this has happened in practice.

The first section analyses the pattern of labour demand, comparing the scale and composition of employment trends in the cities during the 1990s with earlier decades and the rest of the country. Despite the growth of service industries, streamlining of local government, standardisation of local taxes on business and a more consensual approach to urban policy, the pattern of relative and absolute job loss in the cities has continued. The second section considers the consequences for the population, including people's ability to adapt through upskilling, out-migration and outward commuting. The difficulties of 'adjustment' have led to an increasing imbalance between labour supply and demand in the cities – a 'jobs gap' – particularly for men. This shortfall in employment needs to be taken more seriously by the government as a source of hardship and social dislocation and an obstacle to effective economic management and welfare reform.

The focus of this chapter is on the 20 British cities which in 1991 had a population of greater than 250,000. They include eight conurbations with more than three quarters of a million people and 12 free-standing cities with between one quarter and half a million population (Figure 3.1). Together they comprise just less than two fifths of Britain's population and just more than two fifths of its jobs. All other parts of Britain, including smaller cities, towns and rural areas, are grouped together in an all-encompassing category called 'towns and rural areas'.

*Figure 3.1:* **Cities in Britain with population greater than 250,000 (1991)**

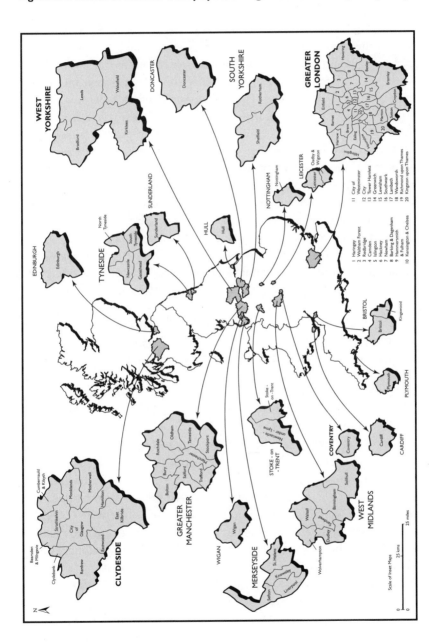

## Patterns of labour demand

During the 1950s, employment in Britain's major cities grew more slowly than in the towns and rural areas. Urban employment began to decline in the 1960s and the scale of decline increased and in the 1970s spread to almost all cities (Table 3.1). The increasing divergence from the rest of the country reflected a growing 'urban–rural shift' in economic activity, coupled with an accelerating process of deindustrialisation and deterioration in national economic fortunes (Fothergill et al, 1985).

Recent commentators have asserted that there has been a revival of cities in the last decade, associated with the growth of high-level business services, global financial markets and the 'knowledge economy'. Cities are alleged to be privileged locations because of their specialised workforces, advanced support services, universities and tele-communications infrastructure (for a review, see Amin and Graham, 1997). Others have argued that the growth of cultural industries, the media, entertainment and other consumption activities have led to a rediscovery of cities because of their high density, social diversity, vitality and 'richness' (see, for example, Comedia and Demos, 1997).

Table 3.1 includes the decade to 1991, a period of employment growth in Britain. The bottom row shows that the gap between cities and other areas widened further in the 1980s, and at a slightly faster rate than in the 1970s. There was very considerable growth of more than 1.1 million jobs (nearly 10 %) in the towns and rural areas, broad stability in the free-standing cities but substantial decline of more than half a million jobs in the conurbations.

Manufacturing made up the bulk of the job losses in the 1960s and 1970s. The decline was steepest in the conurbations, with 1.6 million of such jobs lost during that period. The losses in the free-standing cities for the same period amounted to 0.4 million. In the towns and rural areas, manufacturing jobs increased by half a million in the 1960s but fell back in the 1970s, as manufacturing contracted in the country as a whole. About two thirds of the 1971–81 decline was concentrated in the period 1979-81. This was linked to the sudden raising of interest and exchange rates, which made it difficult for manufacturers to compete abroad and induced a deep recession.

Comparing the 1980s with the 1970s, there was much continuity in the rate of manufacturing decline across each type of area (Table 3.1), although the concentration of the change in the latter part of the 1971-81 period should not be forgotten. The conurbations continued to haemorrhage manufacturing jobs in the 1980s, at roughly twice the rate

**Table 3.1: Changes in employment by area type (1951–91)**

| Change in employment | Conurbations: inner areas 000s | (%) | Conurbations: outer areas 000s | (%) | Free-standing cities 000s | (%) | Towns and rural areas 000s | (%) | Britain 000s | (%) |
|---|---|---|---|---|---|---|---|---|---|---|
| *Manufacturing* | | | | | | | | | | |
| 1951-61 | -143 | (-8.0) | +84 | (+5.0) | -21 | (-2.0) | +453 | (+14.0) | +374 | (+5.0) |
| 1961-71 | -428 | (-26.1) | -217 | (-10.3) | -93 | (-6.2) | +489 | (+12.5) | -255 | (-3.3) |
| 1971-81 | -447 | (-36.8) | -480 | (-32.6) | -311 | (-28.6) | -717 | (-17.2) | -1,929 | (-25.7) |
| 1981-91 | -308 | (-42.9) | -357 | (-33.6) | -193 | (-28.3) | -558 | (-17.8) | -1,407 | (-25.2) |
| *Services* | | | | | | | | | | |
| 1951-61 | +205 | (6.2) | +164 | (+8.2) | +166 | (+106) | +714 | (+11.0) | +1,246 | (+9.3) |
| 1961-71 | -272 | (-7.8) | +262 | (+12.1) | +103 | (+5.9) | +1,037 | (+14.4) | +1,125 | (+7.7) |
| 1971-81 | -183 | (-5.7) | +272 | (+11.2) | +144 | (+7.8) | +1,261 | (+15.3) | +1,457 | (+9.2) |
| 1981-91 | -84 | (-2.8) | +190 | (+7.0) | +173 | (+8.7) | +1,712 | (+18.0) | +1,983 | (+11.5) |
| *Total* | | | | | | | | | | |
| 1951-61 | +43 | (+1.0) | +231 | (+6.0) | +140 | (+6.0) | +1,060 | (+10.0) | +1,490 | (+6.9) |
| 1961-71 | -643 | (-14.8) | +19 | (+0.6) | +54 | (+2.4) | +1,022 | (+8.5) | +320 | (+1.4) |
| 1971-81 | -538 | (-14.6) | -236 | (-7.1) | -150 | (-5.4) | +404 | (+3.5) | -590 | (-2.5) |
| 1981-91 | -392 | (-10.4) | -167 | (-4.4) | -20 | (-0.7) | +1,154 | (+9.1) | +576 | (+2.5) |

*Note:* These are workplace-based figures. It was not possible to reproduce the exact employment figures generated by the Begg et al (1986) study, so the 1981-91 figures are based on newly-created 1981 employment totals. Public services have also been amalgamated with private services because of problems in securing consistent data on the latter. London is included in the conurbations.

*Source:* Census of Population, Special Workplace Statistics

of towns and rural areas. This continued to be the sector changing most in the cities and the biggest influence on overall employment trends.

Growth in the service industry did not compensate. The increase was very uneven across the country, partly reflecting the linkages that exist between manufacturing and services within local economies. Service employment increased by 18% (1.7 million) in the towns and rural areas during the 1980s but by less than 4% (0.27 million) in the cities. The growth of services in the towns and rural areas accelerated between the 1970s and 1980s but slowed down in the major cities.

## Contemporary patterns

Figure 3.2 shows more recent data, indexed to help compare the different types of area. There was a continuing divergence between the conurbations, free-standing cities and the rest of Britain. Looking through the pattern of peaks and troughs associated with the economic cycle, employment in the conurbations has continued to decline. Meanwhile, employment outside the cities has continued to expand. During the period 1981-96, the cities lost half a million jobs (5% of their 1981 total) while the rest of the country gained more than three times as many (almost 1.7 million, or 15 % of their 1981 total) (Table 3.2).

**Figure 3.2: Change in employment by type of area (1981-96) (1981=100)**

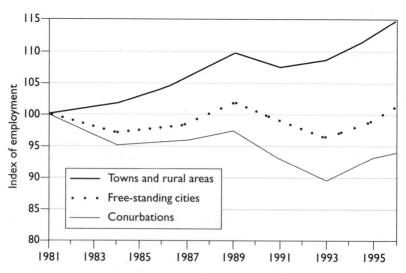

*Source:* Annual Employment Survey, via NOMIS

*Table 3.2:* Changes in employment by sector and area type (1981-96)

| Change in employment | London | | Other conurbations | | Free-standing cities | | Towns and rural areas | | Britain | |
|---|---|---|---|---|---|---|---|---|---|---|
| | 000s | (%) | 000s | (%) | 000s | (%) | 000s | (%) | 000s | (%) |
| Manufacturing | -402 | (-59) | -615 | (-41) | -185 | (-35) | -748 | (-23) | -1,950 | (-32) |
| Finance and business services | +353 | (+52) | +236 | (+55) | +129 | (+74) | +939 | (+95) | +1,657 | (+73) |
| Distribution, hotels and catering | +20 | (+3) | +85 | (+10) | +34 | (+10) | +775 | (+36) | +914 | (+23) |
| Transport and communication | -96 | (-26) | -26 | (-9) | -24 | (-21) | +64 | (+10) | -82 | (-6) |
| Public services | -23 | (-3) | +155 | (+17) | +117 | (+31) | +738 | (+29) | +987 | (+22) |
| Other services | +47 | (+28) | +32 | (+21) | +21 | (+36) | +248 | (+76) | +348 | (+49) |
| Total employment | -212 | (-6) | -289 | (-6) | +19 | (+1) | +1,675 | (+15) | +1,193 | (+6) |

*Note:* Total employment also includes energy, construction and extractive sectors.
*Source:* ONS (Annual Employment Survey) via NOMIS

So, the urban–rural differential in employment has continued to widen. The cities have done less well than the rest of the country in periods of recession and recovery. The period 1993-96 may have prompted some of the recent speculation about a revival of the cities because of the upturn in employment in the cities that occurred then. This seems to be associated with the upswing of the economic cycle rather than representing a reversal of previous trends. The cities' share of national employment (excluding London) fell from 27.4 % in 1993 to 26.8 % in 1996, while the employment level for the rest of the country increased from 58 % to 58.2 %. So, the gap between the cities and other areas still widened during this period.

Sharpening the focus, there has been a continuing divergence between the inner and outer areas of the conurbations since 1981. Employment in the conurbation cores fell by no less than 12% between 1981 and 1996 but by only 1% in the outer areas. Greater London has been different in this respect, with the same rate of decline in employment affecting the inner and outer boroughs. The really striking feature is the great divergence between Greater London and the rest of the South East. Between 1981 and 1996 London lost 212,000 jobs (6%), while the rest of the South East gained 556,000 (15%). This reflected the continued deindustrialisation of London, the strong decentralisation of jobs and growing economic diversity of the South East.

## Sectoral differences

Looking at more recent evidence, the decline of manufacturing continued after 1991. Its direct share of employment in Britain fell from almost 30% (6 million) in 1981 to only 18% (4 million) by 1996. Its indirect contributions to the economy through its extensive backward and forward linkages, its spillovers from technology and disproportionate export earnings add greatly to its significance. Manufacturing's local linkages meant that its faster decline in the cities had adverse knock-on effects for other local sectors.

Looking in more detail at the service sector, Table 3.2 shows that employment growth in almost every major category was greatest in the towns and rural areas and lowest or negative in the conurbations. London's performance was at least as bad as the other conurbations. Its overall percentage decline was the same because the conurbations performed worse in energy, construction and extractive sectors, which are not included as separate categories in the table.

The fastest growing sector of all has been business services, including professional services (such as accounting, marketing, consultancy and legal activities), computing services, recruitment and estate agencies, security services, industrial cleaning and renting of equipment. Many of these services have benefited from sub-contracting by manufacturing and other industries. Increased demand from households for various financial services has also been important, arising from rising incomes and a shift from state welfare to private pensions and health insurance. The fact that employment growth for business services was fastest in the towns and rural areas appears to contradict the idea that cities are particularly good locations for these activities and 'motors' for contemporary forms of economic growth, although more detailed research would help to check this.

Distribution (including retailing), hotel and catering industries serve consumers and businesses, so their performance is responsive to the state of the economy. They have experienced increasing competition in the last decade and have responded by seeking to reduce labour and other costs. Employment has grown steadily since the 1970s, particularly outside the cities. This reflects the decentralisation of population and industry, although other factors may also have been involved. There is little sign that increased private consumption in the form of entertainment, eating out, high-order retailing and tourism have benefited the cities especially, prompting questions of those who state that cultural industries and consumption are the drivers of urban regeneration.

Transport and communications also serve consumers and businesses. They have been subject to considerable reorganisation as a result of privatisation, deregulation and corporate takeovers since the early 1980s. Intense competition and pressure to cut costs have affected levels of employment and led to more flexible patterns of temporary, part-time and sub-contracted staff. Employment in this sector declined slightly in Britain as a whole, and the position of the cities deteriorated compared with the towns and rural areas, where jobs actually increased.

Public services include health, education, public administration and defence. Most are not marketed or sold directly, although there has been growth within private health and education in the last two decades. Employment in public services has been more stable historically than other sectors, including core functions for large population centres (such as hospitals and higher education providers). There was little difference in the growth of public services employment between the free-standing cities and the towns and rural areas during the 1980s and 1990s, although the conurbations lagged behind. Nevertheless, the differential was much less than for other sectors.

Overall, the urban–rural disparity continued to widen across all sectors, against suggestions of a revival in urban fortunes. This consistency suggests that there are general processes at work. Statistical techniques to identify these processes indicate that the particular industrial mix of cities has not caused their poor performance (Turok and Edge, 1999). Local factors seem to be more important, and a major recurring feature is the physical constraint on development in urban areas (Fothergill et al, 1985; Townsend, 1993). In some cases the density of the built environment constrains the increasing floorspace requirements of industry. A lack of investment in redeveloping vacant and derelict land and buildings has limited the space available to accommodate business growth and attract inward investment. Towns and rural areas have had more land available for development, especially 'greenfield' sites with greater amenities, good motorway access and no costs of recycling land.

The cities that have performed relatively well, such as Leeds (in terms of total jobs) and Sunderland (in terms of manufacturing), seem to have been more active than the rest in improving their physical fabric and infrastructure, making serviced land and premises available for economic development, protecting land from retail pressures, and replacing or modernising older buildings. Cities such as Glasgow, Liverpool and Manchester have been doubly penalised by having narrow administrative boundaries that restrict the development of large sites on the edge of the built-up area where there is good access to the strategic road network.

## Changes in employment status and occupation

There have also been differential changes in the composition of employment. Full-time jobs, traditionally for men, fell by nearly 1.5 million (13%) between 1981 and 1996, while part-time jobs, traditionally for women, expanded by over 1.4 million (38%). Part-time jobs for men increased by half a million (almost 90%) for the same period. The growth of almost two million part-time jobs reflects the expansion of service industries and increased female participation in the workforce. It is also linked with the wider trend towards 'flexibility' in the economy, apparent in service providers having irregular labour requirements, especially where direct customer contact is involved.

There was a systematic urban–rural difference in the distribution of gains and losses between 1981 and 1996 (Figure 3.3). The towns and rural areas secured the lion's share of part-time job growth, as well as full-time jobs traditionally done by women. The fundamental problem for the cities has been the loss of full-time traditionally male jobs – the conurbations lost nearly one quarter of their 1981 stock, equivalent to more than half a million jobs. This was strongly linked to the decline of manufacturing. The conurbations also had the smallest proportionate growth of other jobs. The modest growth in traditionally female part-time employment would have done little to offset the effect on household incomes of the loss of full-time male jobs.

*Figure 3.3:* **Change in employment by status (1981-96) (000s)**

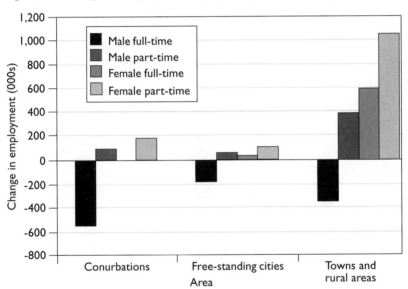

*Source:* Annual Employment Survey, via NOMIS

The changes in broad occupation are equally significant. Manual (blue-collar) jobs in Britain fell by 11% between 1981 and 1991, while non-manual (white-collar) jobs expanded by 16 % (using Census of Population data). Within the non-manual category, professional and managerial jobs increased by 28%, while junior non-manual jobs increased by only 0.6%.

The towns and rural areas gained many more non-manual jobs than the cities and lost far fewer manual jobs (Figure 3.4). Britain's conurbations and cities lost between one fifth and one sixth of their manual jobs during the 1980s. They gained half as many professional and managerial jobs but these are unlikely to have been much of a substitute because upward mobility from the latter to the former is low, especially among men (Elias and Bynner, 1997). The contraction of skilled manual occupations has tended to result in downward movement for men into less skilled, lower paid jobs or unemployment and casual work, especially for those with few qualifications. The opportunities for workers displaced from manual jobs in the cities to find work locally were small, especially as junior non–manual jobs also contracted in the cities.

*Figure 3.4:* **Change in employment by occupation (SEG) (1981-91) (%)**

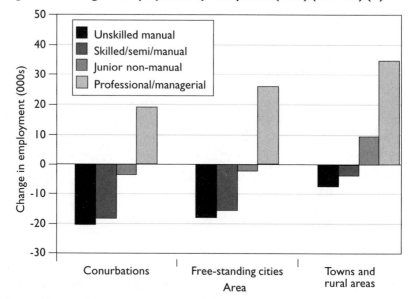

*Source:* Census of Population, 1981 and 1991, Special Workplace Statistics

Manual employment declined in the cities because of the contraction of manufacturing. This was the main source of skilled and semi–skilled manual jobs. Figure 3.5 shows the occupational breakdown for each sector discussed in the previous section. It relates to 1991, after the major decline in manufacturing in the 1980s, yet it shows the continued importance of manufacturing for manual jobs, along with transport and communications. The distribution, hotels and catering sector provides most unskilled manual jobs. The problem for the cities is that employment fell in the transport and communications sector and only increased marginally in distribution, hotels and catering (Table 3.2). Consequently these industries did little to offset the sharp decline in manufacturing. Financial and business services and public services provide relatively few manual jobs, so their growth in the cities provided few accessible opportunities for people displaced from manufacturing.

*Figure 3.5:* **Occupational category (SEG) by industry sector (1991) (%)**

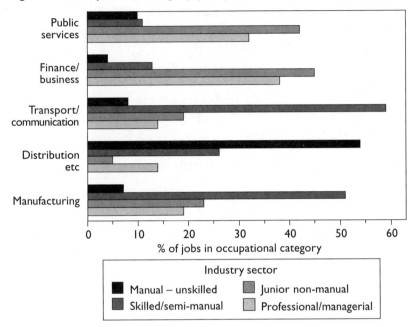

*Source:* Census of Population, Special Workplace Statistics

## Consequences for labour supply

How have people been affected by these changes and how well have market mechanisms reduced the employment disparities? The simplest way of examining the consequences is through the framework of labour market accounts (LMAs). LMAs relate changes in employment to natural (demographic) changes in the size of the workforce, net migration, net commuting, economic participation and changes in recorded unemployment. To calculate these components it is necessary to integrate data from different sources and time periods (Turok and Edge, 1999).

Looking first at the overall pattern of change for men, some 755,000 jobs were lost from the 20 largest cities between 1981 and 1991 (Table 3.3). This was equivalent to 12.2% of the 1981 male workforce. Interestingly, this level of job loss was 25% greater than in the coalfields, where net male job loss was 9.2% for the same period (Beatty et al, 1997a). Despite the urban job losses, the overall level of male unemployment recorded by the Census actually fell by about 78,000 during this period. Table 3.3 helps to account for how and why this happened. The change in unemployment is an arithmetic function of the loss of jobs plus the natural change in the workforce (the growth or decline in the working age population resulting from different sized cohorts entering and leaving this age group), minus net out-migration (people in the workforce moving out of the area in relation to those moving into it), minus changes in net out-commuting (people in the workforce commuting elsewhere to work or reductions in ex-urban residents commuting into the cities), minus the decline in the economically active population, minus people on government training and work experience schemes.

**Table 3.3: Labour market accounts for Britain's cities (1981-91)**

|  |  | Male | | Female | |
|---|---|---|---|---|---|
|  |  | **Number** | **%*** | **Number** | **%*** |
| Loss of employment | | 755,000 | 12.2 | -44,000 | -1.1 |
| PLUS | natural increase in workforce | 134,000 | 2.2 | 59,000 | 1.4 |
| MINUS | net out-migration | 459,000 | 7.4 | 164,000 | 3.9 |
| MINUS | change in net out-commuting | 77,000 | 1.2 | -61,000 | -1.5 |
| MINUS | decline in economic activity rate | 338,000 | 5.4 | -154,000 | -3.7 |
| MINUS | number on government schemes | 93,000 | 1.5 | 59,000 | 1.4 |
| EQUALS | change in unemployment | -78,000 | -1.2 | 7,000 | 0.2 |

*Note:* * As a percentage of the economically active men/women of working age in 1981.

*Source:* Census of Population, 1981 and 1991

## Migration

The single largest response to the loss of jobs was net out-migration. This reduced male labour supply in the cities by up to 459,000, or 7.4% of the 1981 economically active male population. This is likely to be an overestimate by up to two or three percentage points because of underenumeration in the 1991 Census of Population (Turok and Edge, 1999; Beatty et al, 1997a). In fact underenumeration is likely to affect the precise figure for most components of the LMAs, particularly for men, although probably not their order of magnitude and size in relation to each other. Little can be done about this in practice, because of the lack of other evidence. All published research on the subject agrees that net out-migration from the major cities in recent decades has been substantial.

The effectiveness of migration as an adjustment mechanism depends on who moves out. Other research has shown that migration is weakest among manual workers, the unemployed and economically inactive people of working age. Most migrants from cities are "people in higher-paid white-collar work and of younger working age ... (out-migration) is a selective process that favours better-off people" (Champion, 1998, p 73; see also Atkins et al, 1996). They are typically people with jobs who own their own homes moving elsewhere to live and/or work, or young adults leaving to study or work in other places. Residential preferences feature prominently, since this type of migration is not just a response to job loss.

The composition of *net* migration is more important than the characteristics of those who move out, since migration is a two-way process with substantial in- and out-flows. Recent research on the conurbations has established that there is "a strong positive relationship between social class and the rate of net out-migration to the rest of Britain, with the professional category recording the highest rates of net loss and the two groups of manual workers (skilled and others) recording the lowest" (Champion and Ford, 1998, p i). The clear implication is that migration is a poor adjustment mechanism for urban residents vulnerable to unemployment.

Another problem with migration concerns the cumulative environmental, economic and social consequences for the areas left behind, including surplus housing, over-capacity in schools, under-used community infrastructure, general neighbourhood decline and ultimate abandonment. These issues are becoming increasingly important and costly to the public purse in many northern cities (Power and Mumford, 1999).

## Economic participation

The second largest response by men to the decline in labour demand was a reduction in the economic activity rate. This reduced male labour supply in the cities by up to one third of a million, or 5.4% of the 1981 workforce. These were people who apparently withdrew from either employment or recorded unemployment. The 5.4% figure is not much less than that of 6.8% found by Beatty et al (1997a) for the coalfields. They argue that most of these people were not really inactive and out of the workforce – that labour supply had not actually been reduced by this amount. They were better described as the 'hidden unemployed', many of whom were available for and seeking work, but who transferred to the category of sickness (or incapacity benefits) because of the difficulty in finding work and because the welfare payments are slightly higher for some of them since they are not means-tested.

The existence and spatial incidence of hidden unemployment is vital for national employment programmes, urban and regional policy, and judgments about the state of the labour market for the purposes of macro-economic management. The Labour government has shown signs of recognising the growth of inactivity and hidden unemployment in the context of welfare reform (see, for example, Secretary of State for Social Security, 1998). However, its analysis has focused on the characteristics of the groups affected (such as lone parents, young people, older men and people on incapacity benefit) and the specific factors thought to be responsible for their difficulty in securing employment (such as family breakdown, benefit dependency, lack of work incentives and motivation, low skills and detachment from the labour market). The circumstances of each group are typically analysed in isolation from the others, so separate explanations emerge which usually focus on supply-side obstacles. They also often confuse the symptoms of problems with their causes.

There are many ways in which the geographical distribution of particular groups coincide. For instance, areas with a high incidence of lone parents tend to have high proportions of youth unemployment, long-term sickness, workless households, and so on (Turok and Webster, 1998). This distribution is related to that for recorded unemployment and the decline in male employment, indicating that an essential part of the explanation for the growth of these phenomena is bound to be the deficient demand for labour, which is greatest in the cities and coalfields. A recent study which compared the ratio of unfilled job vacancies (a measure of labour demand) to the level of recorded unemployment (labour supply) in winter 1997 for Travel-to-Work areas concluded: "Buoyant labour markets tend to be semi-urban or sub-urban in nature while inner cities, old industrial conurbations and remote rural areas remain depressed. The 'boom' areas occupy a swathe of semi-urban Britain running from the Home Counties to the Welsh Borders ..." (Employment Policy Institute, 1998, p 8).

Registered unemployment statistics, recently published by the Office for National Statistics (ONS), for Local Authority Areas (and corrected for errors caused by imbalances between in- and out-commuting) show that the major urban areas have by far the highest rates of claimant unemployment in the country (Webster, 1999a). They include Merseyside, Inner London, Teeside, Manchester, Clydeside, Tyneside, Hull and Birmingham. Monthly reports from the House of Commons Library on unemployment by constituency show that most of these cities and their hinterlands also experienced increases in recorded unemployment throughout 1998, while towns and rural areas dominated by services, particularly in the South of England, saw steady reductions in unemployment for the same year (Webster, 1999b).

The Labour Force Survey has confirmed a large increase in economic inactivity among older male manual workers in cities during the last two decades:

> Inactivity has risen for all male groups, but is concentrated amongst those aged 50 and over and among the least skilled (and) in high unemployment regions, typically urban areas.... One in three men with no formal educational qualifications are now inactive, up from just 5% in 1979. (Gregg and Wadsworth, 1998, p 9, p 3)

It also shows that some sections of the supposedly inactive population are seeking employment and some do manage to get jobs, leading to the conclusion that "current measures (of unemployment) may fail to account for a significant body of individuals who could be considered as part of the potential labour force" (Gregg and Wadsworth, 1998, p 9).

More extensive research on the geography of inactivity has confirmed that it is highest in the inner cities and coalfields. This research reiterated the need to broaden the definition of unemployment to include some of the inactive: "In general, the greater the degree of labour market disadvantage in an area, the smaller the proportion of people who would like to work who are included within conventional definitions of unemployment" (Green and Owen, 1998, p ix). Our research found that the rate of increase in inactivity was highest in cities where job loss was greatest, such as Liverpool, Glasgow, Manchester, Newcastle and Doncaster (Turok and Edge, 1999).

Beatty et al (1997b) tried to produce systematic estimates of 'real' unemployment for every area of Britain, including some people who are officially classed as inactive but are actually seeking work. The conurbation cores and coalfields came out highest with real male unemployment rates of 25-35% in January 1997, while some of the medium-sized towns of South East England emerged lowest with rates of only around 4-5%. Liverpool's estimate was 37.4%, Glasgow 35.3% and Manchester 33.8%, compared with the official male claimant count rates of 20.7%, 16.7% and 19.6% respectively.

All this evidence suggests that declining demand for labour has been a powerful influence on rising inactivity. It also indicates that the reduction in the economic activity rate is a deceptive response to job loss, since many of those classed as inactive should properly be regarded as unemployed. In any case, inactivity is an unsatisfactory adjustment mechanism in many ways because of its adverse consequences for the health, welfare and income of the individuals and communities most affected.

## Government schemes

The third major response to job loss is characterised by the number of men engaged in temporary government programmes such as Youth Training and Employment Training. Most were likely to be seeking employment but participating in these programmes because of the lack of available jobs. People on these schemes were not identified as a separate category in 1981 but were split among the numbers in employment and education. The programmes expanded during the 1980s as unemployment rose, so it seems reasonable to include them as a separate category in 1991. If the total increase in inactivity plus those on government schemes were added to recorded male unemployment, it would be raised by 430,000 or 7% higher than it appeared to be in 1991.

## Net out-commuting

There was only a small increase in net outward commuting for men (1.2%). This suggests that outward commuting was not a significant response to employment decline. Other research on the 1991 Census has confirmed the "high dependence of inner city residents upon inner city job opportunities.... The low levels of 'reverse commuting' by city residents to satellite employment centres show that rural economic growth is not of much benefit to the urban workforce" (Atkins et al, 1996, p 125, p 6). This applies even more strongly to manual workers, since they are less likely to be car owners and therefore commute shorter distances than others on average. Research in Glasgow has shown the importance of distance as an employment barrier, particularly for residents of deprived housing estates seeking access to jobs in the outer conurbation (Glasgow City Council, 1996).

Most research on the subject of spatial obstacles to employment has been undertaken in the USA. The issue has gained urgency by recent US welfare reforms, since strict time-limits on benefits oblige welfare recipients to find 'entry-level' jobs. A recent review concluded that: "there is a 'spatial mismatch' between where workers live and where jobs are located, and low-income workers often have no easy way to travel between home and work" (Pugh, 1998, p 1). In terms of policy: "Federal, state and local leaders must recognise that spatial mismatch is not inevitable, and they must cease thinking of low-income job access as an issue having to do with mobility. The goal must be to bring jobs and people closer together, through controlling sprawl, increasing affordable housing in the suburbs and strengthening urban economies" (Pugh, 1998, p 3).

## Female labour market accounts

The LMAs for women show a very different pattern. First, the number of jobs actually increased during the 1981-91 period, albeit by a modest 44,000. Unemployment also increased very slightly overall, although this is mainly attributable to the disproportionate influence of London, where unemployment increased against the general trend. Second, there was growth in economic participation among women. This increased labour supply in the cities by 154,000, or 3.7% of the 1981 workforce. The growth in female economic activity rates tended to be strongest where job growth was greatest, in cities such as Plymouth, Bristol, West Yorkshire and Cardiff. This suggests a demand-led explanation, with women being drawn into the workforce by the availability of jobs.

Net out-migration was still significant for women – in apparent contradiction to the increase in employment. This may be because other factors influenced these decisions, including the migration behaviour of their partners and their residential preferences. The disaggregated figures indicate that cities with large job losses affecting women had greater increases in net out-migration (particularly Merseyside, Clydeside and Greater Manchester), whereas cities with job gains had little change in net out-migration (Plymouth, Cardiff, Bristol and Edinburgh) (Turok and Edge, 1999). In general, changes in net out-migration offset the effect of rising economic activity rates on the overall level of female labour supply.

There was an increase in net inward commuting to the cities of

61,000 (a more appropriate way of representing the decline in net outward commuting of 61,000). This was also in contrast to the pattern for men, but consistent perhaps with net out-migration and commuting back to work. The disaggregated figures showed that cities with a relatively large gain in female employment were more likely to have an increase in net inward commuting (such as Cardiff and Edinburgh). Cities with large job losses experienced a decline in net inward commuting (particularly Merseyside).

## Contrast with towns and rural areas

The pattern of employment change and its labour market consequences were very different outside the major cities. Table 3.4 presents the LMAs for the towns and rural areas. Some of the differences from Table 3.3 are very striking and the contrast helps to illuminate the adverse situation in the cities. For instance, male employment increased very slightly outside the major cities, but fell sharply within them. Female employment increased very substantially outside the major cities, but very little within them.

*Table 3.4*: **Labour market accounts for Britain's towns and rural areas (1981-91)**

|  |  | Male | | Female | |
|---|---|---|---|---|---|
|  |  | **Number** | **%*** | **Number** | **%*** |
| Loss of employment |  | -13,000 | -0.1 | -959,000 | -16.8 |
| PLUS | natural increase in workforce† | 204,000 | 2.2 | 97,000 | 1.7 |
| MINUS | net out-migration | -247,000 | -2.7 | -226,000 | -4.0 |
| MINUS | change in net out-commuting | -16,000 | -0.2 | 150,000 | 2.6 |
| MINUS | decline in economic activity rate | 374,000 | 4.0 | -865,000 | -15.1 |
| MINUS | number on government schemes | 120,000 | 1.3 | 74,000 | 1.3 |
| EQUALS | change in unemployment | -40,000 | -0.4 | 5,000 | 0.1 |

*Note:* *As a % of the economically active men/women of working age in 1981.

† The natural increase in the workforce figures were not available for all areas, so average rates of increase were used, based on the rates for the cities in Table 3.3 and for the Rural Development Areas (RDAs) (Beatty and Fothergill, 1997), which were very similar anyway.

*Source:* Census of Population, 1981 and 1991

The responses to these shifts obviously differed as well. There was net in-migration to the towns and rural areas, the converse of net out-migration from the cities. The female economic activity rate increased dramatically in the towns and rural areas as more women were drawn into the workforce by the rising demand for labour. The male economic activity rate actually fell, probably because of the declining demand for manual labour, although the latter was not as great as in the cities (see Figure 3.4).

Changes in net commuting were small for men, but larger for women and in an outward direction. This is surprising considering the relative trends in female employment in and outside the major cities. It is possible that some of the women migrants from the cities retained their jobs there and commuted back to work. The disaggregated results showed that the cities that experienced an increase in net inward commuting also had relatively large gains in female employment. Changes in recorded unemployment were negligible and the rates of increase in people on government schemes were only slightly less than in the cities.

The static overall employment and unemployment levels for men in the towns and rural areas obscured significant changes in the components of labour supply – an increase in net in-migration, a reduction in the economic activity rate and a rise in hidden unemployment. Together with the evidence in Figure 3.4, this suggests that some groups may have been benefiting (such as professional and managerial workers) while others were losing out (such as manual workers). The substantial growth in female employment was not translated into lower unemployment because of the sharp rise in economic participation and smaller increase in net in-migration.

## Conclusions and implications

Long-standing economic disparities between Britain's cities and other parts of the country have continued to widen during the 1990s. The conurbation cores have experienced the steepest decline, particularly in full-time male employment. The loss of manual jobs may be the most important single issue facing the cities. Two processes appear to have been at work – deindustrialisation and a broader-based urban–rural shift affecting all the main economic sectors. So the cities have secured a disproportionately small share of the growth in services.

The heavy loss of male employment has been accompanied by substantial net out-migration, some increase in net out-commuting and a big decline in the economic activity rate. So, recorded urban unemployment is not as high as it would otherwise have been, although it is still the highest in the country. Adjustment is not a satisfactory way to dissipate job loss because out-migration is socially-selective and imposes costs on the areas left behind. Commuting elsewhere to work is not viable on a significant scale in most cities. Retraining and upskilling can have limited impact on unemployment in a context of generally deficient labour demand. The rise in economic inactivity has impacted disproportionately on older manual workers and disguised the reality of higher unemployment. Estimates suggest that real unemployment has risen to a very high level in the conurbation cores.

There appears to be a lack of understanding of the economic divergence between the major cities and other parts of the country among many national policy makers. In the fields of housing and land-use planning, there has been renewed interest in recent years in redirecting physical development towards the cities and constraining it in the countryside, largely for environmental and political reasons. However, there appears to have been less interest in or willingness to tackle the crucial employment and economic dimensions. For example, the Urban Task Force set up by the Department of Environment, Transport and the Regions (DETR) under Lord Rogers was charged with recommending ways of regenerating cities based on three principles: "design excellence, social inclusion and environmental responsibility" (Rogers, 1999, p 2). The importance of a stronger economic base was omitted and there are few references to the issue of employment in the interim report. Housing is asserted to be "the regeneration driver" along with local services such as education, police and health (Rogers, 1999, p 3). The need to increase the quantity of suitable employment opportunities in order to raise local incomes, reduce poverty and retain and attract the population was not mentioned.

Other government policies which address the overarching issues of unemployment, welfare reform and macro-economic management show little apparent awareness of urban–rural disparities. Although it has recently been acknowledged that the number of people wanting work is more than double the level of registered unemployment, the significance of geographical differences has been neglected. For the labour market to function effectively and to allow the economy to grow more quickly without running into constraints, locational imbalances between labour supply and demand need to be addressed alongside the issues of education, training, 'passive' welfare benefits and childcare. The recent statement that "when the economy moved into the recovery phase, labour market bottlenecks, skill shortages and wage inflation stalled recovery while worklessness remained at unacceptable levels" (HM Treasury, 1998b, p 52) lacked any recognition that geographical inequalities may have been part of the explanation. There is a strong economic, social and environmental case to be made for relative economic expansion in the conurbations.

For many years, central government has perceived the challenges of urban areas as essentially social and confined to specific neighbourhoods. This emerged once again in the report of the Prime Minister's Social Exclusion Unit (1998) which introduced the New Deal for Communities (see Chapter Six). Similarly, an important DETR paper stated that: "The rationale for this (urban regeneration) is largely social" (DETR, 1997, para 2.2). Such views are echoed in the Treasury:

> Unemployment, poor educational attainment and benefit dependency often interact with other social problems such as bad housing, crime and substance misuse to create a vicious circle of disadvantage. The concentrations of disadvantage and deprivation in small and specific areas are of particular concern as some of the worst effects of worklessness and low pay are felt by children. (HM Treasury, 1997, p 47)

There seems to be little recognition of the economic and employment dimensions of urban problems, or of the city-wide context for neighbourhood decline and regeneration. With the current emphasis on neighbourhood initiatives and the wide jurisdiction of the emerging Regional Development Agencies (RDAs), there is a danger that cities may become something of a blind spot in policy terms.

An important implication of this research is the need for action to increase labour demand in and around the cities, particularly for blue-collar workers. Many of those who are recorded as inactive and on incapacity and other benefits "would work if they had the opportunity and incentive to do so" (HM Treasury, 1997, p 46). Spatial targeting of economic development in areas where the rate of worklessness is highest would be efficient in several respects. In some cases this may need to be supported by other measures to reduce additional obstacles people face, including racial and other forms of discrimination, inflexibilities in the benefits system and possible lack of self-confidence and up-to-date vocational skills. Current government programmes to get people off welfare and into work concentrate excessively on supply-side issues – personal motivation, behaviour and low level skills. In the major cities and coalfields the New Deal implies pushing all workless groups into jobs in local labour markets that are already experiencing an over-supply of labour (Turok and Webster, 1998).

The New Deal is likely to prove less effective in areas with high unemployment than in tight labour markets with a shortage of labour. First year monitoring results show that the New Deal has been consistently least successful at getting people into jobs in the major cities (Bivand, 1999b). The long-term consequences for such cities and their poorest neighbourhoods could be serious in terms of individual hardship, growth of the underground economy and the loss of income to communities if mainstream employment does not expand and welfare benefits are pared back over time. Social security is an important social and spatial stabiliser, without which "cumulative forces of decline may be set in motion which are likely to be difficult to check once they gain momentum" (MacKay, 1998, p 59).

In many old industrial cities the most important single mechanism for expanding labour demand and creating appropriate employment probably involves investment in land improvement, strategic sites and premises, and modern infrastructure to accommodate business expansion and attract inward investment. A pragmatic approach might mean the promotion of sites within and on the edge of built-up areas, depending on land availability, the road and rail network, other essential infrastructure and proximity to high unemployment neighbourhoods. The long-term impact would be improved by extending and enhancing the provision of services to help new and existing firms develop and expand, including advice and training in growth management, export promotion, supply chain and cluster development, technological support and reinvestment. The government recently endorsed an unusually comprehensive set of proposals from the DETR Coalfields Task Force for revitalising coalfield communities (DETR, 1998a, 1998b). They were to be 'kick-started' by reclaiming key sites for development and providing suitable infrastructure to attract investment and create additional employment. Something with similar ambition and breadth of vision is needed for Britain's cities.

## Acknowledgements

This chapter draws on a longer report (Turok and Edge, 1999). The author is grateful to the Joseph Rowntree Foundation for its financial support, the ESRC for support under the Cities Programme, Nicola Edge for extensive research support, and Nick Bailey, Tina Beatty, Iain Begg, Tony Champion, Steve Fothergill, Anne Green, John Low,

Alan Townsend and David Webster for their advice and comments on a draft report. The usual disclaimers apply.

## References

Amin, A. and Graham, S. (1997) 'The ordinary city', *Transactions of the Institute of British Geographers*, vol 22, pp 411-29.

Atkins, D., Champion, T,. Coombes, M., Dorling, D. and Woodward, R. (1996) *Urban trends in England: Latest evidence from the 1991 Census*, London: HMSO.

Beatty, C. and Fothergill, S. (1997) *Unemployment and the labour market in rural development areas*, Salisbury: Rural Development Commission.

Beatty, C., Fothergill, S. and Lawless, P. (1997a) 'Geographical variation in the labour-market adjustment process: the UK coalfields 1981-91', *Environment and Planning A*, vol 29, pp 2041-60.

Beatty, C., Fothergill, S., Gore, T. and Herrington, A. (1997b) *The real level of unemployment*, Sheffield: CRESR, Sheffield Hallam University.

Begg, I., Moore, B. and Rhodes, J. (1986) 'Economic and social change in urban Britain', in V. Hausner (ed) *Critical issues in urban economic development, volume I*, Oxford: Oxford University Press.

Bivand, P. (1999a) 'Unemployment up but employment continues to rise', *Working Brief*, issue 104, May, pp 26-7.

Bivand, P. (1999b) 'New Deal one year on', *Working Brief*, issue 104, May, pp 8-13.

Champion, A.G. (1998) *Urban exodus*, London: Council for the Protection of Rural England.

Champion, A.G. and Ford, T. (1998) *The social selectivity of migration flows affecting Britain's large conurbations: An analysis of the regional migration tables of the 1981 and 1991 Censuses*, ESRC Cities Programme Project on Migration, Working Paper 1, Newcastle: Department of Geography, University of Newcastle.

Comedia and Demos (1997) *The richness of cities*, Working Papers 1-12, London: Comedia/Demos.

DETR (Department of the Environment, Transport and the Regions) (1997) *Regeneration programmes – The way forward*, Discussion Paper, London: DETR.

DETR (1998a) *Making the difference: A new start for England's coalfield communities*, The Coalfields Task Force Report, London: DETR.

DETR (1998b) *Making the difference: The government's response to the Coalfields Task Force Report*, London: DETR.

Elias, P. and Bynner, J. (1997) 'Intermediate skills and occupational mobility', *Policy Studies*, vol 18, pp 101-24.

Employment Policy Institute (1998) *Employment Audit*, Summer, London.

Fothergill, S., Kitson, M. and Monk, S. (1985) *Urban industrial change: The causes of the urban-rural contrast in manufacturing employment trends*, DoE, London: HMSO.

Glasgow City Council (1996) *Glasgow's Housing Plan 1996: Changing problems and a changing agenda*, Glasgow: Glasgow City Council.

Green, A.E. and Owen, D. (1998) *Where are the jobless?: Changing unemployment and non-employment in cities and regions*, Bristol: The Policy Press.

Gregg, P. and Wadsworth, J. (1998) 'Unemployment and non-employment: unpacking economic inactivity', *Employment Policy Institute Economic Report*, vol 12, no 6.

HM Treasury (1997) *Pre-Budget report*, Cm 3804, London: The Stationery Office.

HM Treasury (1998a) *New ambitions for Britain: Financial statement and Budget report*, HC 620, London: The Stationery Office.

HM Treasury (1998b) *Pre-Budget report*, Cm 4076, London: The Stationery Office.

MacKay, R. (1998) 'Unemployment as exclusion, unemployment as choice', in P. Lawless, R. Martin and S. Hardy (eds) *Unemployment and social exclusion: Landscapes of labour inequality*, London: Jessica Kingsley, pp 49-68.

Power, A. and Mumford, K. (1999) *The slow death of great cities? Urban abandonment or urban renaissance*, York: Joseph Rowntree Foundation.

Pugh, M. (1998) *Barriers to work: The spatial divide between jobs and welfare recipients in metropolitan areas*, Discussion Paper, Washington, DC: Brookings Centre on Urban and Metropolitan Policy.

Rogers, R. (1999) *Preface: Urban renaissance: Sharing the vision 01.99*, Summary of Responses to the Urban Task Force Prospectus, London: DETR.

Secretary of State for Social Security (1998) *A new contract for welfare: Principles into practice*, Cm 4101, London: The Stationery Office.

SEU (Social Exclusion Unit) (1998) *Bringing Britain together: A national strategy for neighbourhood renewal*, Cm 4045, London: The Stationery Office.

Townsend, A. (1993) 'The urban-rural cycle in the Thatcher growth years', *Transactions of the Institute of British Geographers*, no 18, pp 207-21.

Turok, I. and Edge, N. (1999) *The jobs gap in Britain's cities: Employment, loss and labour market consequences*, Bristol: The Policy Press.

Turok, I. and Webster, D. (1998) 'The New Deal: jeopardised by the geography of unemployment?', *Local Economy*, vol 12, no 4, pp 309-28.

Webster, D. (1999a) 'The cities' unemployment crisis: corrected claimant unemployment rates for local authorities for January 1999', Published on the internet at www.mailbase.ac.uk/lists/unemployment-research/

Webster, D. (1999b) 'Monetary policy and unemployment: macro-economic fallacies and geographical realities', Memorandum of evidence submitted to the House of Lords Select Committee on the Monetary Policy Committee of the Bank of England, February.

# FOUR

# Educational inequalities and Education Action Zones

*Ian Plewis*

## Introduction

Our knowledge of the extent and changing nature of educational inequalities in Britain is patchy and our understanding of the causes of these inequalities much more so. This chapter will discuss just what data are available to assess inequalities before considering three of the policies of the present government which have a bearing, either directly or indirectly, on these inequalities. The first of these policies is the publication of schools' results on attainments in tests and examinations, the second is setting targets for attainments, and the third, the one which receives most attention in this chapter, is the creation of Education Action Zones (EAZs). The chapter will then consider some of the issues which have to be faced when evaluating policies such as EAZs and will end with conclusions about information gaps and research needs.

Throughout the chapter, reference is made to educational inequalities, rather than to educational inequality, and the focus is on inequalities of outcome, notably pupils' performance in tests and examinations. This is not to downplay the importance of other outcomes such as self-esteem and social responsibility, although these are more difficult to measure, nor is it to ignore the importance of inequalities of 'process' – the way in which different groups are treated within the education system – which might contribute to inequalities of outcome. Inequalities of process include factors such as school exclusions, streaming and setting arrangements within schools, and expectations held by teachers about different groups of pupils. However, it is the case in British society, as in Western society generally, that performance in tests and examinations determines entry into higher education which, in turn, has a strong bearing on life chances.

The three inequalities in performance to receive most attention are: gender inequality, ethnic group inequality and inequality between social classes or, more generally, socioeconomic circumstances. Another division, which has not been widely studied, but which is becoming increasingly important with rapid demographic changes such as the rise in one-parent families, is inequality between family types. Inequality by generation, or by birth cohort, is also important both in its own right and, especially, to describe trends in inequalities. Are, for example, social class differences widening over time? The absence of systematic data on trends in educational inequalities is a serious problem for anyone trying to monitor the effects of government policies of all types.

## Data sources

There are no data sources which permit the simultaneous analysis of educational inequalities for all five social divisions described above. Instead, we have a number of patches which, if sewn together, would add up to less than a full quilt. This chapter is not about reviewing all the evidence; indeed, much of the work to produce the evidence remains to be done. Instead, it will indicate where relevant data can be found and how these data have been, and might be used.

There is one inequality we do know quite a lot about and that is gender inequality. This is because all the official data on national assessment and examination performance are given separately for boys and girls. The evidence on gender differences, and how they have changed over time, is reviewed by Arnot et al (1998). In recent years, concerns about the achievements of girls have been overtaken by concerns about boys' performance, especially in literacy. One important point to bear in mind when comparing male and female performance is that although boys generally do less well up to the age of 16, they tend to show greater variability in outcome than girls. For example, in 1995 in A level Mathematics, 28.1% of males achieved grade A but 13.8% got fail grades (N and U). The corresponding figures for females were 26.7% and 11.3% (SCAA, 1996).

With regard to inequalities between ethnic groups, there are a number of local research studies but a paucity of national data. Since the publication of the Swann Report (1985), the issue of a national system to monitor the education performance of all ethnic groups has been discussed within the Department for Education and Employment (DfEE) but never resolved. As the review by Gillborn and Gipps (1996) points out, "to repay the investment of time and resources it is essential, first, that monitoring exercises are sufficiently detailed to produce useful information and, second, that the results are used to good effect". The need for improvement in this area is clear (p 79). There are data from the 1991 Census, which included an ethnic question for the first time, although the education data are limited to staying-on rates (analysed by Drew et al, 1997) and qualifications above A level (analysed by Owen et al, 1997). The Higher Education Statistics Agency and UCAS (the Universities and Colleges Admissions Service) do give some breakdowns by ethnic group. The Youth Cohort Surveys – a series of repeated cross-sections – have also yielded valuable detail, albeit from rather low response rates (Payne, 1998).

On the whole, we have to rely on rather old data for information on social class differences in educational outcomes. Most of these data come from the national birth cohorts – the National Survey of Health and Development (whose members were aged 16 in 1962), the National Child Development Study (NCDS) (whose members were 16 in 1974) and the 1970 British Cohort Study (whose members were 16 in 1986). The General Household Survey (GHS) and the Labour Force Survey (LFS) both collect data on educational qualifications for people older than 16 and these could, with care, be exploited to give some information on trends in class inequalities. The Office for National Statistics (ONS) Longitudinal Study (LS) could also be used. It is important, in any analysis, for variables such as social class to be truly exogeneous. In other words, it is not helpful to correlate, for example, adults' educational attainments with their own social class because, if based on an occupational classification, social class is influenced by education qualifications. Instead, both adults' and pupils' attainments must be related to their parents' socioeconomic circumstances. Although there can be little doubt that social class differences exist, we know rather little about their current extent or recent trends.

The GHS and LFS can also be used to describe age, or cohort, differences, as can the 1996 survey of adult literacy (Carey et al, 1997). However, some caution is needed when comparing the performance of different cohorts because the instruments used to measure outcomes change with time along with the outcomes themselves, making the interpretation of change difficult – see Plewis (1998a) for more details.

Not only are each of the above inequalities of interest in their own right, they are also potentially important in combination. So, for example, we know that boys perform less well than girls in public examinations at age 16, and we know that pupils from working-class backgrounds do less well than middle-class pupils. However, we do not know whether working-class boys are further behind working-class girls than middle-class boys are behind middle-class girls. In other words, there could be an additional penalty for being a working-class boy, conceptualised as a statistical interaction between gender and social class. Other statistical interactions are also plausible, between gender and ethnic group for example (Tizard et al, 1988). It is because there could be interactions of this type that data should be collected so that all inequalities can be considered together, rather than each being examined separately. Another reason for analysing inequalities together is that there are associations between, for example, social class and family structure, and it is important to disentangle their separate effects.

## Government policies

The present government is committed to raising educational standards. However, current policy documents and ministerial statements put much less emphasis on the need to reduce educational inequalities, other than an implicit belief that these inequalities will become smaller if standards are raised. This section considers three of the ways in which the government hopes to raise standards: publishing tables of schools' performance in tests and examinations, setting targets for local education authorities (LEAs) and schools, and creating Education Action Zones. It is argued that none of these policies will necessarily reduce inequalities even if successfully implemented, and that they are not guaranteed to raise standards either.

### League tables

The decision of the previous Conservative government to publish tables of schools' performance, which were, as intended, translated by the media into 'league' tables, was widely criticised at the time. Despite persistent and trenchant criticism, the policy has been retained by the Labour administration. The main criticisms of the policy (Goldstein, 1998) are that it ignores the powerful influence of a school's intake on its results, that it takes no account of a school's achievements in areas other than test and examination performance, that it ignores uncertainty arising from the vagaries of sampling, that it ignores the effects of pupil mobility such as the leeching effects of fee-charging schools and the arrival of refugees and that it ignores the possibility that schools are more effective for some groups of pupils and in some subject areas, than for others.

There have been some moves recently (DfEE, 1998) towards

judgements based on what is known as a 'value-added' approach. In other words, an allowance is made for the differing socioeconomic circumstances faced by schools as represented by the proportion of their pupils eligible for free school meals (FSM). Although a slight improvement on comparisons based on raw results, eligibility for FSM is an incomplete control for intake. It is certainly not the case that schools with equal proportions of pupils eligible for FSM are 'similar' schools in the way that the DfEE (and the Office for Standards in Education [OFSTED] and the Qualifications and Curriculum Authority [QCA]) suppose. Even though these slightly less unfair comparisons have now received official blessing, there is no suggestion from the government that league tables might be scrapped.

The league tables have a clear, built-in bias against schools in disadvantaged areas, where educational performance is lower because socioeconomic circumstances are worse. This bias is likely to increase inequality if schools adopt certain policies designed to try to push them up the league table. One way of doing this at the secondary level is for schools to concentrate their resources on pupils most likely to achieve exam success, particularly the success represented by five A to C grades at GCSE. Another way is for schools to have selection policies which favour pupils most likely to do well in tests and exams. Schools low in the league tables, which are perceived to be poor schools, are likely to suffer from poor staff morale and to have difficulty recruiting the more able teachers. The pressures on school managers created by the league tables are not likely to be in the best interests of these pupils in most need of extra attention. In addition to these pressures on schools to act in ways that will increase inequalities, parents who can afford to change where they live are encouraged to move near to schools high in the league tables, further increasing segregated communities and unequal school outcomes.

Perhaps the real value of the league tables is to turn them around and regard them as one indicator of social inequality. In other words, we might think of league tables not as an outcome of schooling as at present, but as a reflection of area-based poverty. Differences in results between schools, and between LEAs, map well onto inequalities in family resources which in turn map onto the inequalities in outcome.

## Targets

The education White Paper (DfEE, 1997a) states that by 2002 the government expects that 80% of pupils aged 11 (the end of Key Stage

2) will be at Level 4 in English with a corresponding figure of 75% for mathematics. The data for 1999 shows that these targets were reached by 69% of pupils in English and 70% in mathematics. Setting targets in this way raises a number of questions: why have these particular targets been chosen?; how are the targets to be achieved?; what value can we put on them if they are achieved?; and what effects will setting targets have on teaching and learning?

The government has handed down its Key Stage 2 targets to each LEA, giving some variation between LEAs to allow for differing social circumstances. In turn, each LEA will set a target for each of its primary schools, and it will be up to the head of the school to 'deliver' these targets. Each of the players in the system will have to make decisions about how to organise the resources available to them in order to try to reach their targets. It would not be surprising if some LEAs set high targets for schools in more favoured areas and concentrated their resources on these schools. Similarly, some heads and teachers will be tempted to concentrate on those pupils most likely to reach the desired level, paying less attention to those pupils who are far behind. For example, in English, in both 1997 and 1999, 7% of pupils had not reached Level 3. These pupils may well be ones who are seen by their teachers to have less potential, and they are likely to be concentrated in disadvantaged social groups. The extra government resources which were allocated early in 1999 for 'booster' Year 6 classes are clearly intended to help schools meet their targets of getting a certain percentage of their pupils to Level 4, and may well reinforce the tendency to ignore pupils performing below, or only just at, Level 3.

Consequently, as Plewis (1998b) shows, it is possible to raise standards overall, but also to increase inequality. Consider the following hypothetical situation. Suppose pupils are divided into three social groups with 35% in the top group, 50% in the middle group and 15% in the bottom group. Table 4.1 shows how the percentages reaching at least Level 4 rise slightly from time 1 to time 2 for the top group (from 90 to 98%), substantially for the middle group (from 55 to 90%) and not at all for the bottom group (7% at both time points). In other words, standards might have risen for groups one and two but not for the bottom group. Therefore, in this example, educational inequality has widened. Standards have, however, risen – from 60% at time 1 (before the targets policy) to 80% at time 2 (after the targets policy).

*Table 4.1:* **Hypothetical percentages achieving at least Level 4, at two points in time by social class group**

|  | Social class | | | |
|  | 1 | 2 | 3 | Total |
| --- | --- | --- | --- | --- |
| Distribution (%) | 35 | 50 | 15 | 100 |
| Pupils achieving Level 4 and above |  |  |  |  |
| Time 1 (%) | 90 | 55 | 7 | 60 |
| Time 2 (%) | 98 | 90 | 7 | 80 |

There are useful targets of attainment to aim for. Setting out explicitly to reduce the gaps between ethnic groups and social classes is both legitimate and, importantly, measurable. However, these targets do not figure in government plans. It is difficult to see how the combination of a policy driven by targets, reinforced by the publication of schools' results, and allied with the ability of richer parents to pay for their children to be educated in the better resourced independent sector, can have anything but a negative effect on inequalities.

## Education Action Zones

The government has so far set up 25 Education Action Zones (EAZs). These started to come into operation in September 1998, and there are plans for more. The existing zones each cover approximately 15 primary and three secondary schools. Each zone receives about £1 million a year in extra resources, three quarters of which will come from the public budget, with the other quarter expected to be raised from private sponsors. The zones are spread across England with three (Herefordshire, Norfolk and North Somerset) in predominantly rural areas. According to the 1997 White Paper, they were to be "set up in areas with a mix of underperforming schools and the highest levels of disadvantage" (DfEE, 1997a, p 39). To quote the Secretary of State, "they will provide new and exciting ways for schools, LEAs, parents, business and community organisations, to work together to raise standards" (DfEE, 1997b, p 2). As well as being an important part of the government's education policy, the EAZ idea has wider ramifications in that it has been identified as a "forerunner for the future of public services in the next century" and as an exemplar of a "third way" in welfare provision (Byers, in Rafferty, 1998; Hodge, 1998). There has been considerable opposition to the idea from some of the teaching unions, partly because of their hostility to the involvement of for-profit organisations in state education, and partly because of the threat to nationally negotiated pay scales.

Ironically, EAZs might be regarded as a 1960s solution to a 1990s problem. In the late 1960s, Education Priority Areas (EPAs), with their origins in the Plowden Report (1967) into primary education, and the associated research suggesting that there were clusters of disadvantage, were set up with aims similar to the proposed EAZs. There are differences between the EPA idea and the EAZ policy (for example, EPAs were never formally designated as such by the Department of Education and Science and they were restricted to the urban primary sector); nevertheless, they are both predicated on the idea that poor educational performance of *pupils* can be tackled at an *area* level. However, EPAs were not a great success. One of the reasons for this lack of success can be ascribed to the 'ecological fallacy'. As part of the EPA research in London, Barnes and Lucas (1975) created a six point risk index for individual pupils, and divided primary schools into two groups. These were EPA schools (accounting for 14% of pupils) and the rest. They showed that 6% of those pupils at least risk attended EPA schools and 72% of those at most risk did not attend EPA schools. In other words, some pupils living in favourable circumstances attended EPA schools and, very importantly, the majority of disadvantaged pupils did not attend EPA schools.

We can illustrate the ecological fallacy in another way. If we use the proportion of pupils eligible for FSMs as an indicator, there are about 12 times as many primary schools serving advantaged areas (no more than 20% eligible) as there are serving disadvantaged areas (more than 50% eligible) (DfEE, 1998). If the proportion of poor pupils in disadvantaged schools is six times the proportion of poor pupils in advantaged schools, then there will be twice as many poor pupils attending advantaged schools as there are poor pupils attending disadvantaged schools. If we assume, using Eurostat (1997) data, that one third of pupils are living in poverty, then directing resources at disadvantaged schools will inadvertently give a further benefit to about 7% of the pupils who are not poor but who attend these schools. In other words, a proportion of the resources directed at EAZ schools will benefit already advantaged pupils whereas the majority of disadvantaged pupils will receive nothing extra.

The EPA research was conducted in the early 1970s and only referred to London primary schools. It is possible that there are more concentrated pockets of disadvantage outside London. It is also possible that disadvantage has become geographically more concentrated during the last 25 years. However, there is evidence from the 1991 Census (Simpson, 1996) which is in line with the EPA research in that the 14% (50 out of 366) of English districts with the lowest percentage car ownership contain only 35% of all English households without a car, and the top 18% of car-owning districts contain 7% of all carless households.

We can also draw on evidence from school effectiveness research to support the view that although schools do vary in their outcomes, this variation is not especially large. The majority of between school variability in outcome can be accounted for by variability in intake. There is a lot more variability in attainment within schools than there is between schools, or as Gray (1998) puts it, "most schools have pupils who are doing well with respect to national norms as well as pupils who are doing badly" (p 5). Again, this implies that targeting aggregates such as schools and areas, rather than those individuals and families in most need, might not be very successful.

The extra resources to be directed at the proposed EAZs are miniscule. In 1997/98, total public expenditure on education in England was more than £30 billion. Hence, the three quarters of a million pounds extra for each Zone amounts in total to just 0.06% of total expenditure. If we assume that the 25 Zones together comprise 75 secondary schools and 375 primary schools then the Zones will cover about 2% of all schools (and hence about the same proportion of pupils) in England. Bearing in mind the estimate that one third of all children live in poverty, then even if all the pupils living in EAZs were living in poverty (which they won't be), only a small proportion of poor children will benefit from any extra resources. On this basis, it is difficult to see how the introduction of a small number of less than generously funded EAZs can have much effect either on standards, or on educational inequalities.

There is merit in a redistributive policy which allocates relatively more resources to those groups identified as disadvantaged and it is possible that individual EAZs will choose to focus on trying to reduce educational inequalities. The difficulty lies in deciding how much more, relatively, the disadvantaged are to receive, and what the balance should be between individual targeting and group targeting of the type represented by EAZs. It is perfectly possible to squander resources, as suggested above, unless careful consideration is given to the optimal policy. When overall resources are scarce and no new resources for education are being made available, the removal of resources from some schools or areas into others may have an overall deleterious effect. This might be especially problematic for schools beyond the EAZ borders but within the same LEA.

There have been similar programmes to the EAZs in at least two other European countries: France and the Netherlands. The French Zones d'Education Prioritaire (ZEPs) started in 1981; there are 563 of them, covering 10% of all pupils. A total of 70 priority areas were set up in the Netherlands in 1986 under the Education Priority Policy (OVB). There, some attempt was made to direct resources towards disadvantaged pupils, rather than just to schools with disadvantaged pupils, in that schools received extra funding depending on the number of disadvantaged pupils in them. However, the amounts involved were rather small and the evidence from the evaluations of the OVB programme suggests that it had little effect on reducing inequalities. Evaluative evidence from the French programme also points to only slight effects on pupils' educational attainments.

## Evaluating area-based interventions

New Labour proclaims the need for evidence-based policy, which we must take to mean that policy initiatives are to be supported by research evidence and that policies introduced on a trial basis are to be evaluated in as rigorous a way as possible. The evidence from the EPA project outlined in the previous section suggests that, a priori, it is unlikely that the EAZs will succeed in their aim of raising standards, even within their own boundaries. On the other hand, it could be argued that the content of the EAZ policy is sufficiently different from the EPA idea that it might be more effective. The only way of establishing its effectiveness is to set up a carefully designed and controlled study from the outset. Unfortunately, and in marked contrast to the Dutch OVB project, this has not been done. Instead, the first tranche of EAZs are in place and all that has been funded so far by way of evaluation is a rather small project to collect baseline data. Consequently, many of the important questions about the effects of the EAZ policy might now be difficult to answer. At the very least, a long-term evaluation, even if restricted to looking just at attainment, needs to:

* encompass the heterogeneity of EAZs, both intended and unintended;
* collect *longitudinal* data at each of three levels – pupil, school and Zone – to analyse pupils' progress properly;
* collect comparable data from carefully selected control schools in similar areas.

These criteria are likely to apply, in a similar way, to the evaluation of other types of area-based evaluations.

## Conclusions

Educational inequalities are pervasive and far-reaching and it would be ingenuous to suppose that they can be eradicated easily. The first step on the road to their eradication is to collect relevant data so that we know how large they are and, very importantly, how they are changing with time. Unfortunately, most official education statistics are not broken down by social groupings. Hence, we know less about educational inequalities, and how they are changing, than we do, for example, about inequalities in health. Ideally, we need a monitoring system which is national in scope, large enough to pick up detailed ethnic differences and their interactions with gender and social class, longitudinal so that we can see how inequalities vary over the course of schooling and beyond, and at the pupil level to avoid the perils of aggregation, and the ecological fallacy.

We do have a monitoring system of a sort at present and one which is primarily concerned to monitor the performance of schools and LEAs (mostly, it seems, to punish those which are viewed as unsatisfactory). Regrettably, the punishments – in the form of 'naming and shaming' schools with disadvantaged intakes, and LEAs in poor areas – are based on inadequate data and poorly conceptualised statistical analyses. Perhaps the proposal from the DfEE for an education identifier for all pupils (rather like an NHS number) could form the basis of a more thoughtful and informative approach to statistical monitoring. However, even a monitoring system targeted at inequalities is only a prelude to action, not an end in itself.

Although the statistical base is limited, there is, nevertheless, evidence from studies such as the three birth cohorts (and their second generations) to inform us that there are substantial differences in educational attainments by social class, ethnic group and gender. The effects of these inequalities on children's life chances mean, in turn, that the road towards equality based on equality of opportunity is bound to be blocked until these systematic differences are substantially reduced. It is argued here that the government's policies, and their new programmes, well-intentioned as they may be, will do little to reduce inequalities and may well exacerbate them.

One of the depressing aspects of the way new policies are being formulated is that there is no evidence that the government is aware of, or willing to learn from, the experiences of the past, or of our European partners. A substantial amount of research resources were devoted to the EPA idea. Partly as a result of that and related research, it is possible to conclude that spatially and institutionally based interventions of this type, however imaginatively planned, are unlikely to solve the deep-seated problems they are aiming to address. The same types of argument apply to Health Action Zones (see Chapter Seven by Davey Smith and Gordon) and other similar schemes such as the Priority Estates Project (see Chapter Six by Pantazis).

The arguments marshalled here against EAZ-type interventions do not imply that there is no place for educational interventions of any type. Interventions that are targeted directly at pupils with specific problems can work, but even interventions that are successful in the short run often need to be reinforced continually to maintain their effectiveness. Different strategies might be needed, depending on the inequality to be addressed. Policies designed to tackle different types of gender inequalities – for example, the relatively poor performance of boys at 16, or the under-representation of women in science disciplines in higher education – will not necessarily help with the problems created by poverty. On the other hand, a reduction in social class inequality might also have a beneficial effect on ethnic inequalities.

Perhaps the best way to raise all educational standards, and not only those related to pupils' performance in national assessments and public examinations, is to create a public education service which achieves excellence in all areas of the country. A really worthwhile target would be one which aimed for such excellence so that as a result the private sector would start to fade away. However, probably the most effective way of tackling those educational inequalities which arise from poverty is to tackle the causes of poverty among families with children.

## References

Arnot, M., Gray, J., James, M., Rudduck, J. with Duveen, G. (1998) *Recent research on gender and educational performance*, London: OFSTED.

Barnes, J.H. and Lucas, H. (1975) 'Positive discrimination in education: individuals, groups and institutions', in J.H. Barnes (ed) *Educational priority, vol 3*, London: HMSO, pp 237-87.

Carey, S., Low, S. and Hansbro, J. (1997) *Adult literacy in Britain*, London: ONS.

DfEE (Department for Education and Employment) (1997a) *Excellence in schools*, London: The Stationery Office.

DfEE (1997b) *Education Action Zones: An introduction*, London: DfEE.

DfEE (1998) *The Autumn Package (Key Stage 2)*, London: DfEE.

Drew, D., Gray, J. and Sporton, D. (1997) 'Ethnic differences in the educational participation of 16-19 year-olds', in V. Karn (ed) *Ethnicity in the 1991 Census (Vol 4)*, London: The Stationery Office, pp 17-28.

Gillborn, D. and Gipps, C. (1996) *Recent research on the achievements of ethnic minority pupils*, London: OFSTED.

Goldstein, H. (1998) 'Performance indicators in education', in D. Dorling and S. Simpson (eds) *Statistics in society*, London: Arnold, pp 281-6.

Gray, J. (1998) *The contribution of educational research to the cause of school improvement*, London: Institute of Education.

Hodge, M. (1998) 'A pragmatic ideology', *Times Educational Supplement*, 12 June, p 15.

Owen, C., Mortimore, P. and Phoenix, A. (1997) 'Higher education qualifications', in V. Karn (ed) *Ethnicity in the 1991 Census (Vol 4)*, London: The Stationery Office, pp 1-16.

Payne, J. (1998) *Routes at sixteen: Trends and choices in the nineties*, Research Report 55, London: DfEE.

Plewis, I. (1998a) 'What's worth comparing in education', in D. Dorling and S. Simpson (eds) *Statistics in society*, London: Arnold, pp 273-80.

Plewis, I. (1998b) 'Inequalities, targets and zones', *New Economy*, no 5, pp 104-8.

Plowden Report (1967) *Children and their primary schools*, London: HMSO.

Rafferty, F. (1998) 'Action Zones will pilot new ideas', *Times Educational Supplement*, 6 February, p 4.

SCAA (School Curriculum and Assessment Authority) (1996) *GCE results analysis*, London: SCAA.

Simpson, S. (1996) 'Resource allocation by measures of relative social need in geographical areas: the relevance of the signed $\chi^2$, the percentage, and the raw count', *Environment and Planning A*, no 28, pp 537-54.

Swann Report (1985) *Education for all: The Report of the Committee of Enquiry into the Education of Children from Ethnic Minority Groups,* Cmnd 9453, London: HMSO.

Tizard, B., Blatchford, P., Burke, J., Farquhar, C. and Plewis, I. (1988) *Young children at school in the inner city,* Hove: Lawrence Erlbaum.

# FIVE

# How can we end inequalities in housing?

*Alan Murie*

## Introduction

Housing is prominent in images of poverty, homelessness, poor health and poor education. Deprived estates and their problems of crime and unemployment have become increasingly important in debates about poverty (see Chapter Six) and the poverty and savings 'traps' are strongly affected by the operation of Housing Benefit and policies towards rents. In spite of this, housing has been nowhere near the top of the policy agenda and has increasingly been seen as part of the problem rather than a solution. During the last 20 years, the housing policy agenda has actively operated to increase inequality. The promotion of home ownership and the changed financial regime for social rented housing have contributed to an increasing concentration of lower income groups in council and housing association property. The residualisation of these tenures and the active deregulation of the private-rented sector have left a more unequal housing system. This is reflected in the increased spatial concentration of deprived households living in cities and towns.

At the end of the 1990s, there is some renewed interest in housing issues. While housing itself is not at the top of the agenda, the concerns about health and education have increasingly identified housing as a key element affecting demand and performance in these areas. At the same time, policies to get people into the labour market and expand employability, increasingly come up against the issue of residualised housing. Housing itself has not been at the top of the policy agenda of the Labour government but it has an important place in the emerging discussion of social exclusion. Two of the three initial priorities identified for the Social Exclusion Unit, following its creation in December 1997, relate to housing: rough sleepers and the worst estates. The recognition of housing's past is a welcome development. However, this chapter will argue that the nature of the response is insufficient and that it could be inappropriate.

## Background

The traditional debate about housing inequality focused on a series of circumstances which threatened life chances: unfitness, overcrowding, sharing, and a lack of amenities. These circumstances have by no means been eliminated. However, enormous progress was made in the three decades after 1946 in reducing the number of households and dwellings affected by such circumstances. Tables 5.1 and 5.2 set out the key statistics related to the conventional measures of housing problems and housing shortage at a national level. It is the reduction in traditional problems shown here, as well as the growing preoccupation with home ownership, which moved the policy agenda away from its previous concerns. In governments' views, progress had been significant: the post-war housing problem had largely been solved and was now concentrated in specific localities, especially in the private-rented sector, and particularly affected minority ethnic groups and low-income households generally. This general policy shift has been outlined elsewhere (Malpass and Murie, 1999) but is illustrated by the Labour government's housing policy White Paper of 1965:

> Once the country has overcome its huge social problem of slumdom and obsolescence and met the need of the great cities for more houses to let at moderate rents, the programme of subsidised council housing should decrease. The plans now are to expand the public programme to meet exceptional needs. This is born partly of a short-term necessity, partly of the conditions inherent in modern urban life. The expansion of building for owner-occupation, on the other hand, is normal; it reflects a long-term social advance which should gradually pervade every region. (Great Britain, 1965)

Wider economic problems led the government to cut back the building programme as part of the package of public expenditure reductions which followed the devaluation of sterling in November 1967. Public sector completions fell away sharply after 1968 and the reduction in slum clearance activity, foreshadowed in the White Paper of 1968, *Old houses into new homes* (Great Britain, 1968), marked the end of the period of high levels of construction and the beginning of a shift towards rehabilitation and improvement of existing dwellings. Although presented as a switch of resources, it has been shown subsequently that the new policy represented a major reduction in public investment in housing (Merrett, 1979).

The abandonment of high-output policy can be explained in terms of wider economic problems, but it was also affected by the easing of the overall housing shortage. As Table 5.2 shows, by the late 1960s, the total number of dwellings was broadly equivalent to the number of households. Ministers were able to present the national housing shortage as over – what remained was a series of 'local shortages'.

*Table 5.1:* **Households unsatisfactorily housed, England and Wales (1951-76) (000s)**

|  | 1951 | 1961 | 1971 | 1976 |
|---|---|---|---|---|
| Multi-person sharing households | 1,442 | 582 | 380 | 275 |
| Single-person sharing households | 430 | 448 | 440 | 375 |
| Concealed households* | 935 | 702 | 426 | 360 |
| Overcrowded households† | 664 | 415 | 226 | 150 |
| Households in dwellings below standard‡ | 7,500 | 4,700 | 2,846 | 1,650 |

*Notes:* *Married couples or one-parent families living as part of another household.

† Living at densities above 1.5 persons per room.

‡ Unfit or lacking one or more basic amenities.

*Sources:* Great Britain (1977a, Table 1); Great Britain (1977b, Table 1.22); Lansley (1979, Table 3.3)

*Table 5.2:* **Households and dwellings in England and Wales (1951-76) (000s)**

|  | 1951 | 1961 | 1971 | 1976 |
|---|---|---|---|---|
| Total dwellings | 12,530 | 14,646 | 17,024 | 18,100 |
| Total households | 13,259 | 14,724 | 16,779 | 17,600 |
| Deficiency (-) or surplus (+) | -729 | -78 | +245 | +500 |

*Sources:* 1951-71: Great Britain (1977a, p 15, Table 1.5); 1976: Great Britain (1977b, p 10)

## Housing conditions

The period since the early 1970s has been one in which the promotion of home ownership, privatisation and a shift from bricks and mortar subsidy to Housing Benefit dominated housing policy. House condition problems have received less attention. Although they have changed, with issues such as dampness and disrepair displacing lack of basic amenities, they have persisted. They remain central to housing inequality and, for example, debates about housing and health (see Marsh et al, 1999). With little new council house building since 1980 and the disposal of the best council housing through the Right to Buy scheme of the Thatcher government, the quality, condition and attractiveness of the council stock has been adversely affected. Nevertheless, house condition problems remain more severe in other tenures. Tables 5.3 and 5.4 show that the private-rented sector continues to have the greatest concentration of problems and the owner-occupied sector has the largest number of dwellings with problems.

The 1996 English House Condition Survey (EHCS) distinguishes three standards of disrepair (DETR, 1998).

- urgent repairs are those required to prevent further significant deterioration in the short term;
- repairs and replacements include urgent repairs together with additional visible work required within five years;
- comprehensive repairs include the above, together with any replacements assessed as being needed within the next 10 years.

The 1996 EHCS found a backlog of outstanding urgent repairs costing an estimated £26 billion to remedy. On average, this amounted to £1,280 per dwelling (Table 5.3) but the extent of disrepair is highly skewed, with most dwellings having lower than average costs. The backlog of repairs and replacements was £37 billion and comprehensive repairs £69 billion. In broad terms, privately-rented dwellings are the most likely to be in a state of poor repair and their average repair cost is considerably higher than in other tenures. The private-rented sector accounts for around 14% of the backlog of comprehensive repairs although only 9% of dwellings are in this sector. As the owner-occupied stock is the largest, it accounts for around 73% of all outstanding repairs, although 69% of dwellings are in this sector. The local authority sector has considerably lower average repair costs than either of the private tenures and accounts for 11% of the backlog of disrepair, although it represents 17% of all dwellings in 1996. The Registered Social Landlord

(RSL) sector has the lowest average repair costs, and accounts for only 1% of the bill although 5% of dwellings are owned by RSLs. Although the EHCS may underestimate repair costs in the social-rented sector to a greater extent than in the private sector because of the profile of building types in social renting (see DETR, 1998, Appendix D, for further details), these estimates give a reasonable profile of the scale and distribution of backlog repairs.

*Table 5.3:* **The backlog of disrepair by tenure, England (1996)**

|  | | | Tenure | | |
| --- | --- | --- | --- | --- | --- |
|  | Owner-occupied | Private rented | Local authority rented | RSL rented | All tenures |
| % of stock in 1996 | 69.0 | 9.3 | 17.0 | 4.6 | 100 |
| *Urgent repairs* | | | | | |
| Average per dwelling (£) | 1,250 | 2,370 | 920 | 610 | 1,280 |
| Aggregate across whole stock (£ billion) | 18 | 4 | 3 | 1 | 26 |
| % of total | 68 | 17 | 12 | 2 | 100 |
| *Repairs and replacements* | | | | | |
| Average per dwelling (£) | 1,850 | 3,250 | 1,200 | 770 | 1,830 |
| Aggregate across whole stock (£ billion) | 26 | 6 | 4 | 1 | 37 |
| % of total | 70 | 17 | 11 | 2.0 | 100 |
| *Comprehensive repairs* | | | | | |
| Average per dwelling (£) | 3,620 | 5,030 | 2,240 | 1,310 | 3,240 |
| Aggregate across whole stock (£ billion) | 51 | 9 | 8 | 1 | 69 |
| % of total | 73 | 14 | 11 | 2 | 100 |

*Source:* DETR (1998)

The 1996 EHCS provides a wealth of further detail on disrepair for each tenure by dwelling age, type, size and type of area and highlights the characteristics of households living in poorer condition properties. Dwelling age and size are major factors associated with repair costs in the private and RSL sectors. In the local authority sector, dwelling type is also important, with high rise flats and other dwellings built using non-traditional construction methods often having high costs.

The 1996 EHCS report (DETR, 1998) also contains data on the availability of modern facilities and amenities in the housing stock. Table 5.4 summarises data on central heating systems, electrical systems, and kitchen and bathroom facilities. In overall terms a majority of dwellings have modernised amenities but there are significant minorities of dwellings which lack particular facilities. Some 4% of dwellings lack a modern kitchen (facilities installed after 1964), 11% a modern bathroom (facilities installed after 1964), 14% a modern central heating system, and 2% a modern electrical system (PVC wiring, modern 13 amp sockets and modern light fittings). Local authority and privately-rented dwellings are more likely to lack modern facilities than owner-occupied or RSL dwellings. Central heating is the main problem in the private-rented sector while bathrooms are the main local authority sector problem.

*Table 5.4:* **Summary of modern facilities by tenure, England (1996)**

| | Owner-occupied | Private rented | Local authority rented | RSL rented | All tenures |
|---|---|---|---|---|---|
| All dwellings | 13,928.0 | 2,032.0 | 3,470.0 | 9,41.0 | 20,371.0 |
| *Unmodernised kitchen facilities* | | | | | |
| Dwellings (000s) | 456.0 | 149.0 | 247.9 | 22.0 | 874.9 |
| % of dwellings in tenure | 3.3 | 7.3 | 7.1 | 2.3 | 4.3 |
| % of all dwellings lacking facility | 52.1 | 17.0 | 28.3 | 2.5 | 100.0 |
| *Unmodernised bathroom facilities* | | | | | |
| Dwellings (000s) | 1,221.1 | 217.1 | 680.0 | 57.0 | 2,175.2 |
| % of dwellings in tenure | 8.8 | 10.7 | 19.6 | 6.1 | 10.7 |
| % of all dwellings lacking facility | 56.1 | 10.0 | 31.3 | 2.6 | 100.0 |
| *Unmodernised central heating system* | | | | | |
| Dwellings (000s) | 1,494.3 | 511.0 | 644.9 | 97.4 | 2,747.7 |
| % of dwellings in tenure | 10.7 | 25.2 | 18.6 | 10.4 | 13.5 |
| % of all dwellings lacking facility | 54.4 | 18.6 | 23.5 | 3.5 | 100.0 |
| *Unmodernised electrical system* | | | | | |
| Dwellings (000s) | 322.6 | 42.2 | 37.1 | 5.0 | 406.9 |
| % of dwellings in tenure | 2.3 | 2.1 | 1.1 | 0.5 | 2.0 |
| % of all dwellings lacking facility | 79.3 | 10.4 | 9.1 | 1.2 | 100.0 |

*Source:* DETR (1998)

In overall terms, the pattern of disrepair in the housing stock in England has changed considerably in recent decades. The most serious problems of maintenance and disrepair have traditionally been found in the private-rented sector. However, as the number of dwellings in that sector has declined, maintenance problems have become more apparent elsewhere. While the concentration of maintenance problems is greatest in the private-rented sector, numerically it is now more significant within the owner-occupied sector. In both of these sectors, maintenance problems are associated with patterns of ownership and patterns of use but also with the age structure of the housing stock and the neglect of maintenance over long periods for a variety of reasons.

In the owner-occupied sector, disrepair problems are particularly found in the pre-1919 housing stock, much of which was transferred from private landlords at some stage in its existence. While maintenance problems in the local authority and RSL sectors are not so likely to be reflected in large costs associated with disrepair, dissatisfaction with maintenance in the social rented sector is significant.

## Homelessness

The data on house conditions in 1996 challenges the view that the housing problem has largely been solved. However, the concerns about housing inequality relate to a wider agenda and, most immediately, to access to housing. Changes in the structure of the housing market have affected the capacity of some households to gain access to good quality dwellings. Changing concerns about homelessness and access to different parts of the housing system have been central to debates.

The changing significance of homelessness can be simply illustrated. In 1979, 70,232 households were accepted as homeless by local authorities in Great Britain under the Housing (Homeless Persons) Act. By 1991, the number had risen to 178,867. By 1996, there had been a fall to 131,139. Just as significant as this, was the rising number of homeless households housed in temporary accommodation. Such accommodation, especially that in Bed & Breakfast hotels, was insecure, sub-standard, unsafe and expensive. At the end of 1980, 1,330 households in England were in Bed & Breakfast hotels and a total of 4,710 in some form of temporary accommodation. At the end of 1991, these figures were 12,150 and 20,140 respectively, and in 1996 4,020 and 13,610.

The two main reasons for acceptance as 'homeless' were the breakdown of sharing arrangements with relatives and friends or the breakdown of a relationship with a partner. Social and demographic trends are key elements in homelessness. Although there are flaws in homelessness legislation, the lack of additional resources to meet need and the wider direction of housing policy since the mid-1970s have resulted in households which might previously have been housed from general waiting lists now becoming homeless. Homeless people have received a growing share of new allocations to council and housing association properties but the household characteristics of the homeless people allocated housing were very similar to those at the top of general waiting lists.

Homelessness legislation had always excluded the majority of non-family households from rights to more than advice and assistance in obtaining housing. By the late 1990s this feature, changes in the housing market and in legislation, left the private-rented sector, with all its quality deficiencies, continuing to play a key role in housing homeless people not accepted by local authorities. Homeless people generally falling outside the priority categories for rehousing by local authorities are single persons and couples without children and are widely referred to as single homeless people (Anderson et al, 1993). Single homeless persons were affected by a 'hostels initiative' to improve the standard of temporary accommodation for single homeless people and a 'rough sleepers initiative' which channelled new resources to schemes designed for roofless people. Both of these measures had some success but the levels of single homelessness and its impact on health and well-being remain at an historically high level.

Changes in the labour market and demographic processes, especially relationship breakdown, were prominent in the causes of homelessness. Lack of security of accommodation and action by landlords to regain possession were also important elements. The continued deregulation of the private-rented sector has made these problems of insecurity greater but has had little impact on encouraging landlords to invest in properties or improve housing conditions.

## Residualisation of council housing

By the end of the 1990s, the issues which increasingly dominate the housing agenda are neither house conditions nor homelessness. Much greater reference is being made to the long-term restructuring of the housing market and the increasing concentration of low-income groups in the social-rented sector and in the least desirable housing in that sector. Concentrations of poverty and high turnover are now more frequent features of the housing system and are key elements of housing inequality, with consequences for those in the social rented sector and other deprived neighbourhoods. The decline of the private-rented sector and the encouragement of owner-occupation over a long period of time have changed choices and perceptions in housing. Social, economic and demographic change have increased inequalities generally, and those with least bargaining power have increasingly been funnelled towards council housing and the worst estates in terms of reputation, stigma and dwelling type. This pattern of change has been widely referred to as the 'residualisation of council housing' (Forrest and Murie, 1983).

The statistics of residualisation show that, in 1954, some 21% of national assistance recipients were council tenants; in 1967, 45% of all recipients of Supplementary Benefit were council tenants and, in 1979, the comparable figure was 61%. In the period 1967-79, council housing had increased from housing 29% of households to 32%. The concentration of lower income households in the tenure had increased. Family Expenditure Survey (FES) data shows that, in 1963, council tenants accounted for 26% of households in the bottom three income deciles. The comparable figures for 1972 and 1979 were 41% and 47% (Murie, 1983). Operating against this background, the Right to Buy policies of the 1980s served to residualise the tenure even further. Between 1980 and 1991, the proportion of council tenants who were in the lowest three income deciles rose from 44% to 65%.

Forrest and Murie (1990) have identified other features of the changing social profile of council housing:

- a decline in the proportion of economically active heads of households;
- a decline in the proportion of multiple-earner households;
- a decline in the proportion of higher-income households;
- a declining level of car ownership;
- a declining family housing role;
- an increase in the proportion of households with no earners;
- an increase in the proportion of unskilled manual workers;
- an increase in the proportion of non-married households;
- an increase in the proportion of households headed by women;
- an increase in the proportion of households with older people and of single elderly households;
- an increasing role in housing persons aged under 25;
- an increasing role in housing those receiving Income Support;
- an increasing role in housing those with the lowest incomes;
- a declining dwelling stock and rate of new building;
- an ageing dwelling stock;
- a declining proportion of three- to four-bedroom houses in the stock and among newly built dwellings;
- an increasing proportion of flats and small houses;
- an increasing proportion of lettings to homeless persons.

In its early and expanding years, council housing consisted almost exclusively of modern, traditionally-built dwellings with much higher standards than applied in the sector which dominated the housing market, that of private-rented dwellings. Council housing was accessible to a wide section of households which would not have been able to obtain such good quality housing in the private sector. In this way, it formed an important element in redistribution and breaking the link between poor housing and low income. In the 1990s, council housing is much more mixed in age, design, type, condition and desirability. Over time, the characteristics of households in the council sector have changed from the affluent, employed working-class family to a low-income, benefit-dependent group including disproportionate numbers of elderly persons and lone-parent families. Housing is both a product and contributory factor in determining inequality. What is emerging is a compound, reinforcing pattern of multiple deprivation which is persistent over time and concentrated in particular areas because of the role of housing. It is resistant to traditional policy interventions and partly generated through public policy.

## Housing and social exclusion

The process of residualisation has been associated with wider processes of social exclusion and this can be summarised as follows:
* Households entering the housing market have differential choices and bargaining powers. Those without jobs and with family responsibilities and those with special needs and outside the labour market graduate towards the rented sectors.
* Those with least choice graduate towards the least desirable dwellings and areas.
* Households living in these areas are dependent on local facilities and low demand housing areas tend to be poorly served by other services. Consequently, those living in deprived areas are less able to build satisfactory homes or avail themselves of opportunities which could increase their incomes and bargaining power and enable them to move on.

The term 'social exclusion' is generally used to refer to more than just income poverty. It is used to relate to a wider range of resources and citizenship rights and emphasises the compound, persistent, resistant and concentrated nature of deprivation. It also focuses on the processes of exclusion and the roles of actors and agencies rather than simply on outputs.

As used by the government, the term social exclusion is seen as:

> ... a shorthand label for what can happen when individuals or areas suffer from a combination of linked problems such as unemployment, poor skills, low incomes, poor housing, high crime environments, bad health and family breakdown. (SEU, 1998)

Housing is included in this definition and identified in the initial remit of the Social Exclusion Unit both in relation to rough sleeping and the worst estates. Rough sleeping relates to the traditional housing agenda in which homelessness and the lack of adequate housing are seen as contributing to disadvantage and represent a threat to health and security. However, the current debate involves a move from this traditional debate towards one also concerned with neighbourhood resources and instability.

To focus the policy agenda on the worst estates would appear to follow quite naturally from the account of residualisation presented above. The disproportionate concentration of poor people in council housing and the social-rented sector would suggest that to target those experiencing social exclusion you would target council housing. The spiral of decline and stigma and adverse labelling clearly affects many large council estates. However, this is too simple. Research which has mapped deprivation shows a strong link with housing tenure but does not show that it is safe to assume that mapping council housing is the same as mapping where the most disadvantaged live (Lee et al, 1995). The structure of the housing market in London (with very high affordability thresholds for home ownership) may mean that the most disadvantaged sections of the community are most likely to be found in council housing. However, they will also be found in mixed tenure estates, in housing association dwellings, and in the private-rented sector. In the Midlands and the North of England, where a higher proportion of the housing stock is in the private sector and average house prices are lower, a significant proportion of low-income households are in the private sector. This is particularly true among ethnic minority communities where the early experience of discrimination in housing led to concentration of households in owner-occupation and where preferred areas of residence tend to be dominated by the private sector. An agenda which equates social exclusion with council housing will actively discriminate against significant proportions of disadvantaged groups. In many parts of the country there is a far greater proportion of deprived 'white' households living in council housing than of equally deprived 'non-white' households and a focus on council housing favours 'white' households (Lee and Murie, 1997).

The conditions in low priced and easy access private sector and mixed tenure neighbourhoods with deprived populations are comparable with those on council estates. They have differences, just as different council estates have differences, in terms of access to services, levels of crime and the fear of crime and other factors. These neighbourhoods are more like council estates than they are like affluent enclaves of owner-occupation. The private-rented sector continues to provide the poorest quality housing and to house many of those with the least bargaining power in the economy and society. The owner-occupied sector, especially in some cities, has a disproportionate role in housing elderly people, low-income groups, ethnic minority groups and many of those who are in relative poverty.

## Responses

Much of the debate about residualisation and spatial concentrations of poverty (at least partly as a result of housing processes) demonstrates that while housing situations are consequences of low income and bargaining power, they also actively disadvantage households. The 'passive' view of housing, as the receptacle for inequalities created elsewhere, gives too little weight to the extent to which where people live and what they live in affects their access to employment, education and other resources as well as their health, wealth and ability to change residence.

Within cities, where you live increasingly affects your life chances, both directly and indirectly, and the concentration of poverty relates to the operation of the housing market. This links to the work of the Social Exclusion Unit, with its initial emphasis on the worst estates, and to a wider literature which is preoccupied with problems in the council housing sector and which makes little or no reference to problems elsewhere. For example, research carried out for the Department of the Environment (DoE) identified 1,370 deprived council estates and appears to have informed the early thinking of government ministers (DoE, 1997). This research adopted an approach which was bound to identify council areas rather than equally deprived mixed tenure areas and is an insufficient basis for the development of a housing strategy or a strategy related to social exclusion (Lee and Murie, 1998). A number of fallacies emerge from this and other contributions:

- There is an ecological fallacy that targeting areas is the most effective way of reaching deprived groups. The evidence suggests the opposite and the arguments for targeting areas must relate to a belief that households living in such areas are more likely to experience prolonged social exclusion than those living elsewhere.
- There is a second fallacy which relates to housing tenure. This is the fallacy that the targeting of the social-rented sector everywhere would involve targeting the most deprived groups. Again, the evidence is that targeting the private-rented sector and the lower end of the owner-occupied sector will often be more important than targeting social-rented housing. The tenurial fallacy grows out of a limited perspective perhaps dominated by work on the London housing market.
- A third fallacy relates to the place given to housing management, both in explanations of housing inequality and the concentration of poorer people in different tenures and parts of cities and in policy solutions designed to respond to this. Again, the thinking of the Social Exclusion Unit would appear initially to have been influenced by this (see Chapter Six). The key question is whether housing management initiatives on the worst estates will make a significant impact on housing inequality. On the basis of existing evidence, the answer would be 'no'. The last 20 years has seen various well-intentioned initiatives designed to target the worst estates. The evidence is that their impact is short-lived, that there is a tendency to be overwhelmed by developments in the society and economy outside the estate and that interventions in one estate tend to move problems and people elsewhere. The approach does not remove the problems which underlie the worst estates relating to lack of choice, to poverty, to low demand and to high turnover (see, for example, Foster and Hope, 1993). The basic reasons why concentrations of deprived people emerge on particular estates are not addressed by management initiatives focused on a limited number of selected estates.

The recognition that social exclusion is not contained purely within the social-rented sector suggests that the solution to the problem does not simply rest in tenure diversification or privatisation or in housing management. There would still be concentrations·of people with the least choice living in the housing which is least desirable and the consequences of this are likely to be as damaging as at present. Instead, what is needed is a policy agenda which builds up from an analysis of cities and deprivation and adopts a more wide-ranging approach to housing interventions, including action in the private-rented sector and in relation to urban renewal.

Addressing issues of housing inequality, especially those related to concentrations of deprivation, requires an agenda which moves beyond housing management into housing finance and the structure of the incentives which funnel different households to different parts of the market. This relates to rent levels, Housing Benefit and the poverty and savings traps, and to wider systems of housing finance and subsidy. Effective engagement with problems of inequality in housing requires a parallel engagement with regeneration of incomes and employment. However, it is important not to take this argument too far and to argue that 'getting jobs and incomes right' means that the housing system will sort itself out. Issues about housing standards and access continue to need to be addressed through strategies for renewal and investment. At the end of the 1990s, there is increasing concern about low demand for certain types of properties and a high turnover of residents is a factor affecting the success of schools and other services in a given area. Strategies are required to deal with poverty, to alter housing finance and to regenerate housing stock. There is a need for investment and renewal in the housing stock to replace the least desirable housing and to ensure that those on the lowest incomes are not excluded from the housing standards and neighbourhoods which the rest of the population chooses to live in.

National policy interventions will be imprecise and blunt instruments in dealing with very different circumstances in different places. At the same time, local strategies cannot just be about council housing and need to be based on a proper analysis of where concentrations of poverty exist, and on the different problems in different tenures, and experienced by different social groups.

**Notes**

Statistical material on housing is available in the HMSO annual and quarterly *Housing and Construction Statistics*.

In recent years a valuable annual collection, entitled *Housing Finance Review*, has been edited by S. Wilcox for the Joseph Rowntree Foundation.

# References

Anderson, I., Kemp, P. and Quilgars, D. (1993) *Single homeless people*, London: HMSO.

DETR (Department of the Environment, Transport and the Regions) (1998) *English House Condition Survey 1996*, London: The Stationery Office.

DoE (Department of the Environment) (1997) *Mapping local authority estates using the index of local conditions*, London: HMSO.

Forrest, R. and Murie, A. (1983) 'Residualisation and council housing: aspects of the changing social relations of housing tenure', *Journal of Social Policy*, vol 12, no 4, pp 453-68.

Forrest, R. and Murie, A. (1990) *Residualisation and council housing: A statistical update*, Bristol: SAUS Publications.

Foster, J. and Hope, T. (1993) *Housing community and crime: The impact of the Priority Estates Project*, Home Office Research Study No 131, London: HMSO.

Great Britain (1965) *The Housing Programme 1965-70*, Cmnd 2838, London: HMSO.

Great Britain (1968) *Old houses into new homes*, London: HMSO.

Great Britain (1977a) *Housing policy*, Cmnd 6851, London: HMSO.

Great Britain (1977b) *Housing policy: Technical volume Part 1*, London: HMSO.

Lansley, S. (1979) *Housing and public policy*, Beckenham: Croom Helm.

Lee, P. and Murie, A. (1997) *Poverty, housing tenure and social exclusion*, Bristol: The Policy Press.

Lee, P. and Murie, A. (1998) 'Targetting social exclusion', *New Economy*, vol 5, no 2, pp 89-93.

Lee, P., Murie, A. and Gordon, D. (1995) *Area measures of deprivation*, Birmingham: CURS, University of Birmingham.

Malpass, P. and Murie, A. (1999) *Housing policy and practice* (5th edn), London: Macmillan.

Marsh, A., Gordon, D., Pantazis, C. and Heslop, P. (1999) *Home Sweet Home? The impact of poor housing on health*, Bristol: The Policy Press.

Merrett, S. (1979) *State housing in Britain*, London: Routledge and Kegan Paul.

Murie, A. (1983) *Housing inequality and deprivation*, London: Heinemann.

SEU (Social Exclusion Unit) (1998) *Bringing Britain together: A national strategy for neighbourhood renewal*, London: The Stationery Office.

# SIX

# Tackling inequalities in crime and social harm

*Christina Pantazis*

## Introduction

New Labour's landslide victory in the 1997 Election has been partly attributed to the way in which it fought on the issues of 'law and order'. Its adoption of a populist stance on these issues helped convince the electorate that it was the natural party of 'law and order' – a title which had been rigorously held by the Conservatives for nearly 20 years. Margaret Thatcher, in the 1979 Election, was especially successful in breaking the cross-party consensus on crime by questioning Labour's commitment to the rule of law, in particular to striking trade unions. For many years, until the transformation of the Labour Party, particularly under Tony Blair, the Labour Party was portrayed as being 'soft on crime'. Its policies on crime and its premise that rising crime is linked to growing unemployment, poverty and inequality, was contrasted with the hardline and populist approach taken by the Conservatives. However, the appointment of Tony Blair to Shadow Home Secretary in 1992 changed that perception – with his famous soundbite of New Labour's promise to "be tough on crime, tough on the causes of crime".

Invoking the third way approach (see Chapter One) New Labour has adopted a twin stance to deal with the problem of crime. Like the Conservatives, New Labour sees an important role for punishing offenders. Punishment not only acts as a deterrent to potential criminals, it also means that people take responsibility for their actions: "Recognising that there are underlying causes of crime is in no way to excuse or condone offending. Individuals must be held responsible for their own behaviour, and must be brought to justice and punished when they commit an offence" (Labour Party, 1996, p 6).

Like Old Labour, New Labour promises to be tough on the causes of crime. However, while Old Labour stresses factors relating to poverty, unemployment and racism to explain crime, New Labour prioritises factors relating to upbringing over broader social and economic explanations. This was clearly demonstrated in the Labour Party's document *Tackling the causes of crime* (1996), where it lists the causes of crime in the following order: parenting, schools and truancy, drug and alcohol abuse, lack of facilities for young people, unemployment, low income, and recession, homelessness and the treatment of the mentally ill. New Labour's belief that the roots of crime lie firmly within the family is in accordance with Conservative thinking about the causes of crime. However, unlike the Conservatives, New Labour does at least partially recognise the role of social and material deprivation:" ... all too often the factors we identify are interlinked in pockets of deprivation" (Labour Party, 1996, p 9).

Nevertheless, Labour's new approach towards crime has involved a substantial retreat from Old Labour's thinking (Brownlee, 1998). Not only has New Labour distanced itself from the civil disobedience issues, such as the anti-road protests that took place during the 1990s, it supports the anti-trade union legislation introduced by the Conservatives. It has also instigated attacks on the most vulnerable groups of people. For example, the Shadow Home Secretary Jack Straw in 1995 proposed a crackdown on 'winos' and 'squeegee merchants' cleaning car windscreens at traffic lights. Encouraged by the zero-tolerance policies of the New York Police Department (NYPD), Straw urged that the streets be reclaimed "for the law-abiding citizen" from the "aggressive begging of winos and squeegee merchants" (Straw, cited in Travis, 1995). In 1997, the Prime Minister Tony Blair added to the vilification of the homeless by stating that it was "right to be intolerant of people homeless on the street" (Blair, cited in Travis and Meikle, 1997)[1]. New Labour has endorsed zero-tolerance strategies not in response to homelessness as a pressing social problem that needs to be eradicated but, rather, in response to homelessness as a public protection issue, and in order to stem the apparent link between disorder and crime:

> The rising tide of disorder is blighting our streets, neighbourhoods, parks, towns and city centres. Incivility and harassment, public drunkenness, graffiti and vandalism all affect our ability to use open spaces and enjoy a quiet life in our own homes. Moreover, crime and disorder are linked. Disorder can lead to a vicious circle of community decline in which those who are able to move away do

so, whilst those who remain learn to avoid certain streets and parks. This leads to a breakdown in community ties and reduction in natural social controls tipping an area further into decline, economic dislocation and crime. (Labour Party, 1996, p 4)

New Labour's support for New York's zero-tolerance policing strategies broke strikingly with Old Labour thinking, which stressed broad social and economic measures to control low-level criminal behaviour (Downes and Morgan, 1997).

In its 1997 election manifesto, New Labour accused the Conservatives of letting crime spiral and also of letting criminals get away with crime (Labour Party, 1997). They continued to press for their "tough on crime and tough on the causes of crime" approach to law and order by insisting on individual responsibility for crime, and by pledging to attack the causes of crime by introducing measures to relieve social deprivation. However, in terms of the proposals that were pledged in the manifesto, it is clear that New Labour's commitments lie more with being tough on crime rather than on being tough on the causes of crime. For example, the manifesto promised continued support for the police, reform of the youth justice system to improve the speed at which children are dealt with, and improved sentencing by ensuring greater consistency and stricter punishments for repeat offenders. New Labour also promised to introduce measures to deal with threatening and disruptive criminal neighbours and young children who are let out at night. Furthermore, policies to deal with the links between crime and drugs were the only ones specifically mentioned in the crime section of the manifesto to deal with the causes of crime.

Once in power New Labour wasted little time before introducing the 1998 Crime and Disorder Act. This has created new draconian measures to combat anti-social behaviour and includes orders that can be used against 'criminal neighbours' as young as 10 who cause 'harassment, alarm or distress'. Although they are civil orders, any breach of them can result in imprisonment of up to five years. Local authorities have also been given the power to operate a local child curfew scheme under which a curfew notice may be given banning children below a specified age (under the age of 10) from being in a public place during specific hours unless they are under the control of a responsible person aged 18 or over. The government has also implemented the 1997 Crime (Sentences) Act introduced by the Conservatives which created automatic life sentencing for a second conviction for serious sexual or violent offences.

However, it would be unfair to paint New Labour as a reincarnation of the Conservatives. In many respects, its policies on crime and criminal justice have been more progressive than those introduced under the previous Conservative governments. For example, the 1998 Crime and Disorder Act made racist attacks a separate criminal offence. The government has also introduced measures on social exclusion, including improvements in education and the Welfare to Work scheme in recognition of the links between deprivation and crime. This suggests that New Labour has not completely ignored the social causes of crime. This is most evident in its New Deal for Communities programme which aims to improve safety in Britain's poorest neighbourhoods through regeneration. Launched in September 1998, John Prescott called it the most ambitious government programme ever conceived to bridge the gap between the poor and the rich, while Blair invoked Benjamin Disraeli's memory in his launch speech at the Holly Street Estate in London's Borough of Hackney (see Hetherington, 1998).

## New Deal for Communities

Details of the New Deal for Communities are contained in the Social Exclusion Unit's (SEU's) third report *Bringing Britain together: A national strategy for neighbourhood renewal* (1998). The report's main purpose is to show how to develop integrated and sustainable approaches to the problems of the poorest neighbourhoods. The report describes how crime is just one of the symptoms of a range of social problems suffered by the people living in the poorest areas in the following way: "these neighbourhoods are places where unemployment is endemic; crime, drugs, vandalism are rife; and public and private-sector services are second-rate or completely absent" (p 2). Evidence is cited from the London Research Centre showing the heavy concentration of violent crime in London's boroughs according to the Index of Local Conditions (p 12), and other research is used to show that burglary and drug use are also higher in poor areas. Evidence is also advanced to show that high rates of crime exist in areas which also have higher rates of unemployment, lone-parent households, households on benefit, people with low literacy, poor housing, as well as a higher proportion of people from ethnic minority groups.

During the next three years New Deal for Communities will inject £800 million into the worst-off local communities to deal with specific problems such as unemployment, sub-standard housing, poor access to public and private services, poor health and crime and drugs. The programme has initially involved 17 pathfinder areas that have been selected because of the severity of the problems suffered. In addition, the government has created 18 cross-cutting action teams involving 10 Whitehall departments, outside experts and community workers to draw up plans for tackling the underlying problems of regenerating local economies, improving housing and neighbourhood management, enhancing prospects for young people, increasing access to services and making the government work better.

Neighbourhood and housing management are seen as key to solving the problems of vacant properties and crime and disorder (SEU, 1998). The SEU's report suggests that neighbourhoods should have a management board whose remit will be to identify local needs and ensure a more 'joined-up' service planning and delivery. 'Super-caretakers' will provide on-the-spot housing management to deal with the turnover of housing, graffiti and vandalism, and neighbourhood wardens will supplement their work. A flavour of the type of management favoured by the Unit is provided with the various examples of good practice. According to the report, 'super-caretakers' on the Broadwater Farm Estate (in Tottenham, North London) have kept the estate virtually free of litter, refuse and graffiti. Similarly, Pride in Pennywell's drive to improve community safety through a rigorous enforcement of tenancy conditions, high profile police and council actions against offenders, physical crime prevention and youth diversionary schemes are reported as having contributed to the reduction in crime on this estate in Sutherland.

New Deal for Communities has been welcomed by various statutory and voluntary agencies (Allen, 1999) and academics (see Power, 1999) as an ambitious programme that attempts to tackle the concentration of inequalities in certain neighbourhoods. Combined with the Sure Start programme which will inject £540 million into children's services and the Single Regeneration Programmes which will involve a further £2 billion, the 50 most deprived districts are being guaranteed a major regeneration programme. Nevertheless doubts have been raised, including the fact that the programme is limited to 17 pilots (or 50 projects by 2002), and that the funds available for each of the pathfinder areas are quite limited (for example, Hackney's scheme alone has been costed at £97 million). Some academics have criticised the extent to which the report might be conceptualising the problems of poor neighbourhoods as problems that are bound up with the underclass (see Chapter Five). For example, Watt and Jacobs (1999) have described the report's discussion of housing problems as being underpinned by a 'moral underclass' discourse (MUD).

## Dealing with the underclass

MUD is just one of the three approaches identified by Levitas (1998) as embodying the ubiquitous concept of social exclusion. The three approaches are:

> ... a redistributionist discourse (RED) developed in British critical social policy, whose prime concern is poverty; a moral underclass discourse (MUD) which centres on the moral and behavioural delinquency of the excluded themselves; and a social integrationist discourse (SID) whose central focus is on paid work. (Levitas, 1998, p 7)

MUD combines references to the underclass and to a culture of dependency. While the underclass refers to a group that is below or separated from other social classes by either structural conditions or cultural attitudes, the culture of dependency arises not from the poverty trap in which people find themselves but from the disincentives provided by the welfare state. Thus MUD is:

> ... a gendered discourse with many forerunners, whose demons are criminally-inclined, unemployable young men and sexually and socially irresponsible single mothers, for whom paid work is necessary as a social discipline, but whose (self-)exclusion, and thus potential inclusion, is moral and cultural. (Levitas, 1998, p 8)

The framework for understanding the contested meaning of social exclusion provided by Levitas was applied by Watt and Jacobs to the SEU's report (1998). Their focus was on the presentation of issues relating to 'poor neighbourhoods' and 'housing problems' and how these were being identified with crime and disorder issues. Their conclusion was that, despite all three discourses being evident in the report, the discussion of poor housing was dominated by MUD concerns.

> ... the *root* of the housing problem is not defined as the systematic under-funding of local authority housing in combination with the growth of poverty (as in RED), or lack of work opportunities (as in SID), but is instead crime and anti-social behaviour. The problems

of housing, and social housing in particular, in poor neighbourhoods are in effect being redefined in terms of crime and anti-social behaviour. (Watt and Jacobs, 1999, p 14)

According to Watt and Jacobs, despite MUD concerns being present throughout the report, they become more explicit when the report moves on to discussing social housing (council and housing association properties). In discussing the problems of social housing the agenda becomes one of 'surplus' housing, which is then linked to "crime, anti-social behaviour and wasteful public expenditure" (1999, p 13). Crime is linked to 'unpopular housing': "One of the most striking developments in some poor neighbourhoods today is the phenomenon of low demand and neighbourhood abandonment. Crime and severe anti-social behaviour is often at the root of the problem" (SEU, 1998, p 66). In other words, the SEU locates the problem of empty housing on crime and disorder rather than on other factors such as people migrating out of cities in search of employment (see Chapter Three).

The way the problems of social housing and crime and disorder have been brought together in the SEU report is characteristic of the way in which social housing has generally been depicted during the last 25 years or so. For example, Murray (1990), the Right-wing American underclass theorist, claims that there are entire neighbourhoods differing from the rest of the population in their attitude to 'illegitimacy', employment and criminality. Similarly, Hall discusses the Broadwater Farm Estate that saw rioting which resulted in the death of a policeman in October 1985 in the clear context of the underclass:

A prize-winning urban-renewal project of 1970.... It degenerated into a hard-to-let estate, with a large number of problem tenants – particularly, young unmarried black mothers and their children; by 1980, the project was more than half black. A virtual no-go area for the police, it was brought back to life through a remarkable community effort led by one of the black tenants.... Then, her absence, and that of other key leaders, helped to precipitate a new wave of crime and thus, indirectly, the triggering of the riot. (Hall, 1988, p 398)

The work of Watt and Jacobs (1999) is important for highlighting the extent to which New Labour is defining the problems of poor neighbourhoods, particularly areas dominated by social housing, in terms of the underclass. Crime and disorder are depicted as the central factors which explain surplus housing on estates and, therefore, the decline of these neighbourhoods. One solution to the problems of 'problem estates', or 'sink estates' as they are often called, is claimed to be improved management – and this is characteristic of a second approach to social housing.

## Improving neighbourhoods through better management

A second approach to social housing focuses on the relevance of housing management, in particular the extent to which 'problem estates' are bound up with poor council services and the consequential disillusionment of tenants on those estates (see Chapter Five). This approach is most clearly associated with the work of Professor Anne Power of the London School of Economics (LSE), who is currently a member of the SEU. Power was instrumental in initiating the Department of the Environment (DoE) sponsored Priority Estates Project (PEP) of the late 1970s. The PEP model seeks to reverse the deterioration of estates through measures based on the principles of estate-based management and tenant involvement. The scheme involves a local estate-based office with, for example, a local repairs team and a caretaker to clean and maintain open spaces. Although crime prevention is not the main goal of the PEP, the intention is that victimisation and fear of crime are reduced as a consequence of changes occurring as a result of, or coincidentally with, measures implemented by the PEP (Foster and Hope, 1993).

The Home Office and the DoE commissioned research on the impact of the PEP on crime and community life (Foster and Hope, 1993). The progress of two new PEPs (one was in the London Borough of Tower Hamlets and the other was in the City of Kingston-upon-Hull) was investigated over three years and involved the selection of two control estates in each of the cities so that comparisons could be made. The research showed that the PEP had produced ambiguous and contradictory results. Although both crime and perceptions of safety among the Bengali residents fell on the London PEP estate, the crime rate fell by a greater degree on the London control estate. On the Hull estate the combined effect of the PEP with a tenant turnover produced intensification both of social control and criminality. The authors of the report claimed that:

> ... despite a programme of improvements to the security of the tower
> blocks, and better management of the estate, the newcomers – that

is, the young, childless poor – displaced many of the previous, elderly residents and attracted crime to themselves, both as perpetrators and victims, concentrating crime in their part of the estate. (Foster and Hope, 1993, p ix)

One of the key conclusions of the research was that "the capacity of the PEP model to bring about community organisation and involvement may be affected by the rate of population turnover and the degree of social and cultural heterogeneity within the community" (Foster and Hope, 1993, p x). In other words, improvements in management alone failed to reduce crime and fear of crime on these estates. With the emphasis on management, there is a danger that the New Deal will fail to bring about the expected reductions in crime and fear of crime on the poorest estates.

## New Labour and 'Left Realism'

New Labour's policies on crime and criminal justice are intellectually rooted in the 'Left Realist' criminological paradigm (see Taylor, 1981; Kinsey et al, 1986; Lea and Young, 1993). Although the origins of 'Left Realism' stem from the mid-1970s, it gained momentum following the victory of the Conservative Party at the 1979 Election – an election in which 'law and order' issues had a high profile. 'Left Realism' began as a critique of radical or critical approaches to deviancy and social control with its emphasis on prioritising the crimes of the state, and its supposedly sympathetic approach to deviants. According to 'Left Realist' supporters, it was this approach that allowed the Conservatives to hijack the issue of law and order in the 1979 Election (Downes, 1983). Over the years 'Left Realism' has developed from existing as a critique of Left-wing criminology to providing a more fully-fledged theoretical approach to the problem of crime. Its starting point is that crime is a socialist issue, which requires the 'political Left' to reassess the issue of law and order by taking working-class crime more seriously (Lea and Young, 1993). Crime needs to be taken more seriously because its consequences have a greater impact on the poor (Lea and Young, 1993). It is argued that not only does crime have a greater impact on poor people, but also that the majority of crime is intra-group and not inter-group – the main target of working-class crime is the working class itself, not the middle or upper classes:

> We are not equally threatened by crime as the right would assume; neither are the rich the sole targets of crime as left-wing romantics would presume. The poor suffer disproportionately from all the more serious forms of crime, the middle income brackets suffer more than the rich, the rich suffer only in terms of the least serious forms of crime.... (Lea and Young, 1993, pp 47-8)

Throughout the 1980s 'Left Realist' criminologists began putting into practice their theoretical endeavours to take working-class crime more seriously by conducting local crime surveys. With Labour-controlled councils often providing the financial support, local crime surveys were carried out in places such as Islington and Liverpool with the intention of discovering the true extent of crime against poor and socially disadvantaged groups – such as women and ethnic minorities and poor people (Kinsey, 1984; Jones et al, 1986; Anderson et al, 1990). These surveys have been important in establishing the social and geographical focus of victimisation. They have also made several methodological advances to the study of victimisation by better preparing interviewers through improved training, so that the respondent's willingness to answer sensitive information is maximised, and by adopting wider definitions of certain offences than pure legalistic terms. For instance, the 1986 Islington Crime Survey used four categories of sexual crime, rather than the usual one (Jones et al, 1986).

However, these surveys have, in part, failed to achieve what they set out to uncover. In particular, they do not lend support to the 'Left Realist' claim that poor people are more likely to be at risk from crime than the rest of the population. For instance, while the 1984 Merseyside Crime Survey demonstrates that crime is greatest for the people living in the 'poorest' council housing, the 1986 Islington Crime Survey shows that the victims of most types of crime (burglary, vandalism, theft from the person) are predominantly higher income households. This survey also found that women in higher income groups have disproportionately higher risks of sexual assault. But rather than address these contradictory findings the 'Left Realists' have chosen to ignore them.

A second issue is that while these surveys have tapped into the crimes against poor people and other socially disadvantaged groups, they have done so at the expense of examining other types of harms (such as ill-health and work injuries) that may be more prevalent in their lives. By restricting coverage to 'street crimes' or conventionally defined crimes, these surveys perpetuate a narrow conceptualisation of harm. The result is that they encompass the harmful activities of poor people but exclude many of the harmful activities of the rich and powerful. For example, in these surveys people have been asked about their experience of burglary but not about being missold an endowment mortgage; being mugged but not about whether they have experienced pension fraud; being violently attacked by a stranger but not about being 'injured' at work, and so on.

A more fruitful approach may be to consider crime in the context of a range of other harms people experience during their life cycle. The study of social harm or 'zemia' is in its infancy but it has enormous potential to reveal the extent of and inter-connections between various harms that people experience (Hillyard et al, 1999). The Poverty and Social Exclusion Survey of Britain is the first to put this approach into practice by asking people directly about their experience of various harms – some of which are criminal but many others (such as work injuries, food poisoning) may not be criminal (see Bradshaw et al, 1998).

The remaining part of this chapter re-analyses British Crime Survey (BCS) data to consider the extent of inequalities in harm – both criminal and non-criminal – among individuals, as well as the extent to which people worry about these harms. The purpose is to discuss inequalities in crime in the context of other harms in order to assess its relative significance, and therefore to judge the extent to which New Labour is prioritising criminal harm over other types of harm which poor people may experience a greater share of.

## Mapping the extent of social harm

The BCS is considered to be the most reliable guide to the extent and nature of crime in England and Wales since it overcomes many of the shortcomings associated with crime recorded by the police[2]. It also provides information on other related issues such as perceptions of safety and concerns about victimisation. The analysis presented in this chapter is drawn from secondary analysis of the 1994 BCS which involved interviews with 14,500 people aged 16 and above. To find out what types of people experience crime, the 1994 BCS asked respondents questions about other non-criminal incidents that they may have also experienced in the previous year, as well as how worried they were about them.

## Inequalities in crime, fear and location: unpacking the evidence

There is a plethora of research on the link between crime and poor areas stretching as far back as the 19th century with Henry Mayhew's (1862) comprehensive survey of Victorian London which provided detail on various 'rookeries' (slum criminal quarters). In the latter half of the 20th century, research based on local areas has linked crime with poor neighbourhoods in Sheffield (Baldwin et al, 1976) and more recently Liverpool (Hirshfield and Bowers, 1996). On the other hand, national survey statistics based on combined sweeps of the BCS indicate a more complicated reality. Using the ACORN classification of neighbourhoods, the Home Office found that there are significant levels of crime in both poor and better-off areas (Mayhew and Maung, 1992; Mirrlees et al, 1998). Furthermore, deprived neighbourhoods are not equally crime-ridden. For example, data from the combined 1984, 1988 and 1992 British Crime Surveys show that 'agricultural' areas and 'older terraced housing' – areas typically containing many low-income households – have respectively very low and average burglary and robbery rates (Mayhew and Maung, 1992).

This section considers in more detail the variation in the risks of victimisation in different ACORN neighbourhoods (see Appendix A at the end of this chapter), and confirms that the risk of being victimised is highly dependent on where you live. Figure 6.1 shows that crime is significantly higher in 'striving' areas (neighbourhoods with local authority and multi-ethnic, low-income households) but also in 'rising' areas (urban, and inner-city neighbourhoods with affluent professionals, and better-off executives). Rising areas have the highest proportion of victims of most types of crime, whereas 'striving' areas have a disproportionate number of people who have had their property vandalised (10%). 'Striving' neighbourhoods also have the highest proportions of people who feel unsafe when they are walking alone in their neighbourhood after dark or when they are alone in the house at night (Figure 6.2). In other words, while the risks of victimisation can be equally high in some rich and some poor areas, the risk of feeling unsafe is much greater in poor areas.

*Figure 6.1:* **Proportion of the population experiencing crime (1993) (%)**

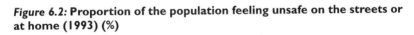

*Source:* 1994 BCS

*Figure 6.2:* **Proportion of the population feeling unsafe on the streets or at home (1993) (%)**

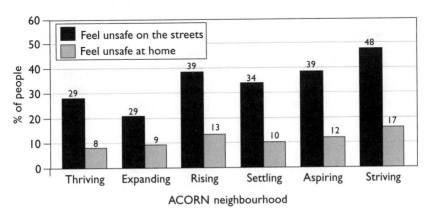

*Source:* 1994 BCS

The simplistic notion that crime and poverty are linked is further undermined when we consider the issue of whether the predominant victims in deprived areas are people who are themselves living in circumstances of poverty. It is misleading to assume that 'poor' people only live in 'poor' areas, or that better-off people do not also live in 'poor' areas (Lee et al, 1995). By avoiding the assumption that individuals have the same characteristics as the areas in which they live, the dangers inherent in the 'ecological fallacy' – in which inferences about relationships at the individual level are made on the basis of aggregate data obtained at the area level – may be overcome (Robinson, 1950). Taking account of the ecological fallacy means that we are in a better position to examine how inequalities in victimisation are distributed across different groups in different areas. Many of the early ecology studies of juvenile delinquency fell into the trap of the ecological fallacy (Polk, 1957; Willie, 1967). For example, inappropriate conclusions were made about British immigrants and their propensity to commit crime based on recorded crime data that showed that crime was highest in areas with an immigrant population (Wallis and Maliphant, 1967). With the relative absence of the ecological fallacy within the criminological discussions (for a review see Baldwin et al, 1976), there is a danger that current assumptions about poverty and crime may be failing to take into account the full effects of the fallacy (Pantazis and Gordon, 1998).

Accordingly we move on to consider the extent to which inequalities in crime vary between different income households *within* the areas. Figure 6.3 illustrates the risk of experiencing crime among poor and rich households according to the neighbourhood type. Contrary to the common assumption about the link between poverty and crime, victimisation risks are greater for higher income individuals – regardless of neighbourhood type. Figure 6.3 shows that for both rich and poor people victimisation risks are higher in 'striving' areas. However, the risks of crime are significantly greater for higher income people. Three in every four people in the highest household income category suffered from some form of criminal victimisation in the previous year (78%). This compares with 41% of the poorest individuals.

**Figure 6.3: Proportion of the population experiencing total crime (1993) (%)**

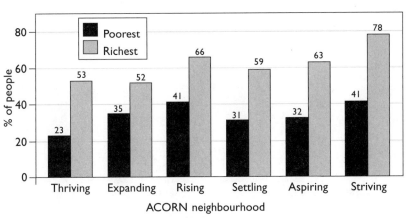

*Source:* 1994 BCS

One of the main factors explaining the vast difference in the victimisation experience between the richest and poorest people is vehicle ownership. Vehicle ownership is significantly higher in richer households and the fact that it forms a large proportion of total crime explains why richer individuals experience more crime. However, even when vehicle-related crime is removed from total crime, the data indicates that the richest still experience a higher victimisation rate – although the gap does narrow (Figure 6.4).

While the data show that crime is positively related with income, so that as household income rises so does crime risk, the reverse is true when we consider people's perceptions of safety. Figure 6.5 shows that poor people are more likely to feel unsafe when alone on the streets regardless of where they live. Out of all neighbourhoods, 'striving' areas contain the highest proportion of poor people who feel unsafe (59%). However, the greatest disparities between people's perceptions of safety can be found in 'thriving' areas (suburban/rural/retirement neighbourhoods with wealthy people). In these types of neighbourhood, the poorest individuals are 2.5 times as likely to feel unsafe on the streets compared with the richest individuals.

**Figure 6.4: Proportion of the population experiencing crime, excluding vehicle-related car crime (1993) (%)**

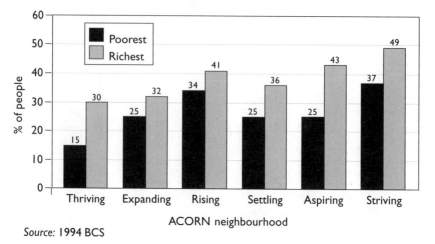

*Source:* 1994 BCS

**Figure 6.5: Proportion of the population feeling unsafe on the streets (1993) (%)**

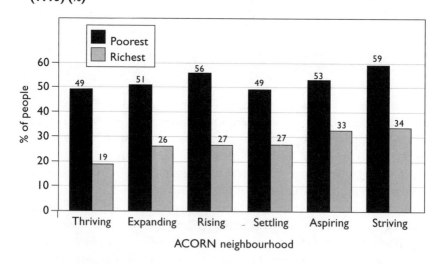

*Source:* 1994 BCS

Figure 6.6 shows the proportion of people in poor and rich households who are worried about being victimised in relation to a range of conventional crimes. People in poor households are more prone to worrying about becoming the victims of crime although, in comparison with the global measures (fear on the streets or at home), there is less variance between people in different income households. The starkest difference is in relation to mugging: 57% of poor people worry about being mugged compared with only 37% of rich people. Poor people are also more likely than rich people to worry about becoming a victim of rape, public insults or having their vehicle stolen. The fact that they are equally likely to worry about thefts from the car and burglary is a surprising result given the fact that the effects of victimisation involving property loss may be greater for poor households.

**Figure 6.6: Proportion of the population worried about specific types of crime (1993) (%)**

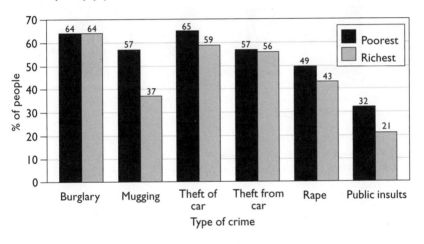

*Source:* 1994 BCS

## Inequalities in non-criminal harm

Having considered the extent of criminal harm experienced by poor people, we move on to examine the range of other social harms which they may be more prone to suffering. Figure 6.7 shows the population's experience of a range of non-criminal harms. Poor individuals are more likely than the rich to be victims of these selected non-criminal harms. There are significant inequalities between poor and rich people in relation to an illness occurring in the household. More than three times as many poor people said that they or someone else in their household had been seriously ill in the previous year. The main wage earner losing their job in the previous year affected twice as many poor people as it did rich people. On the other hand, there were more rich individuals affected by a road accident – and this is probably related to the higher prevalence of vehicle ownership among the better-off.

**Figure 6.7: Proportion of the population experiencing non-criminal harms (1993) (%)**

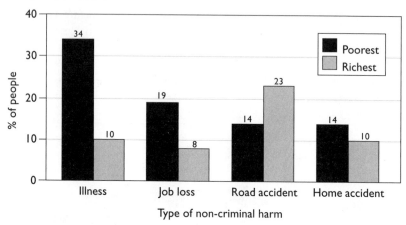

*Source:* 1994 BCS

Poor people are more likely than rich people to worry about non-criminal harms (see Figure 6.8). They worry more in relation to falling ill; an illness occurring in the household; financial debts; a wage earner losing their job; and themselves or somebody else having an accident at home. The one anomaly – worry about themselves or somebody else in their household having a road accident – is likely to be related to the fact that the poor have fewer cars than the rest of the population. With few exceptions, people in the poorest income households are more likely to worry about becoming a victim in relation to a range of crimes and are also more likely to worry about a number of other non-criminal harms. To this effect, anxiety about crime and victimisation can be seen as part of a long chain of insecurities that may be experienced more acutely by people living in poverty. Illness in the household features at the top of the hierarchy of insecurities among people living in circumstances of poverty. Concern about an illness occurring in the household overshadows the worry about becoming a victim of crime.

**Figure 6.8: Proportion of the population worried about non-criminal harms (1993) (%)**

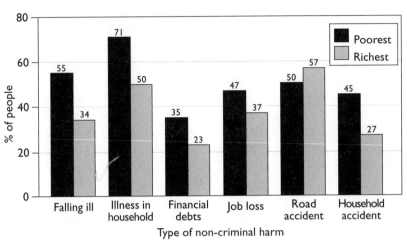

*Source:* 1994 BCS

## Conclusions

This chapter has examined New Labour's approach to crime and punishment. Tony Blair's famous soundbite about being "tough on crime and tough on the causes of crime" is in reality focused much more on punishment rather than tackling the causes of crime. One of its key policies to deal with the causes of crime, the New Deal for Communities – which attempts to regenerate poor communities – has been criticised for seeing the problems of poor neighbourhoods as problems that are bound up with the underclass. Its proposals on using management structures and practices to deal with the problems of crime and disorder may end in failure as previous experiments have demonstrated.

The social harm approach adopted in this chapter has sought to offer a wider assessment of the broad and diverse range of harms that people living on the poorest incomes experience disproportionately. It has unveiled a complicated picture that undermines the consensus among New Labour politicians and Left-Realist criminologists concerning the links between poverty and crime. Poor areas do suffer from intolerable levels of crime, but so do some better-off areas. Furthermore, the main targets of offenders tend to be better-off individuals who have more property and which is also of greater value. But this is not to deny that the impact of crime affects everyone equally. Poor people are much more concerned about crime than the rich – regardless of where they live. The implication of this is that poor people's perception of safety is influenced more by their income status than by the level of deprivation of their neighbourhood. The lesson of this for government is that if it is serious about reducing insecurity among people then it ought to target resources at the individual level (eg by raising income levels). A second lesson is that while people living in poverty may not be the predominant victims of criminal harm they are clearly the main victims of other social harms. If New Labour is concerned with tackling social inequalities then it must be "tough on social harm and tough on the causes of social harm".

**Notes**

[1] Blair retracted this statement by claiming that he was referring not to the homeless, but to homelessness (Blair, 1997). This, however, tended to contradict the full text of the interview which read:

> Obviously some people will interpret this in a way which is harsh and unpleasant, but I think the basic principle is here to say: yes it is right to be intolerant of people homeless on the streets. But the way to deal with that is you make sure that when those people come off the streets that you're doing the other part of the equation. You're providing them with somewhere to go. (Blair, cited in MacAskill, 1997)

[2] Nevertheless, crime surveys like the BCS cannot possibly claim to offer a complete account of the extent and nature of crime and fear of crime (see Pantazis and Gordon, 1998 and Pantazis: forthcoming)

**References**

Allen, R. (1999) *Safety through regeneration*, Safer Society No 2, London: NACRO.

Anderson, S., Grieve Smith, C., Kinsey, R. and Wood, J. (1990) *The Edinburgh Crime Survey, First Report*, Edinburgh: Scottish Office.

Baldwin, J., Bottoms, A. with Walker, M. (1976) *The urban criminal: A study in Sheffield*, London: Tavistock.

Blair, T. (1997) 'War on the streets', *The Guardian*, 8 January, p 17.

Bradshaw, J., Gordon, D., Levitas, R., Middleton, S., Pantazis, C., Payne, S. and Townsend, P. (1998) *Perceptions of poverty and social exclusion*, Bristol: Townsend Centre for International Poverty Research, University of Bristol.

Brownlee, I. (1998) 'New Labour – new penology? Punitive rhetoric and the limits of managerialism in criminal justice policy', *Journal of Law and Society*, vol 25, no 3, pp 313-35.

CACI (1997) *ACORN User Guide*, London: CACI Ltd.

Downes, D. (1983) *Law and order: Theft of an issue*, London: Fabian Society.

Downes, D. and Morgan, R. (1997) 'Dumping the "hostages to fortune"? The politics of law and order in post-war Britain', in M. Maguire, R. Morgan and R. Reiner (eds) *The Oxford handbook of criminology*, London: Oxford University Press.

Foster, J. and Hope, T. (1993) *Housing, community and crime: The impact of the Priory Estate Project*, London: HMSO.

Hall, P. (1988) *Cities of tomorrow*, Oxford: Basil Blackwell.

Hetherington, P. (1998) 'Blair pledges programme to bridge the gap between the rich and poor', *The Guardian*, 16 September.

Hillyard, P., Pantazis, C. and Gordon, D. (1999) *Zemiology: Beyond criminology?*, Unpublished conference proceedings, 12-13 February.

Hirshfield, A. and Bowers, K. (1996) 'The geography of crime and disadvantage: an English case study', Paper presented at the 5th International Seminar on Environmental Criminology and Crime Analysis, Tokyo, Japan, 1-3 July.

Jones, T., Maclean, B. and Young, J. (1986) *The Islington Crime Survey*, Aldershot: Gower.

Kinsey, R. (1984) *First Report on the Merseyside Crime Survey*, Liverpool: Merseyside County Council.

Kinsey, R., Lea, J. and Young, J. (1986) *Losing the fight against crime*, Oxford: Blackwell.

Labour Party (1996) *Tackling the causes of crime*, London: Labour Party.

Labour Party (1997) *New Labour: Because Britain deserves better*, London: Labour Party.

Lea, J. and Young, J. (1993) *What is to be done about law and order* (2nd edn), London: Pluto Press.

Lee, P., Murie, A. and Gordon, D. (1995) *Area measures of deprivation*, Birmingham: CURS, University of Birmingham.

Levitas, R. (1998) *The inclusive society?*, London: Macmillan.

MacAskill, E. (1997) 'Blair opts for zero tolerance,' *The Guardian*, 7 January.

Mayhew, H. (1851-62) (reprinted 1967) *London Labour and the London poor* (four volumes), London: Frank Cass.

Mayhew, P. and Maung, N. (1992) *Surveying crime: Findings from the 1992 British Crime Survey*, Home Office Research and Statistics Department, Research Findings No 2, London: HMSO.

Mirrlees, C., Budd, T., Partridge, S. and Mayhew, P. (1998) *The 1998 British Crime Survey*, Issue 21/98, London: Home Office Research, Development and Statistics Department.

Murray, C. (1990) *The emerging British underclass*, London: Institute of Economic Affairs.

Pantazis, C. (forthcoming) 'Fear of crime, vulnerability and poverty', *British Journal of Criminology*.

Pantazis, C. and Gordon, D. (1998) 'Are crime and fear of crime more likely to be experienced by the "poor"?', in D. Dorling and S. Simpson (eds) *Statistics in society*, London: Arnold, pp 198-212.

Polk, K. (1957) 'Juvenile delinquency and social areas', *Social Problems*, no 5, pp 214-17.

Power, A. (1999) 'Pool of resources', *The Guardian*, 3 February.

Robinson, W. (1950) 'Ecological correlations and the behaviour of individuals', *American Sociological Review*, no 15, pp 351-7.

SEU (Social Exclusion Unit) (1998) *Bringing Britain together: A national strategy for neighbourhood renewal*, London: The Stationery Office.

Taylor, I. (1981) *Law and order, arguments for socialism*, London: Macmillan.

Travis, A. (1995) 'Straw takes on "addicts and winos"', *The Guardian*, 5 September.

Travis, A. and Meikle, J. (1997) 'Parties squabble over street cred', *The Guardian*, 8 January.

Wallis, C. and Maliphant, R. (1967) 'Delinquent areas in the County of London: ecological factors', *British Journal of Criminology*, vol 7, pp 250-84.

Watt, P. and Jacobs, K. (1999) 'Discourses of social exclusion: an analysis of "Bringing Britain together: a national strategy for neighbourhood renewal"', Discourse and Policy Change Conference, University of Glasgow, 3-4 February.

Willie, C.V. (1967) 'The relative contribution of family status and economic status to juvenile delinquency', *Social Problems*, vol 14, pp 326-35.

## Appendix A: ACORN classification

| ACORN categories | Groups | % of GB popul- ation | % population in England and Wales (1994 BCS) |
|---|---|---|---|
| Thriving | 1. Wealthy achievers, suburban areas | 19.8 | 21.1 |
| | 2. Affluent greys, rural area | | |
| | 3. Prosperous pensioners, retirement area | | |
| Expanding | 4. Affluent executives, rural communities | 11.6 | 10.3 |
| | 5 Well-off workers, family areas | | |
| Rising | 6. Affluent urbanites, town and city areas | 7.8 | 7.6 |
| | 7 Prosperous professionals, metropolitan areas | | |
| | 8. Better-off executives, inner-city areas | | |
| Settling | 9. Comfortable middle-agers, mature homeowning areas | 24.0 | 27.7 |
| | 10. Skilled workers, homeowning areas | | |
| Aspiring | 11. New homeowners, mature communities | 13.7 | 14.0 |
| | 12. White-collar workers, better-off ethnic areas | | |
| Striving | 13. Older people, less prosperous areas | 22.6 | 19.3 |
| | 14. Council estate residents, better-off homes | | |
| | 15 Council estate residents, high unemployment | | |
| | 16. Council estate residents, greatest hardship | | |
| | 17. People in multi-ethnic, low-income areas | | |

*Notes:* The ACORN classification has been developed from a wide range of data items from the 1991 Census (CACI, 1997). Key factors such as home ownership, health, employment, ethnicity and life-style are all used to produce a picture of neighbourhood area types. The ACORN classification consists of 54 types, which are amalgamated into 17 groups, and into six categories.

*Source:* 1994 BCS: core sample: weighted data ($n$=32,875)

# SEVEN

# Poverty across the life-course and health

*George Davey Smith and David Gordon*

## Introduction: poverty, inequality and health

The Black Report is justly celebrated for the attention it drew to the persistence of health inequalities after the introduction of the National Health Service (NHS) and for the framework of explanations for health inequalities it advanced (Davey Smith et al, 1994). Since the appearance of the Black Report, much of the focus of research into socioeconomic differentials in health has related to the continuous gradient of improving health from the bottom to the top of the socioeconomic hierarchy (Davey Smith et al, 1990a; Macintyre, 1994; Marmot, 1994). This focus on inequality and health represents a move from an earlier focus on poverty and health (M'Gonigle and Kirby, 1936; Titmuss, 1943) in which the poor health status of the most socially disadvantaged was the major concern. In terms of explanations for inequalities in health, the Black Report's categorisation of statistical artefact, selection, behavioural/ cultural and material factors has been developed into a set of considerations regarding the accumulation of exposures acting across the life-course and how, together, they produce the sizeable differentials in health status which are seen today.

## Deprivation at different stages of the life-course and health: aetiological considerations

Several studies have demonstrated that lifetime social circumstances are strongly related to morbidity and mortality in adulthood (Mare, 1990; Davey Smith et al, 1997; Lynch et al, 1997; Power et al, 1998). For example, Figure 7.1 demonstrates that cumulative social class (indexed by the number of occasions from childhood to adulthood an individual was in a manual social class location) together with the deprivation level of current area of residence, are powerful predictors of mortality risk. Childhood and adult social circumstances make independent contributions to the risk of dying. Cumulative experience during adult life is also important. Individuals with average or higher income who experience fluctuating reductions to low income levels have higher mortality rates than those who remain on average or high incomes (McDonough et al, 1997). The highest mortality rates by a considerable degree are seen among those with persistently low incomes.

***Figure 7.1:* All cause mortality by cumulative social class and deprivation category**

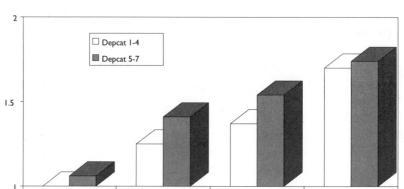

*Note:* 3M represents men with fathers in manual occupations, whose first job on labour market entry was manual and whose job in middle age was manual; 3NM represents men whose fathers were in a non-manual job, whose first job at labour market entry was non-manual and who were in a non-manual job in middle age. The intermediate categories fall between these. 'Depcat' refers to deprivation category of current area of residence.

*Source:* Davey Smith et al (1997)

Socioeconomic inequalities in health should be considered against the background of broad secular changes and international differences in health status and mortality risk. During the 20th century, there have been very sizeable declines in mortality in most industrialised countries, with infant mortality rates in the 1990s being only 5% of those at the turn of the century in England and Wales, for example. For one- to four-year-olds, the reduction is even more dramatic: mortality rates for the 1990s are 2% of those at the turn of the century. Even among the middle-aged there have been substantial reductions, with end of the 20th century mortality rates being around one fifth to one third of the rates seen at the beginning of the century (Charlton and Murphy, 1997). It is likely that the factors which have contributed to the sizeable reductions in mortality are also those which contribute to the current differentials in mortality between socioeconomic groups.

If our understanding of the factors generating socioeconomic differentials in health is to be advanced, we need to consider the particular factors that contribute to international differences, secular trends and socioeconomic differentials in particular causes of ill-health. Some illustrative cases are given here.

Internationally, stomach cancer is a major cause of mortality, being one of the most common cancers seen in developing countries and, in earlier times, in developed countries. Stroke mortality shows a similar geographical and temporal distribution to stomach cancer mortality and also has declined dramatically during this century. Among middle-aged men and women in England and Wales, stroke mortality at the beginning of the 20th century was up to seven times higher than at the end of the century (Charlton and Murphy, 1997). The declines in stroke and stomach cancer in England and Wales contributed to the declines in mortality among post-childhood age groups. The risk of these diseases seems to be established mainly in childhood. People migrating from high to low stomach cancer areas after childhood take with them the risk of stomach cancer of the place they have migrated from (Coggon et al, 1990). Cohort effects can be seen in the mortality trends, in support of this conclusion (Hansson et al, 1991). Data from a large prospective study in Scotland (Davey Smith et al, 1997, 1998) demonstrate that stomach cancer and stroke risk are associated more strongly with parental socioeconomic position – and hence socioeconomic circumstances in childhood – than to socioeconomic position in adult life. It is suggested that the material conditions of existence at the time the people currently dying of stomach cancer and stroke were born are important factors underlying current risk for these conditions. Adverse socioeconomic circumstances in childhood favour *Helicobacter pylori* acquisition (Mendall et al, 1992) and *Helicobacter pylori* infection appears to be an important cause of stomach cancer (Forman et al, 1991). Declining rates of *Helicobacter pylori* infection have accompanied improving social conditions during the century (Banatvala et al, 1993) and thus may underlie the falling rates of stomach cancer mortality. Infections acquired in childhood may also be important factors in producing the risk of stroke in adult life. Current morbidity and mortality patterns for these conditions are related directly to poverty-associated factors experienced in early life, such as overcrowding and hygiene practices.

For other important causes of morbidity and mortality in adulthood, socially patterned exposures acting in early life appear to interact with, or accumulate with, later life exposures. Morbidity and mortality from respiratory disease in adulthood is related to housing conditions and infections acquired in childhood. Smoking and occupational exposures in later life then influence disease risk, in association with these earlier life factors (Mann et al, 1992). In the case of diabetes, hypertension and coronary heart disease, low birthweight – which is strongly socially patterned and related to intergenerational experiences as well as maternal nutrition – interacts with obesity in later life (increasingly prevalent among people in unfavourable social circumstances) to produce elevated disease risk (Phillips et al, 1994; Leon et al, 1996; Frankel et al, 1996; Lithell et al, 1996). Large differences in relative and absolute risk for various forms of morbidity can be demonstrated when groups are defined by clusters of socially patterned adverse exposures acting throughout life. These exposures include health-related behaviours, such as dietary patterns and smoking, and the effects of psychosocial exposures, such as job insecurity.

Poverty can influence health through a broad range of factors acting during the life-course. These include such embodied features as low birthweight, height, obesity and lung function. There is increasing evidence of intergenerational influences on these attributes and the influence of nutrition (Gunnell et al, 1998) and infection in early life should be given more attention. The extent to which health-related behaviours are constrained by structural factors should be acknowledged when considering the underlying determinants (rather than proximal mechanisms) of health inequalities (Graham, 1988; Davey Smith and Brunner, 1997). Parsimonious explanations would be based on the assumption that broad secular changes in biologically plausible aspects of the material conditions of people's existences underlie the broad secular changes in health, the substantial differences in health status between countries and the socioeconomic differentials in health within countries. Alternative explanations should be sought when it is apparent that such material conditions of existence fail to account for health differentials. It is clear that biologically plausible mechanisms linking the experience of poverty to many particular health problems exist (of which only illustrative examples are given above, due to space limitations) and that the proportion of the burden of disease and ill-health in a population which may be attributable to poverty-related exposures is likely to be considerable.

## Poverty across the life-course in Britain

Any consideration of how the cumulative experience of poverty across the life-course can influence health requires an operational definition of poverty. It is sometimes stated that poverty no longer exists in Britain (see Chapter One), generally on the grounds that consumer durable ownership is now high even among the lowest income groups (see Table 7.1). This statement fails to acknowledge that technological change and innovation can both generate the availability of such durables and lead to them becoming necessities for meaningful participation in society (Gordon and Pantazis, 1997).

*Table 7.1:* **Access that the bottom decile income group has to consumer durables (%)**

| Individuals in household with access to a: | 1962-63 | 1972-73 | 1982-83 | 1992-93 |
|---|---|---|---|---|
| telephone | 8 | 20 | 58 | 78 |
| washing machine | – | 54 | 79 | 89 |
| refrigerator or fridge-freezer | – | 52 | 95 | 99 |
| car | – | 26 | 44 | 56 |
| video cassette recorder | – | – | – | 68 |
| central heating | – | 20 | 46 | 73 |

*Source:* Goodman et al (1997)

If video ownership is taken to refute the existence of poverty (as, famously, it was by Peter Lilley) then we are forced to consider whether 100% of the population was in poverty in the 1930s. As overall communication and personal transport facilities improve, then the need to have access to them for social participation, for being able to compete in the labour market, and for fulfilling domestic obligations, is increased. The notion that an inability to meet the material and social needs, which are recognised as essential within a society, is a meaningful definition of poverty allows for the distinction between poverty and inequality to be made. The European Commission has produced a definition of poverty which is broadly in line with this reasoning:

> ... the poor shall be taken to mean persons, families and groups of
> persons whose resources (material, cultural and social) are so limited
> as to exclude them from the minimum acceptable way of life in the
> Member State in which they live. (EEC, 1995)

In the UK, the pioneering *Breadline Britain* surveys of 1983 and 1990
(Mack and Lansley, 1985; Gordon and Pantazis, 1997) obtained data on
the perceptions from a sample of the general public on social necessities.
Being unable, through lack of resources, to afford three or more of the
items which more than half of the public consider to be social necessities,
was taken to indicate being in poverty. By this definition, the *Breadline
Britain* survey estimated that 20% of households (approximately 11 million
people) fell below the poverty line in 1990. Attempts to make similar
estimates for previous periods suggested that there was a continuing
decline in relative poverty between the 1930s and 1970s, which then
reversed and was followed by substantial increases during the 1980s and
1990s. This accords with research examining trends in low-income
families (defined by those falling below the Supplementary Benefit or
Income Support level) between 1961 and 1993 (Goodman et al, 1997).
The *Breadline Britain* estimate of the prevalence of poverty in 1990 closely
approximates to estimates based on the numbers on or below the
Supplementary Benefit and Income Support level and proportion of
the population having below 50% of the national average income. All
three methods give estimates of between 11 and 14 million people
falling below these cut-offs.

Poverty is distributed unevenly across the population. The highest
prevalence is seen among lone parents, of whom 41% fall below the
poverty line. For other families with children, 23% fall below the line
whereas, for other non-pensioner households, the equivalent figure is
14%. Similar figures are seen when looking at the percentage of family
types with incomes below half the national average (Table 7.2).

It is families with children who are most likely to remain in the
lowest income category over time and experience persistent poverty
(Table 7.3). Women are over-represented among those experiencing
poverty, with 24% falling below the threshold in the *Breadline Britain*
survey in contrast to 17% of men (Gordon and Pantazis, 1997).

*Table 7.2:* **Percentage of family types with incomes below half the contemporary mean**

| | Before housing costs | | After housing costs | |
|---|---|---|---|---|
| Family type | 1979 | 1992-93 | 1979 | 1992-93 |
| Pensioner couple | 16 | 25 | 21 | 26 |
| Single pensioner | 16 | 25 | 12 | 36 |
| Couple with children | 7 | 20 | 8 | 24 |
| Couple without children | 4 | 10 | 5 | 12 |
| Single with children | 16 | 43 | 19 | 58 |
| Single without children | 6 | 18 | 7 | 22 |
| All family types | 8 | 20 | 9 | 25 |

*Source:* Goodman et al (1997)

*Table 7.3:* **Characteristics of individuals remaining in the bottom income quintile for more than three years and of individuals escaping from the bottom income quintile at some point during a three-year period**

| Wave I family type | Of those permanently in bottom quintile (%) | Of those who escaped at some point (%) |
|---|---|---|
| Couple pensioner | 11 | 10 |
| Single pensioner | 14 | 14 |
| Couple with children | 40 | 38 |
| Couple without children | 4 | 13 |
| Single with children | 24 | 12 |
| Single without children | 6 | 13 |
| Total | 100 | 100 |

*Source:* Goodman et al (1997)

Examining life-course experiences of poverty demonstrates that women are particularly likely to be in poverty when they are responsible for bringing up children. Because of this unequal distribution of poverty between household types and across the life-course, 33% of children in Britain were living in households below the poverty line in 1993-94. This has increased from 10% in 1979. The British situation with respect to child poverty and income inequality is particularly poor (Tables 7.4 and 7.5). If we consider that the concomitants of poverty – poor nutrition, over-crowded, damp or inadequately heated housing, an increased risk of infections, lack of appropriate psychosocial stimulation and inability to maintain cleanliness – are of particular importance during pre-natal, infant and childhood life, then the current distribution and trends in poverty bode ill for health trends in the future.

***Table 7.4:*** **Increases in child poverty rate (1967-92)**

| | |
|---|---|
| More than 30% | UK, USA |
| 10-15% | Norway |
| 5-10% | Netherlands, Belgium, Germany |
| Approximately 0% | Australia, Spain, France |
| Decreases | Sweden, Denmark, Finland, Canada, Italy |

*Source:* Lynch and Kaplan (1997)

***Table 7.5:*** **Increases in income inequality (1967-92)**

| | |
|---|---|
| More than 30% | UK |
| 16-29% | USA, Sweden |
| 10-15% | Australia, Denmark |
| 5-10% | Norway, Netherlands, Belgium |
| Approximately 0% | Spain, France, Finland, Canada, Germany |
| Decreases | Italy |

*Source:* Lynch and Kaplan (1997)

Another dramatic change in the distribution of poverty has been the rapid growth of the long-term sick and disabled among those receiving Income Support (Goodman and Webb, 1991). It is probable that this reflects a disguised form of unemployment, where individuals are encouraged to acquire this category as it allows for more reasonable treatment by the benefit system. The effects of such self-labelling have not been investigated but could clearly be detrimental to the psychosocial functioning of individuals. This hidden unemployment also draws attention to the influence of insecurity at work on health, where a wide range of subjective and objective health measures are seen to deteriorate during periods of job insecurity (Ferrie et al, 1995). Incomes are also becoming subject to considerably greater uncertainty than was previously the case and income insecurity, as well as job insecurity may be detrimental to health (McDonough et al, 1997).

# Which policies could reduce ill-health caused by poverty?

The current fashion in policy making in the health arena is for 'evidence-based' recommendations. While these are highly appropriate for clinical interventions targeting individuals, with regard to population health a demand for randomised or experimental evidence leads to an overemphasis on changing individuals' health-related behaviour (Frankel and Davey Smith, 1997). The research review commissioned for the Variations in Health subgroup of the Chief Medical Officer's Health of the Nation Working Group in 1995 (Arblaster et al, 1995) applied evidence-based medicine principles to the issue of socioeconomic inequalities in health and therefore failed to recognise that inequalities in health are determined by economic and social conditions and not by the inadequate implementation of results from randomised controlled trials (RCTs).

It is important to consider the major indicators of mortality and morbidity risk in industrialised countries: gender, poverty, smoking and constitution (including genetic profile). Life expectancy differences between men and women are 5.6 years; between Social Class I and Social Class V, 5.2 years in men and 3.4 years in women (differences would be greater if more refined socioeconomic categories were used (Davey Smith et al, 1990b); and between smokers and never smokers around five years. Life expectancy differences generated by genetic and other constitutional factors have not been formally estimated, but are likely to be substantial (Sorensen et al, 1988). In none of these cases have RCTs demonstrated their importance with respect to life expectancy (and in the case of gender and genetic factors this would not be possible). The only unifactorial RCT of smoking cessation strategies found no significant effect on mortality (Rose and Colwell, 1992), yet the response to the lack of RCT evidence in this case has, rightly, not been to abandon serious efforts to reduce smoking. The same should be the case with efforts to reduce the health burdens of poverty and inequality.

There are two legitimate responses to the evidence that widening income inequalities and increasing proportions of (especially) children living in poverty generate increasing socioeconomic health differentials and threaten to arrest future secular improvements in health. The first response argues that large income inequalities are necessary for economic growth through, for example, the incentives of large increases in income for those already on high incomes leading to improved productivity and overall economic performance. In this case, the health effects of widening disparities in income and the increasing prevalence of poverty may be considered an unfortunate – but necessary – price to pay for national prosperity, which itself will ultimately lead to an improved health profile. While the evidence suggests that inequality is not necessary for economic growth – indeed it points the other way (see Figure 7.2; see also Hutton, 1996) – this position can be advanced and the economic evidence debated.

**Figure 7.2: Income inequality around 1980 and labour productivity growth between 1979 and 1990**

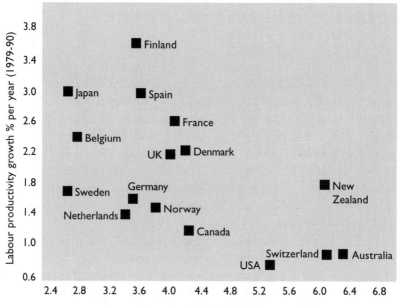

*Source:* Glynn and Miliband (1994)

The second legitimate response is to implement a fiscal programme aimed at arresting and reversing the increasing trend in income inequalities, in order to decrease socioeconomic health differentials and remove the threat of future cessation in secular improvements in health. A third option, that of intimating that there is serious concern with inequalities in health and that concerted efforts will be made to reduce such inequalities, without being willing to implement necessary fiscal and other reforms, is not a legitimate response.

# Health Action Zones and area-based health policies

One of the most high profile government policies designed to tackle the problem of inequalities in health was the establishment of 11 Health Action Zones (HAZs) in England in April 1998. The 11 HAZs were Bradford, the East End of London, Lambeth Southwark and Lewisham, Luton, Manchester Salford and Trafford, North Cumbria, Northumberland, Plymouth, Sandwell, the South Yorkshire Coalfield Communities and Tyne and Wear. They will receive extra resources amounting to £4 million in 1998/99 and £30 million in 1999/2000 to spend jointly with local authorities and other participating agencies. The HAZs represent a long-term financial commitment for the government as they are designed to run for seven years (DoH, 1998).

This flagship policy of HAZs as a primary method for reducing inequalities in health had first been announced in a speech by Frank Dobson to the NHS Confederation on 25 June 1997, only one month after Labour's General Election victory. The White Paper *The New NHS: Modern, Dependable*, published on 9 December 1997 (DoH, 1997) claimed that HAZs would "blaze the trail" for modernising the NHS. It said:

> Starting in up to ten areas from April 1998, they will bring together all those in a health authority area or wider, to improve the health of local people. The accent will be on partnership and innovation, finding new ways to tackle health problems and reshape local services. Health Action Zones will be concentrated in areas of pronounced deprivation and poor health, reflecting the Government's commitment to tackle entrenched inequalities. An early task for each Health Action Zone will be to develop clear targets, agreed with the NHS Executive, for measurable improvements every year. (DoH, 1997, 1998)

Despite the lack of any published evidence that HAZs had met these 'clear targets,' a second wave of 15 HAZs was announced on 11 August 1998. These were in Tees, Wakefield, Leeds, Hull and East Riding; Merseyside (St Helens & Knowsley, Liverpool, Wirral, Sefton); Bury & Rochdale; Nottingham; Sheffield; Leicester City; Wolverhampton; Walsall; North Staffordshire; Cornwall; Camden and Islington; Brent (Brent and Harrow Health Authority). Significant additional funding of £293 million for the HAZs over the three years 1999/2002 was announced on 23 April 1999 (DoH, 1999a).

John Denham (Junior Minister for Health) stated: "Health among the poor must improve at a faster rate than the general population. This means tackling ill health that results from poverty where poverty occurs" and that "Health Action Zones are a key part of the Government's drive in tackling health inequalities" (DoH, 1999b).

During 1998 the government announced similar Employment and Education Action Zones. The number of such area-based anti-poverty initiatives exploded during 1999 to include more than 110 Local Authority Areas. In addition to the Action Zones major area-based initiatives now include New Start, Sure Start, Local Government Association New Commitment to Regeneration, Single Regeneration Budget, New Deal for Communities and Better Government for Older People. A new Cabinet Committee may have to be established in order to coordinate and maintain an overview of all these initiatives (Smith, 1999). However, area-based anti-poverty policies such as the Action Zones have a long history of only limited success or even outright failure. The lessons from the 12 Community Development Projects (CDPs) established in 1969 in similar areas of high social need appear to have been ignored (CDP, 1977).

An area-based rather than people-based approach to attacking inequalities in health, poverty and deprivation can only ever provide help for a relatively small minority of people since most 'poor areas' only contain a minority of 'poor' households and a majority of 'non-poor' households (Lee et al, 1995). For example, there are 1.1 million people in the Tyne and Wear HAZ and the overwhelming majority of them are not poor nor do they have bad health. The criteria used to select the areas of greatest health needs are also often very vague (Carstairs, 1994; Taylor, 1998). The HAZs have been allocated on the basis of competitive tender rather than purely on the basis of greatest health needs. The government seems to have learned little from previous failures and ignored "the strongly held view of those working in regeneration and anti-poverty, that resources should be allocated overwhelmingly according to need and not by competition" (Alcock et al, 1998).

The problem of the relative lack of effectiveness of area-based policies has been known and well documented for more than 25 years (Barnes and Lucas, 1975; Townsend, 1979; Robson et al, 1994; Glennerster et al, 1999). Inequalities in health are a national problem that require national solutions. The root cause of inequalities in health is poverty, which area-based policies cannot tackle effectively or efficiently. For example, in the Luton HAZ, the health needs of Asian women will be particularly addressed. There will be a focus on increasing the uptake of cervical screening, the development of a community-based colposcopy service with a female consultant and a partnership between the NHS and the Asian community to address child development problems (DoH, 1998). However, there are far more Asian women in Birmingham than in Luton and Birmingham does not have a HAZ. Similarly, Plymouth HAZ is developing new approaches to improving dental health, particularly in children (DoH, 1998). However, there are far more children with dental health needs in Bristol, Bournemouth and Brighton, which do not have HAZs, than there are in Plymouth.

The HAZs, like other such programmes in the past, will create a flurry of activity at relatively little cost but probably have little lasting impact on inequalities in health (Higgens, 1998). Even if a particular HAZ has some success, it is doubtful that this success could be easily replicated in other areas since it would inevitably be based on local enthusiasm, energy and expertise which may not be present in many other areas.

## Conclusions

Policy options which could influence inequalities in health need to be focused on reducing the proportion of children born into and living in poverty (which will have short-term as well as long-term effects) and reducing inequalities in income within the population more generally. What is needed are national policies, not a disparate collection of local area-based initiatives. Such policies would involve protection of Child Benefit and Income Support levels, an increase in the rent limit on Housing Benefit, the introduction and enforcement of nutritional standards for school meals and the introduction of subsidised childcare and after-school places to enable parents to take up paid work. Various measures should be implemented to reverse the increasing inequalities in income and to reduce wealth differentials. These would help reduce levels of poverty by releasing resources for the anti-poverty measures above. They include continuing reductions in MIRAS; reducing the tax-free savings threshold; removing charitable status from private education and private healthcare; blocking the tax loopholes inherent in company car provision; extending windfall profit taxation; ensuring the collection of inheritance tax (and increasing the rate of such taxation) and abolishing the upper earnings limit for National Insurance. Reversing legislation relating to trade unions and wages councils (which have precipitated increasing income inequalities) and having a national minimum wage at a reasonable level would directly increase the incomes of the lowest paid.

## References

Alcock, P., Craig, C., Lawless, P., Pearson, S. and Robinson, D. (1998) *Inclusive regeneration: Local authorities corporate strategies for tackling disadvantage*, Sheffield: CRESR, Sheffield Hallam University.

Arblaster, L., Entwistle, V., Lambert, M., Froster, M., Sheldon, T. and Watt, I. (1995) *Review of the research on the effectiveness of health service interventions to reduce variations in health*, CRD Report 3, York: NHS Centre for Reviews and Dissemination.

Banatvala, N., Mayo, K., Megraud, F., Jennings, R., Deeks, J.J. and Feldman, R.A. (1993) 'The cohort effect and *Helicobacter pylori*', *Journal of Infectious Diseases*, no 168, pp 219-21.

Barnes, J. and Lucas, H. (1975) *Educational priority*, London: HMSO.

Carstairs, V. (1994) 'Health care needs, deprivation, and the resource allocation formula', in E. Gilman, S. Munday, L. Somervaille and R. Strachan (eds) *Resource allocation and health needs: From research to policy*, London: HMSO.

CDP (Community Development Project) (1977) *Gilding the ghetto: The state and the poverty experiments*, Nottingham: CDP/The Russell Press Limited.

Charlton, J. and Murphy, M. (1997) *The health of adult Britain 1941-1994*, London: The Stationery Office.

Coggon, D., Osmond, C. and Barker, D.J.P. (1990) 'Stomach cancer and migration within England and Wales', *British Journal of Cancer*, no 61, pp 573-4.

Davey Smith, G. and Brunner, E. (1997) 'Socio-economic differentials in health: the role of nutrition', *Proceedings of the Nutrition Society*, no 56, pp 75-90.

Davey Smith, G., Bartley, M. and Blane, D. (1990a) 'The Black Report on socioeconomic inequalities in health 10 years on', *BMJ*, vol 301, pp 373-7.

Davey Smith, G., Bartley, M. and Blane, D. (1994) 'Explanations for socioeconomic differentials in mortality: evidence from Britain and elsewhere', *European Journal of Public Health*, no 4, pp 131-44.

Davey Smith, G., Shipley, M.J. and Rose, G. (1990b) 'The magnitude and causes of socio-economic differentials in mortality: further evidence from the Whitehall study', *Journal of Epidemiology and Community Health*, no 44, pp 265-70.

Davey Smith, G., Hart, C., Blane, D. and Hole, D. (1998) 'Adverse socioeconomic conditions in childhood and cause-specific adult mortality. Prospective observational study', *BMJ*, vol 316, pp 1631-5.

Davey Smith, G., Hart, C., Blane, D., Gillis, C. and Hawthorne, V. (1997) 'Lifetime socioeconomic position and mortality: prospective observational study', *BMJ*, vol 314, pp 547-52.

DoH (Department of Health) (1997) *The New NHS: Modern, Dependable*, London: The Stationery Office.

DoH (1998) 'Frank Dobson gives the go-ahead for first wave of health action zones', Press Release 98/120, Tuesday 31 March.

DoH (1999a) 'Seven million people to benefit from fifteen new Health Action Zones', Press Release 1999/0259, Friday 23 April.

DoH (1999b) 'Health Action Zones invited to apply for £4.5m funding for innovation and fellowship', Press Release 1999/0386, Friday 25 June.

EEC (European Economic Community) (1995) 'On specific community action to combat poverty (Council Decision of 19 December 1984)', *Official Journal of the EEC*, 85/8/EEC, pp 2-24.

Ferrie, J.E., Shipley, M.J., Marmot, M.G., Stansfeld, S. and Davey Smith, G. (1995) 'Health effects of anticipation of job change and non-employment: longitudinal data from the Whitehall II study', *BMJ*, vol 311, pp 1264-9.

Forman, D., Newell, D.G., Fullerton, F. et al (1991) 'Association between infection with *Helicobacter pylori* and risk of gastric cancer: evidence from a prospective investigation', *BMJ*, vol 302, pp 1302-5.

Frankel, S. and Davey Smith, G. (1997) 'Evidence-based medicine and treatment choices', *Lancet*, no 349, p 571.

Frankel, S., Elwood, P., Sweetnam, P., Yarnell, J. and Davey Smith, G. (1996) 'Birthweight, body mass index in middle age, and incident coronary heart disease', *Lancet*, no 348, pp 1478-80.

Glennerster, H., Lupton, R., Noden, P. and Power, A. (1999) *Poverty, social exclusion and neighbourhood: Studying the area bases of social exclusion*, CASE Paper 22, London: London School of Economics.

Glynn, A. and Miliband, D. (1994) *Paying for inequality: The economic cost of social injustices*, London: Rivers Oran Press.

Goodman, A. and Webb, S. (1991) 'Why are there so many long term sick in Britain?', *Economic Journal*, no 101, pp 252-62.

Goodman, A., Johnson, P. and Webb, S. (1997) *Inequality in the UK*, Oxford: Oxford University Press.

Gordon, D. and Pantazis, C. (eds) (1997) *Breadline Britain in the 1990s*, Ashgate: Avebury.

Graham, H. (1988) 'Women and smoking in the United Kingdom: the implications for health promotion', *Health Promotion*, no 3, pp 371-82.

Gunnell, D.J., Davey Smith, G., Frankel, S.J., Nanchahal, K., Braddon, F.E.M. and Peters, T.J. (1998) 'Childhood leg length and adult mortality: follow up of the Carnegie (Boyd Orr) survey of diet and health in pre-war Britain', *Journal of Epidemiology and Community Health*, no 52, pp 142-52.

Hansson, L.-E., Bergström, R., Sparén, P. and Adami, H.-O. (1991) 'The decline in the incidence of stomach cancer in Sweden 1960-1984: a birth cohort phenomenon', *International Journal of Cancer*, no 47, pp 499-503.

Higgens, J. (1998) 'HAZs warning', *Health Service Journal*, 16 April, pp 24-5.

Hutton, W. (1996) *The state we're in*, London: Vintage.

Lee, P., Murie, A. and Gordon, D. (1995) *Area measures of deprivation*, Birmingham: CURS, University of Birmingham.

Leon, D.A., Koupilova, I., Lithell, H.O. et al (1996) 'Failure to realise growth potential in utero and adult obesity in relation to blood pressure in 50 year old Swedish men', *BMJ*, vol 312, pp 401-6.

Lithell, H.O., McKeigue, P.M., Berglund, L., Mohsen, R., Lithell, U.-B. and Leon, D.A. (1996) 'Relation of size at birth to non-insulin dependent diabetes and insulin concentrations in men aged 50-60 years', *BMJ*, vol 312, pp 406-10.

Lynch, J.W. and Kaplan, G.A. (1997) 'Understanding how inequality in the distribution of income affects health', *Journal of Health Psychology*, vol 2, pp 297-314.

Lynch, J.W., Kaplan, G.A. and Shema, S.J. (1997) 'Cumulative impact of sustained economic hardship on physical, cognitive, psychological and social functioning', *North England Journal of Medicine*, no 337, pp 1889-95.

McDonough, P., Duncan, G.J., Williams, D. and House, J. (1997) 'Income dynamics and adult mortality in the United States, 1972 through 1989', *American Journal of Public Health*, no 87, pp 1476-83.

Mack, J. and Lansley, S. (1985) *Poor Britain*, London: Allen and Unwin.

Macintyre, S. (1994) 'Understanding the social patterning of health: the role of the social sciences', *Journal of Public Health Medicine*, vol 16, pp 53-9.

Mann, S.L., Wadsworth, M.E.J. and Colley, J.R.T. (1992) 'Accumulation of factors influencing respiratory illness in members of a national birth cohort and their offspring', *Journal of Epidemiology and Community Health*, no 46, pp 286-92.

Mare, R.D. (1990) 'Socio-economic careers and differential mortality among older men in the United States', in J.Vallin, S. D'Souza and A. Palloni (eds) *Measurement and analysis of mortality: New approaches*, Oxford: Clarendon Press, pp 362-87.

Marmot, M.G. (1994) 'Social differentials in health within and between populations', *Daedalus*, no 123, pp 197-216.

Mendall, M.A., Goggin, P.M., Molineaux, N. et al (1992) 'Childhood living conditions and *Helicobacter pylori* seropositivity in adult life', *Lancet*, no 339, pp 896-7.

M'Gonigle, G.C.M. and Kirby, J. (1936) *Poverty and public health*, London: Golantz.

Phillips, D.I., Barker, D.J., Hales, C.N., Hirst, S. and Osmond, C. (1994) 'Thinness at birth and insulin resistance in adult life', *Diabetologia*, no 37, pp 150-4.

Power, C., Matthews, S. and Manor, O. (1998) 'Inequalities in self-rated health: explanations from different stages of life', *Lancet*, no 351, pp 1009-14.

Robson, B., Bradford, M., Deas, I., Hall, E., Harrison, E., Parkinson, M., Evans, R., Garside, P., Harding, A. and Robinson, F. (1994) *Assessing the impact of urban policy*, London: HMSO.

Rose, G. and Colwell, L. (1992) 'Randomised controlled trial of anti-smoking advice: final (20 year) results', *Journal of Epidemiology and Community Health*, no 46, pp 75-7.

Smith, G.R. (1999) *Area-based initiatives: The rationale for and options for area targeting*, CASE Paper 25, London: London School of Economics.

Sorensen, T.I., Nielsen, G.G., Andersen, P.K. and Teasdale, T.W. (1988) 'Genetic and environmental influences on premature death in adult adoptees', *North England Journal of Medicine*, no 318, pp 727-32.

Taylor, D.H. (1998) 'The natural life of policy indices: geographical problem areas in the US and UK', *Social Science and Medicine*, vol 6, pp 713-25.

Titmuss, R. (1943) *Poverty and wealth*, London: Hamish Hamilton Medical Books.

Townsend, P. (1979) *Poverty in the United Kingdom*, London: Penguin Books.

# EIGHT

# Inequalities in health service provision: how research findings are ignored

*Walter Barker and Colin Chalmers*

Research findings are low down the list of factors that influence government policies. Since governments of every political hue are concerned with present power and future survival, it appears that political considerations, pressure groups, influence pedlars and the media lead in the battle for the government's mind.

Yet, as researchers, we continue to think that our reports would carry considerable weight with government ministers and civil servants, if they would only read them. We need to ask why so much of what we do is ineffective in bringing about change. We talk to each other in the research community but who in government listens?

We try to remain aware of our own prejudices and hidden agendas, working to establish the validity and reliability of our findings. However, there is no such attempt at dispassionate appraisal by a government reactive to pressures and events. Research findings are an embarrassment, offending the emperor by pointing to the lack of research clothing. Even when lip-service is paid to research, the citations are often so selective that the exercise has no intellectual or moral credibility, lacking an independent appraisal of what is cited.

When governments do pursue socially acceptable policies, this is rarely if ever because research has highlighted the disparities and inequalities of current policies. More usually, it is because there is strong political or moral pressure to introduce changes which have political appeal.

This chapter describes a number of specific examples where research findings appear to have been ignored.

# Health inequalities: the awkward genie

Inequalities in health and healthcare remain the awkward genie that will not dematerialise. The Black Report (DHSS, 1980) and the subsequent Townsend and Davidson study (Townsend and Davidson, 1982) showed the reality of the class divide in Britain and the relationship between material poverty, poorer health and worse healthcare (see Chapter Seven). Of seminal importance at the time, it continues to haunt succeeding governments.

The previous administration argued that the cost of meeting the Black recommendations was "quite unrealistic in present or any foreseeable economic circumstances, quite apart from any judgement that may be formed of the effectiveness of such expenditure in dealing with the problems identified" (Patrick Jenkin, Secretary of State, in his Foreword to the Black Report [DHSS, 1980]). The Health Education Council, an irritant to government because of its practice of pointing to poverty, smoking and other contributors to poor health, funded a study which was published seven years later (Whitehead, 1988). This built on the Black hypothesis and revealed new and even stronger evidence of the health divide.

The government of the day reacted as any potentate to a messenger bringing an uncomfortable message. It abolished the Health Education Council and replaced it with a Health Education Authority with a far more restricted remit.

## Continuing to haunt government

The awkward genie of health inequalities continues to haunt government. The 1996 *Health Survey for England* (HMSO, 1998) confirmed that geography, wealth and class still made a difference to people's health. This government announced that the survey would be used to develop policies to enable people to live longer and healthier lives. However, the response in its consultation papers, *Our healthier nation* (DoH, 1998), was limited.

While the previous government failed to acknowledge the widening gap in death rates between the upper and lower social classes, it had set an ambitious 27 health targets to be achieved. The present government has recognised the health divide but reduced the health targets to four. It has also stated that it "does not propose at this stage to set national targets to narrow health inequalities between social classes, different parts of the country, ethnic groups and men and women", although a study on what could be done to reduce inequalities had been commissioned from a former Chief Medical Officer.

Kenneth Caines, Director of the Institute of Health Service Management, claimed in response to the consultation paper that this change of policy indicated that the government had bottled out: "Without measurable targets, even over a long time scale, there will be less pressure for change and less scope to hold them to account".

The targets selected by the government concern heart disease and stroke, cancer, suicides and accidents – each with a major social component. Potential killers such as bronchial and other chest conditions which drastically shorten the lives of many working men, a wide range of maternal health issues with an equally large social divide, teenage pregnancies and child health, have all been omitted. So too have critically important life-style issues such as diet, smoking and exercise – each with its own significant social divide. Lottery rather than government money is to be focused on the benefits of exercise.

It is paradoxical that this and previous governments have generally refused to support health measures which appear to be effective but have not been clearly proven. Meanwhile, those same governments introduce their own far-reaching initiatives with little attempt to demonstrate their effectiveness in advance. A prime example of a massive policy change was GP fundholding. This was introduced without any large-scale research or controlled field testing although governments and departmental administrators invariably demand randomly controlled trials (RCTs) from other innovators. There is an uneasy parallel with the present government's planned introduction of untested large-scale administrative reforms, such as Primary Care Groups and Primary Care Trusts, to replace fundholding.

## Effectiveness measured by activity levels

The cavalier approach to collecting and evaluating evidence is seen in a number of more clearly definable areas of health policy and practice. The previous government made great play of Körner statistics as a way of 'proving' the effectiveness of all health procedures. The whole thinking behind the Körner proposals (DHSS, 1982) was that measuring and comparing activity levels provided strong evidence of effectiveness. In other words, for every million pounds spent by a health authority, how much activity could be produced by the various medical specialities and hospital administrations?

The fifth Körner Report attempted to quantify community health indices by measuring the activity levels of health visitors and others. How many contacts did they have with clients each day, and, with each contact, how many of a range of health-related topics were discussed?

This latter approach was eagerly adopted by health trusts in order to establish their effectiveness credentials in the eyes of the Department of Health (DoH). It resulted in managers reproaching health visitors who did fewer, more strongly focused and targeted home visits, while visitors making multiple brief visits and discussing multiple topics achieved a kind of stakhanovite status for helping push up the health trust's activity statistics. This practice is still pursued in many trusts today, despite criticism by health visiting professionals and others (Barker, 1987, 1992). Opponents pointed to negative consequences and, in particular, the failure of the Körner approach to provide any evidence on outcomes. For the past decade, both governments have asked for evidence on outcomes, meanwhile insisting on the use of activity measures as their criteria for effectiveness.

This is a classic example of Goodhardt's widely quoted principle (Evans, 1995), that once a measured quantity is used for the purposes of allocating resources, it ceases to be of value as an indicator of effectiveness. Practitioners then concentrate on achieving that target regardless of other considerations. This behaviour has occurred throughout the field of government health resource allocation.

More tangible evidence of the damage done by reliance on the unevaluated activity measurement has come recently in the hip operation crisis. For many years, surgeons have protested against the policy of comparing hospitals and individual surgeons by the number of routine operations performed. Hip operations were often cited as a prime and simple example of the usefulness of the Körner indices. However, that activity measurement ignored the quality of the operations and did not include measures of how many replaced hips failed at an early stage, either through surgical incompetence or poor quality prosthetic devices. Meanwhile, the previous government's narrow focus on costs over a number of years led to the import of inadequately tested artificial hip joints. As a consequence there are now an estimated 5,000 hip replacement operations where one defective type of joint was used which may need to be carried out again, at great expense to the Exchequer and trauma to the individuals concerned. Unfortunately, examples such as these do not appear to alter governments' approaches to allocating funds in the light of activity levels rather than evidence-based practice.

## Lip-service to health prevention

Every government's narrow focus on expensive medical care in the acute sector, while giving little more than lip-service to preventive healthcare in the community, is understandable in both research and political terms.

In *research* terms, there is as yet only limited evidence about the effectiveness of preventive health policies. Although many medical procedures also have little or no research to back them, they are dominant as part of daily medical practice and thus regarded as proven and acceptable. It is the 'new' ideas of prevention and complementary medicine – often age-old ones dressed in modern clothing – which are challenged most because they question existing practice. Research into preventive or complementary medical practices does not attract millions from the pharmaceutical companies. Natural procedures and age-old remedies cannot be patented. Aspiring medical researchers do not view these as attractive research areas, given the difficulty of adequately controlled research into holistic procedures involving the patient as an active participant in therapy or treatment.

In *political* terms the choice faced by governments, between community healthcare and acute medical care, is equally one-sided. The political power of organised medicine is immense. Part of the election success of this government must be attributed to the medical profession's hostility to the policies of the previous government. Wheeling beds from St Thomas' Hospital across Westminster Bridge, in full view of the media, and tabloid headlines about closed wards and staff shortages, had and will always have a powerful effect on official thinking. Waiting lists (for surgery or other hospital treatment) are another political threat hanging over the head of every government.

These costly 'hard' indicators are far more potent symbols of powerful government than are community-based alternatives. Governments are unlikely to gain popular approval for allocating funds to community-oriented GP practices on disadvantaged housing estates, to enable them to upgrade their services and premises to the levels found in most advantaged areas, where preventive medicine is becoming ever more popular with the middle classes.

Inside every voter's mind is the image of 'what will happen if I need a bed in an emergency?'. Most voters see health purely as a matter of expert diagnosis and treatment of what has gone wrong. The voiceless millions on the estates get little chance to hear about the real health choices.

Community health suffers as a result. Its potential for putting health more into the hands of families and communities, and reducing the control of the professional, remains a distant hope, especially for those whose education has not given them the insight or confidence to assume control over their own health and that of their children. The dearth of research evidence on complementary medical practices could be seen as another limiting factor but, given the cavalier official approach to research findings in general, perhaps complementary medicine will come into its own once enough middle-class people demand government funding for this form of healthcare.

The clash between community health and acute medical care has come into prominence in the last few years as NHS cutbacks or standstills have meant increasingly difficult choices for the boards of health authorities. The official policy of a decade ago, of slowly withdrawing money from acute services to put more into community health services, was never seriously applied but at least community health held its own. However, the funding crises of the last two or three years have meant that, in many trusts, some of the community services have been reduced or even closed down. As an example, health visitor numbers are at their lowest level for many years.

The continuing bias towards acute healthcare reinforces inequality. Community health services give much attention to the needs of more disadvantaged families. With the gradual reduction of support services, such as home visiting by health visitors, it is the deprived, the car-less, the less aware parents who lose out because many of them cannot compensate by taking their child to the clinic instead. Even when they do go, they lack the confidence and skill to draw maximum advantage from meeting the professional on their own institutional ground.

In effect, the present cutbacks and rationalisation in the NHS broaden rather than reduce inequality.

## Tobacco and cannabis: contradictory responses

The policy stance of successive governments towards smoking offers an astonishing example of how the authorities choose to ignore research findings. Policies on this issue have been torn between the evidence of the cancerous and other ill-effects of smoking, and the valuable income which the tobacco levy brings to the Treasury – not to mention large donations to Party funds. Early evidence on the fatal effects of smoking was published more than 50 years ago and has continued to fill the research journals in each decade. Every UK government wrings its ritual hands about the dangers of smoking but continues to profit handsomely from the levy, while approving massive subsidies for tobacco production in the European Union.

Moving from the giant screen of smoking to the miniature screen of cannabis, there is evidence of the same refusal to look at facts because of their economic or political implications. Here, there is overwhelming anecdotal evidence on the effects of cannabis in relieving pain and spasms in multiple sclerosis (MS) sufferers, who currently have to pay a high charge if they want to buy it illegally. The government has turned down pleas that this banned soft drug should be made available on prescription for the thousands of MS sufferers, despite the urging of a powerful medical deputation.

A bizarre situation arose in which the Home Office until recently refused to grant a licence for research into the effectiveness of cannabis with MS patients. After much hesitation, the government has now agreed to a very limited study.

## Rationing: the Oregon experiment

Health funding takes a significant share of the government budget. It is understandable that the Treasury and health ministers should be cautious about increasing that funding, given that the more that is spent, the greater the demands on the taxpayer. The alternative of explicit rationing is a politically fraught concept, yet it has always existed in some form. For every medical professional, there is a cut-off point above which they consider it is not worth pursuing even 'heroic' procedures.

An example of openly practised rationing can be found in the state of Oregon in the USA. It was decided some years ago that it was socially more acceptable to have the public choose the priorities for treatment, rather than leave it in the hands of medical or administrative professionals. The need for a new policy arose because only a minimal proportion of the state's population was on Medicaid, the Federal government's nationwide programme for subsidising State health costs for low-income families. It was decided to increase the proportion on Medicaid considerably, so as to include all Oregon's poor residents. However, in order to remain within the limits imposed by taxpayers, it became necessary to work out a system which was equitable and effective in the treatments provided.

A great deal of research was undertaken to find out the public's priorities, with medical professionals contributing their expertise by costing hundreds of different treatments. Based on State-wide public polls, a list was prepared which categorised treatments from the most to the least acceptable. A cut-off point is worked out each year in relation to the available health funds. Below that point no State treatment is offered, although, as always, the well-off continue to get their own private treatment. Above that point, everyone on Medicaid is entitled to treatment.

The results are impressive but this remains a highly contentious issue. Many people oppose it on the grounds that rationing healthcare is immoral and that taxpayers' funds should be made to cover whatever treatments are needed. Others prefer the doctors treating the patients to have the freedom to make these decisions. Despite intense lobbying, the Oregon experiment continues, although Congress originally expressed serious reservations (Greenberg, 1991). On balance, it could be argued that equity is better served by such a public and open policy rather than one that is worked out behind closed doors (Smith, 1990).

Oregon seems a far cry from present health policies in the UK, where rationing operates de facto. Firstly, government ministers and health authorities decide on geographical and other health spending priorities. Secondly, doctors make rationing decisions in the light of their own insights and perceptions. While it could be argued that more research is needed if the UK were ever to consider the Oregon approach or any other form of community involvement in rationing decisions, it may be more appropriate to determine first whether there would be the political will to introduce such a policy. There is little point embarking on expensive research that would be routinely ignored.

## BSE – mad government disease

Bovine Spongiform Encephalopathy (BSE) has infected 175,000 cattle and led to the slaughter of two million healthy cattle at an ultimate cost to the government of £4 billion. Of far greater concern, some 25 people have died from a new strain of Creutzfeldt-Jakob disease (CJD), with strong evidence suggesting that their deaths resulted from eating BSE-infected beef.

While the issue of equity does not arise here, the attitude of successive governments to evidence about causation is of deep concern.

The original evidence of a strange affliction of cattle was not taken seriously for years. Time was lost which could, it is claimed, have resulted in earlier decisions about treatment and prevention. The theory was developed that BSE had resulted from feeding cattle a form of meal which included some rendered cattle and other animal remains, in order to increase the feed's protein levels.

Both the previous and present governments argue, on the basis of the scientific advice given to them, that this cause of BSE is, by now, well established and that, given sufficient slaughtering of older cattle, the time will come when BSE no longer exists. Already, the number of new cattle contracting BSE has fallen to a few thousand in 1998 and is likely to decline to about 90 by the year 2000.

## The organo-phosphate theory

The cause for concern comes from counter-evidence that BSE may instead have been caused by an unusually strong organo-phosphate (OP) dip used under government direction, to combat warble fly in the 1980s and early 1990s.

Organo-phosphates have long been known to be dangerous chemicals. In 1956 a scientific committee of the government's Chief Scientist at the time, Lord Zuckerman, warned of the dangers to humans from OPs. Despite a variety of evidence produced subsequently on the potential long-term damage to the central nervous system, OPs were used in the Gulf War to spray both soldiers and their tents in order to eradicate lice and other pests. Recent decisions in courts in Hong Kong, Australia and the UK gave judgements totalling £2 million in compensation to people who were exposed to OPs in the course of their work.

In an extensive newspaper analysis of this issue, Booker and North (*Daily Telegraph*, 1996) review the history of BSE. They cite evidence that many other countries in Europe and the USA also used cattle remains in cattle feed, but none of them, with the exception of Switzerland and Ireland, had shown any significant numbers of BSE cases. Although a complete ban was imposed on feeding animal remains to cattle in 1988, a further 28,000 cattle contracted the disease in subsequent years. The authors of the analysis refute claims from the Ministry of Agriculture, Fisheries and Food (MAFF) that the disease arose in the UK because British animal remains were rendered at a lower temperature than elsewhere. If anything, British rendering standards were more rigorous.

Instead, those authors advance a theory, first proposed by an affected dairy farmer, that it was the government's introduction of compulsory spraying of warble infected cattle with a particularly potent OP dip, known as phosmet, which had led to the outbreak of BSE. Phosmet combines a powerful OP with another chemical, phthalimide, the latter being an active component of thalidomide. Both agents are mutagenic and can damage the nervous system. It is argued that phosmet affected cows as well as their unborn progeny. The authors point out that phosmet was used mainly on dairy cattle and only on some beef cattle. Other beef cattle were treated with a different OP compound. This differentiation is in line with the evidence that it was mainly dairy cattle which contracted BSE.

The OP theory also explains why BSE was concentrated in areas worst affected by warble fly, and why the disease only appeared in Northern Ireland three years later than on the mainland – phosmet was only introduced there three years after its first use in England. In only two other countries in Europe was phosmet licensed and for use in much lower doses than in the UK. Those countries were Switzerland and Ireland, the only other countries to have (relatively minor) outbreaks of BSE.

When the government was finally persuaded to conduct a trial to test the theory that phosmet was responsible for BSE, the Medical Research Council (MRC) funded a research study which did not test phosmet but experimented instead with a different OP compound with different properties from those of phosmet. The conclusions of the MRC study were negative.

Whatever the truth or otherwise of this alternative hypothesis, the previous government's failure to look dispassionately at other theories is in keeping with governments' general unwillingness to take account of research, especially outside research, when determining policy.

Booker and North (1996) believe that the reasons for the government's unwillingness to concede and investigate fully the OP theory of BSE is linked to its concern about the possibility of massive claims if the Gulf War syndrome can be proven to have resulted from the use of OPs for spraying the British soldiers and their tents.

The final, rather quixotic government response to research in this field came in the form of a recently announced ban on beef on the bone, following scientific evidence that there was a remote possibility of about one in a billion of someone contracting CJD from eating beef cooked this way. This unnecessarily prescriptive response – rather than issuing a warning, to enable people to decide for themselves – derives from the same government which annually supports the subsidisation of tobacco production in the European Union at a cost of £700 million per year in taxpayers' money and, in effect, subsidises the cancers which cost tens of thousands of smokers' lives each year.

# The nutritional supplement scandal

Governments' continuing attempts to block public access to meaningful levels of nutritional supplements are among the most scandalous examples of ignoring research findings and taking action which is in support of powerful commercial interests.

These supplements consist of vitamins or minerals extracted from everyday foods or ones that are chemically manufactured to provide identical nutrients. There is heated controversy among nutritionists, as well as medical researchers, as to whether these supplements are effective in prevention or therapy and, if so, to what extent. Linus Pauling's work on Vitamin C won him the Nobel Prize (reviewed in Cameron et al, 1979), but there are still many who refuse to believe that anything other than pharmaceutical drugs can have preventive or therapeutic effects.

There is mounting research evidence that:

- deficiencies of Vitamin A and other identified nutrients are linked to cancers;
- Vitamin E can reduce the risk of heart disease and is a valuable adjunct to surgical operations because of its healing powers;
- deficiency of folate (a B vitamin) is indisputably linked to spina bifida;
- deficiencies of zinc in pregnancy may be linked to other foetal and birth problems;
- magnesium is of central importance in countering pre-eclampsia;
- a great many chronic illnesses show evidence of deficiencies of Vitamin C and other basic nutrients in the blood and diets of those affected.

There are good reasons for concluding that the refining of foods, particularly wheat, and the excessive phosphate fertilisation of crops, have contributed to many of the nutrient deficiencies experienced today. Wide natural variations in individual metabolisms mean that only some people suffer from these deficits if they are not gross; in other words, there are no uniform criteria for dietary requirements, although government guidelines appear to ignore this basic fact.

Governments' repeated attempts to block the usage or popularisation of nutritional supplements and herbal products are almost invariably backed by 'advice' from secretive committees. Virtually all these products are safe even when taken in doses well above recommended levels. Their therapeutic effect comes from intakes above the normal, with users safe in the knowledge that only massively excessive intakes could possibly do them any harm – as can any normal condiment. Even table salt is known to be dangerous in excess.

Statutory records of mortality and morbidity resulting from pharmaceutical drugs show thousands of deaths and cases of serious illness resulting each year from prescribed levels of dosage of what have long been recognised as potentially dangerous substances. In contrast, there are a small handful of cases where the intake of excessive amounts of one or another supplement is suspected of having caused morbidity or, very rarely, death. The man who died after drinking eight pints of carrot juice a day for several years is frequently cited as an example of the 'dangers' of Vitamin A. Pregnant women who eat an excess amount of liver, as well as taking supplements of Vitamin A, have occasionally had malformed infants. These are rare examples of harm which are repeated ad nauseam by those hostile to any supplements.

For many years attempts have been made by the pharmaceutical industry to have nutritional supplements, well-known herbs and other traditional natural remedies controlled by government committees under the same rules as drugs. This means fixing intakes of supplements at very low (and thus ineffective) levels, so as to leave an enormous margin of safety. It also requires their manufacturers – mostly small production units – to embark on RCTs costing hundreds of thousands of pounds for each individual product and for each separate combination of nutrients.

Three specific examples of attempts by government to muzzle the use of natural remedies relate to folate and spina bifida babies, the use of Vitamin B6 and of comfrey. These are explained below.

### Folate and spina bifida babies

Studies in the mid–1960s had suggested a link between B Vitamin folate deficiency and neural tube defects – so much so that many GPs were then recommending folate supplementation to the diets of pregnant women.

Two studies in the 1970s suggested a much stronger link. They were triggered by the work of people such as Professor John Kevany, a leading public health and nutritional expert at Trinity College in Dublin, who pointed to the wealth of animal research establishing a link between insufficient folate intake in the diet in pregnancy and foetal deformities in general. He argued that similar links were likely to exist in the human population. Smithells et al (1980) and Laurence (1982) published supporting evidence from studies totalling more than 900 cases.

Nevertheless, neither the government nor the medical profession as a whole were willing to take this evidence seriously. Despite the obvious advantages to the Treasury from a reduction in spina bifida births, there was a lack of interest in such research and some professional opposition. Any suggestion that folate supplementation of diets would be beneficial was objected to on the grounds that its reputed blocking of awareness of Vitamin B12 deficiency might lead to anaemia (in a very small number of cases). Concerns were also expressed regarding the possible damaging effects of folate on the mother or foetus. In each case, the risk was admitted to be minute.

A further retrospective case control study or prospective matched design could have settled matters swiftly. However, rather than undertake such a study, the MRC proposed and designed a major study (1991) involving 3,000 women in several countries including the UK. All the cases were to be selected on the basis of a previous spina bifida birth. Of the 3,000 women, 750 were to be given a placebo with the expectation that around 40 would produce a second spina bifida foetus which could be terminated should the mother so wish.

When details of this experiment became known, there was great public concern about both the ethics and the efficacy of such a study. However, the then government was unmoved. In a written reply to a fellow MP, the Minister of Health at that time admitted that he was aware of the strength of feelings about the study and of the current evidence. He then cited the MRC's view that it is "... necessary and ethical to carry out a proper controlled trial ..." and that "[they] hope that women who have volunteered to be in the study are probably unlikely to take extra vitamins ...". Thus mothers denied the treatment vitamins were also to be denied any other vitamin supplementation. A curious interpretation of the term 'ethics'!

Fortunately, the evidence on the positive effects of folate in reducing spina bifida mounted so quickly after the commencement of the study that it was abandoned half-way on the grounds that further experimentation could not be justified. It is interesting to note that a well-known breakfast manufacturer has emphasised the folate addition to its product since 1987. We may ask why the government ignored strong public feelings on this matter, and in particular who now bears responsibility for the many babies born with spina bifida in the interim?

## Deaf to the B6 protest

The implications of the government's official stance on the intake of Vitamin B6 is far more serious. It is no longer a matter of over-cautious medical professionals waiting to be convinced, as happened initially with folate.

In 1997, it was suddenly announced by the Food Minister in the present government that, based on advice, he was considering banning the sale of Vitamin B6 in any quantities above 10mg. This ban would apply not only to the vitamin on its own but also to the many hundreds of multivitamin products which contain B6 at levels above 10mg. Quantities up to 50mg could only be purchased from pharmacists and quantities above 50mg would need to be prescribed by GPs.

The research background is most interesting and offers, perhaps, the best example of every government's cavalier approach to evidence. There have been thousands of studies of the administration of Vitamin B6 to humans. Every type of controlled study has been carried out into safety, at levels far higher than normal supplement levels (which range from 25mg to 200mg a day). Clinical studies of women taking these doses for extended periods have shown no deleterious effects. There are many findings of positive effects of Vitamin B6 intake, especially over a range of conditions linked to women's health, pregnancy and pre-menstrual tension (PMT).

Only one study, carried out by Dr K. Dalton and her husband 11 years ago, produced negative findings. They carried out a retrospective telephone survey of some hundreds of women who had previously taken Vitamin B6 but who had gone to Dr Dalton for her hormonal treatment of post-natal depression. When telephoned, a number of these women reported that they had suffered tingling in the upper limbs. This condition had ended once they stopped taking the Vitamin B6. There was no control group and no attempt to validate the reports. The figures cited by Dalton showed no dose-response variation and there was no examination of other medical factors that could have led to the reported condition. The study was published in a little known Swedish journal.

A neurologist and other experts have pointed to a number of possible alternative explanations, including excess consumption of caffeine or alcohol. A recent survey showed that paraesthesia – the reported upper limb condition – occurred more frequently in the general population that in women taking Vitamin B6. There have been no follow-ups or replications of the Dalton findings. One other 20-year-old study administered extremely high dosages of B6 to dogs to determine what happened. These dosages were the equivalent of many grams of Vitamin B6 a day in humans. The expected neural problems arose.

Based on these two studies (the authors of the animal study protested that their findings were being misused), the government's Committee on Toxicity of Food (COT) recommended in 1997 to the Food Minister that a ban be placed on the sale of Vitamin B6 at any levels above 10mg, other than in the controlled conditions referred to above. A reduction factor (ie, a safety margin) of 300 was used to decide on this minimum. The fact that nine of the 15 members of the COT have had their research supported by the pharmaceutical industry or have other links with it must make it more difficult for the committee to be seen as fully independent – a problem faced by many leading researchers in this field today.

There have seldom been such widespread protests from medical professionals. These included a leading professor of toxicology, another professor who is an international authority on B6, nutritional medical experts and many others who have been administering B6 to women at levels up to 200mg a day, with no ill-effects, for periods as much as 15 years. A review by the German Research Council likewise rejected the Dalton study. The COT was presented with 100 significant studies on the positive effects and safety of Vitamin B6 but it stood by its recommendation.

It has been reported that thousands of people have written to the Minister or to their MPs to protest. Interviewed by the media, the Minister responsible stated that he was not prepared to have women die as a result of using large quantities of Vitamin B6, although no opponent has ever suggested that this might happen. Deputations have been to see the Minister, including leading medical experts in this field, but the Minister remains adamant. Recently it was decided that a final decision on this matter would be put off for two years.

## Comfrey, 1,500 years in use, now banned

The 1993 decision of the COT to recommend that the then government ban comfrey was probably a dry run for what is now happening to Vitamin B6 and is likely to happen to other nutritional and herbal products in the years to come.

Comfrey is a common hedgerow plant that has been used for 1,500 years as a herbal remedy and tea, and is also eaten as a vegetable. A variety of research reports have established its effectiveness. Doses of up to 12% by body weight, fed to rodents, produced no abnormalities and enabled the rodents to thrive better than control animals. A medical review of comfrey usage in humans, undertaken following claims about its dangers, concluded that people who have taken or used products containing comfrey have no cause for alarm.

It is reputed to aid healing after bone fractures, wounds and surgical lesions. It has also been used for digestive problems and pain relief in arthritis. It is not even necessary to believe all these claims to be astonished at the means used to ban what appears to be a totally harmless product.

A statement issued by the Society for the Promotion of Nutritional Therapy examined the COT recommendation, in particular the claim that because comfrey contained pyrrolizidine alkaloids (PAs) it could be dangerous. The COT admitted that there was no evidence linking PAs in comfrey to human illness. One of the few studies claiming to show damaging effects reported that when rats were fed this herb at a level equivalent to 28 times body weight, they died of liver tumours. Potatoes and many other substances are also known to contain PAs, sometimes at levels which have caused poisoning but there is no evidence of this having occurred with comfrey.

The government of the day said it was prepared to look at new evidence. The Society sent out 30,000 questionnaires asking for information on the effects of comfrey. Not one respondent reported any ill-health effects. These conclusions were rejected by the COT and the government placed a total ban on comfrey in any form, no matter how small.

## The European alternative

There have been several attempts by committees of the European Commission to place widespread restrictions on the use of supplements, on the grounds of harmonisation with those few countries where supplements are not available for public purchase at health shops and can only be supplied by medical prescription.

If, given the force of Community law, this will offer an easy way out for UK governments and quangos such as the COT, there will be no need to cite little known and totally atypical studies to justify wide-ranging restrictions on the supply of all nutritional supplements and herbal products.

# Women's health is the chief victim

Throughout recent centuries, women's health in the UK has been largely in the hands of men, whether as medical professionals or government administrators. Although not acceptable, there may be understandable reasons why that was so – the education and career barriers faced by women in the past and even to some extent today.

Government and COT requirements for rigid proof of effectiveness and safety of nutritional supplements is likely to be of prime importance in limiting severely women's access to these supplements. Application of this prerequisite is gradually eliminating all meaningful health products available over the counter in supermarkets, health shops and elsewhere. The spurious grounds are that anything associated with health has to be strictly controlled in the interests of the consumer, and made available only from pharmacists or on medical prescription. The result is decreased availability and increased cost. Governments are willing conspirators in this approach, invoking the law whenever requested by the powerful lobbies whose goodwill is essential for their continuing popularity.

It is regrettable that a government with more women MPs than ever in the history of Parliament should be prepared to block products of special value to women, when there is no evidence of harm, and possibly a considerable potential for good. As fewer of these products become available at supermarkets and health stores, women will turn increasingly to their GPs. However, there is already much anecdotal evidence that when working-class women ask their GPs for prescriptions for B6 and zinc (for PMT or post-natal depression), they are often turned down. They do not have the status or knowledge to argue for their needs in the way that middle-class women do. Thus health inequalities will be reinforced even more.

# A sorry tale: where next?

The broad thrust of this chapter is that governments of all political complexions pay little or no attention to research findings, unless to quote selectively from findings favouring a politically desirable line of action. Even the scientific findings on BSE were only taken seriously when a link was made with human deaths and it was clear that the European Union would impose its own restrictions on British beef.

The practice of governments ignoring research is not a matter of minor concern. Even if the work of every researcher in the UK were to stop tomorrow there would be major national issues that needed addressing because of the interface between science and politics.

This brings us to what Radical Statistics is about, and should be about. We are, at the same time, researchers and political activists, though not necessarily affiliated to parties. If our research role disappeared tomorrow, we would still have a commitment to influencing the political process, each in our own way. However, if our radical research role disappeared, it is doubtful whether most of us would have anywhere to go. Statistics in isolation from political, social, economic or any other reality can be sterile; it needs the motivation of purpose to give it life, or radical purpose for those who choose the more difficult option of pioneering new paradigms in health research and in other disciplines.

There are seven brief conclusions to be drawn from this discussion, which are applicable to the Radical Statistics Group.

1   If the hypothesis has been established that governments pay little or no attention to research in some of the limited, defined issues described earlier, there should be serious concern as to whether macro policy decisions are ever informed by research, since the competing pressures at the macro level are even greater than at the street level discussed in these specific examples. That is not a reason to turn away from trying to influence government, but rather a pointer to the fact that we need to be far more skilled politically (spelt with a small 'p'), finding allies in one camp today, in the other tomorrow, in the interests of our radical integrity.

2   Funding is a sine qua non for any meaningful research. We cannot undertake studies into significant issues without some form of support. Being denied funding, as shown earlier, is an effective way for governments to foreclose the debate and make decisions unembarrassed by research conclusions. Perhaps we need to think of grouping ourselves into larger collectives and apply to major foundations for research monies to explore issues publicly, in such a way that governments would hesitate to ignore the conclusions. The lone researcher or small group finds it much more difficult to influence policies than would larger groups of like-minded researchers.

3   It would be simplistic to see our role as one of David versus the Goliath of government, with David enjoying widespread popular support. On many issues, vested professional interest groups side with the government and help to devalue research which challenges existing policy and practice. At least with the professional interest groups, there is some hope of driving a wedge between those who

are willing to listen and maybe agree and those whose professional security and status are the prime purpose of their work. Forming temporary alliances with radical researchers in other professions may be a way of strengthening our and their influence.

4 We need to consider whether our interest in health policies, and the achievement of greater equity, can be helped by encouraging the least advantaged in society to become aware of the potential of many low cost forms of complementary medicine, the 'alternative' scene, which has its own strengths but also its own charlatans, as does medicine itself. As researchers, we can try to contribute to the many 'alternative' health professionals who are keen to evaluate what they achieve, but are not sure how to do so other than through RCTs whose conceptual basis undermines most alternative therapies. Breaking the stranglehold of the narrow medical model may take many years, but we can already find support from those medical professionals who at heart are already on our side and are keen to look at alternatives which, for many conditions, can be more therapeutic and less costly than mainstream practices.

5 If we find little public support for some of the possibilities outlined here, we should remember that many middle-class people are happy with the present role of government, provided it keeps society in reasonable order. Nutrient bans and similar setbacks can be overcome by those with the money or the ability to compensate in other ways, for example, by pressurising their GPs or importing what they need. Our constituency of support is more likely to be found in the vast estates and towerblocks where healthcare is an imposed solution about which people understand little, other than that they are seen somehow to be blamed for their health predicament. Even such people find it hard to accept that it is the wider community, the social structure and its management, which contributes so much to their health problems. How are we to get across that message, without it appearing like outside interference? For example, how many field researchers could be recruited from the ranks of the unemployed or partially employed on such estates, holding out for them not the desired escape into middle-class suburbia, but the possibility of further education, training and involvement so that they can help to transform their own estates in time?

6 It can be hypothesised that governments' unwillingness to consider research findings is possibly the biggest reason why the current inequities in health provision are likely to persist or even increase, as the 'haves' become even more educated and more aware of how to

run the system for their own benefit. The vast share of state welfare resources already enjoyed by this group reflects the similar social class bias within the health service, with private medical care being their refuge when the statutory services cannot meet their needs.

7 Finally, if healthcare and health policies are to become ultimately interwoven with and controlled by local communities, we may need to resurrect the hopes of Alma Ata (WHO, 1978), that almost forgotten world dream of putting local communities in charge of their own health facilities. There are places where this is already a reality – even in the US, where Federal funding of healthcare for deprived communities has had a profound effect on the health and awareness of some of America's most deprived regions, such as the dwellers around the Appalachian Mountains. There, the residents appoint their own healthcare committees which, in turn, recruit doctors and all the required staff. There is no reason why similar structures could not be funded here on an experimental basis, despite the burden of our persisting class system. Until health is owned by the residents of suitably large communities, it will always remain alien, benefiting the professionals who serve the residents while they in turn attempt to exploit the professionals. There is a far better, more radical alternative, whose parameters were set out at Alma Ata 20 years ago.

## References

Barker, W.E. (1987) 'Counting heads', *Senior Nurse*, vol 6, no 1, January, pp 8-10.

Barker, W.E. (1992) 'Measurement of NHS service provision: activity levels or outcomes?', *Radical Statistics*, no 51, Summer, pp 21-9.

Booker, C. and North, R. (1996) 'BSE: but is feed to blame?', *Daily Telegraph*, p 8.

Cameron, E., Pauling, L. and Leibovitz, B. (1979) 'Ascorbic acid and cancer: a review', *Cancer Research*, vol 39, pp 663-81.

DHSS (Department of Health and Social Security) (1980) *Inequalities in health* (Black Report), Report of a Research Working Group chaired by Sir Douglas Black, London: DHSS.

DHSS (1982) *Steering Group on Health Service Information Reports 1-6* (Körner Reports), London: DHSS.

DoH (Department of Health) (1998) *Our healthier nation*, London: HMSO.

Evans, P. (1985) 'Money output and Goodhardt's Law: the US experience', *Review of Economic Statistics*, February, vol 67, p 1-8.

Greenberg, D.S. (1991) 'The Oregon Plan on Capitol Hill', *The Lancet*, no 338, pp 808-9.

HMSO (1998) *Health Survey for England 1996*, London: HMSO.

Laurence, K.M. (1982) 'Prevention of neural tube defects by diet', *Pediatrics*, no 70, pp 648-50.

Medical Research Council Vitamin Study Group (1991) 'Prevention of neural tube defects: results of the Medical Research Council Vitamin Study', *Lancet*, vol 238, pp 131-7.

Smith, R. (1990) 'Rationing health care in America', *BMJ*, vol 300, p 558.

Smithells, R.W. et al (1980) 'Possible prevention of neural tube defects by periconceptual vitamin supplementation', *The Lancet*, no 11, pp 339-40.

Townsend, P. and Davidson, N. (1982) *Inequalities in health: The Black Report*, Pelican Edition, Harmondsworth: Penguin.

Whitehead, M. (1988) *The health divide: Inequalities in health in the 1980's*, London: Health Education Council.

WHO (World Health Organisation) (1978) 'Declaration of Alma Ata', *The Lancet*, no 2, pp 1040-1.

# NINE

# A mortality league table for Cabinet Ministers?

*Danny Dorling*

## Introduction: is it worth reducing inequalities in health?

The set of statistics presented in this chapter attempts to show how closely the distribution of voting mirrors the distribution of premature mortality in Britain. The chapter goes on to show how spatial inequalities in mortality are reflected in the spatial distribution of Members of Parliament (MPs) and, in particular, Cabinet Ministers. It will be argued that, given the unequal life chances of its constituents, reducing inequalities in health in Britain should be a priority for the New Labour government. It may be a little surprising that the Green Paper on health (DoH, 1998) set no explicit targets to reduce the inequalities described here. Similarly the government's *Independent Inquiry into Inequalities in Health* (Acheson, 1998) did not recommend specific targets and did not prioritise its recommendations (Davey Smith et al, 1998). The government has still to respond to the Inquiry's report other than in saying it would form a "key input" to policy, and this was only a press comment from Frank Dobson, the Secretary of State for Health (before running for mayor of London).

The chapter shows that every year analysed in the 1990s 119 people have died unexpectedly and prematurely in Frank Dobson's constituency of Holborn and St Pancras. This is because people aged below 65 in this constituency have a mortality ratio 50% above the national average, the 21st highest in the country and the 2nd highest among the constituencies of Cabinet Ministers. In the 1980s, Holborn and St Pancras had a mortality ratio for this age group that was 38% above the national average, which meant that 49 fewer people aged below 65 died unexpectedly per year compared with the 1990s rate. Inequalities in mortality are increasing, with the effects being seen most clearly among the constituencies of the people who voted for the ministers of the current government. Since Frank Dobson became MP for Holborn and St Pancras in 1979 at least 1,500 more of his constituents (in absolute terms) will have died prematurely than in the average constituency in Britain. The primary reason for this level of inequality in health is inequalities in wealth, most obviously reflected through levels of poverty. In Frank Dobson's constituency 36% of all households and 56% of households with children live in poverty, compared with 21% and 27% nationally (using *Breadline Britain* methodology – see Gordon and Forrest, 1995).

Given such a long legacy of the effects of poverty on ill-health among the Cabinet Minister's constituents, a naïve analyst might expect government policy to have concentrated on the eradication of poverty and inequalities in health in Britain. This chapter concludes by suggesting an electoral explanation as to why reducing inequalities in general may not be a real political priority for this government. Perhaps ministers, and MPs in general, need to be reminded of the extent of inequalities in health, precisely who those inequalities affect, how they are worsening, and why they first fought to gain office.

## British democracy is weakest where people's lives are shortest

Table 9.1 shows the basic statistics on which most of this chapter is based. To construct the table the age-sex standardised mortality ratio (SMR) of each 1997 parliamentary constituency was calculated for people who died below the age of 65 between 1981 and 1992 (see Davey Smith and Dorling, 1996, 1997, for further details). The mortality data is updated later to 1995 for the constituencies of Ministers and Shadow Ministers. Mortality below age 65 is termed premature mortality from here on. All the constituencies of mainland Britain were then ranked and divided into 10 groups – each containing almost the same number of electors. These are termed decile groups from here on. The first decile group is made up of those constituencies which contain the 10% of the electorate living in areas with the highest premature mortality ratios (these constituencies are listed in Table 9.4). The second contains the tenth of the population living in constituencies with the next highest mortality ratios and so on, up to decile 10 which contains the last tenth of the population living in the constituencies with the lowest premature mortality ratios.

*Table 9.1:* **Excess mortality and voting by 10 groups of parliamentary constituencies containing roughly equal electorates**

| Decile group | Adults in 1991 (millions) | Excess deaths 1981-92 per year | Excess deaths | Absten- tions | Conser- vative | Labour | Lib Dem |
|---|---|---|---|---|---|---|---|
| | | | | | Proportion of the electorate voting in May 1997 | | |
| 1 | 4,489,754 | 37% | 5,031 | 36% | 10% | 39% | 8% |
| 2 | 4,519,899 | 21% | 2,804 | 33% | 13% | 41% | 7% |
| 3 | 4,430,633 | 14% | 1,857 | 31% | 15% | 40% | 8% |
| 4 | 4,450,592 | 7% | 925 | 30% | 18% | 40% | 8% |
| 5 | 4,285,230 | 1% | 144 | 28% | 21% | 35% | 11% |
| 6 | 4,337,816 | -4% | -439 | 27% | 26% | 31% | 12% |
| 7 | 4,324,558 | -9% | -1,089 | 26% | 27% | 28% | 15% |
| 8 | 4,312,125 | -13% | -1,579 | 25% | 30% | 24% | 17% |
| 9 | 4,249,041 | -18% | -2,195 | 25% | 32% | 20% | 20% |
| 10 | 4,330,387 | -23% | -2,945 | 24% | 33% | 20% | 18% |
| Britain | 43,730,035 | 2% | 2,514 | 28% | 22% | 32% | 12% |

*Notes:* Adult populations are taken from the estimating with confidence project (and exceed the electorate).

Mortality rates are age–sex standardised SMRs for death below the age of 65, England and Wales=100.

Voting figures do not sum to 100% because of voting for minor parties.

Table 9.1 requires some explanation. When we compare these decile groups of constituencies we are not comparing exactly the same numbers of adults as not all adults in Britain are registered to vote. The second column in Table 9.1, and Figure 9.1, show how many adults actually lived in each decile group in 1991. Note that the 40% of the electorate living in areas with the highest premature mortality ratios (decile groups 1 to 4) contain disproportionate numbers of adults.

The third column in Table 9.1 shows the proportion of premature deaths (below the age of 65 in these areas) which would not have occurred had the mortality ratios in the areas been the same as for England and Wales as a whole. This ranges from there being one third more premature deaths between 1981 and 1992 in decile group 1 than would be expected, to there being one quarter fewer in decile group 10. These statistics are put in another, and more direct, way in the next column in the table, which shows how in the worst decile 5,031 more people die each year below the age of 65 than we would expect under conditions of equality.

***Figure 9.1*: Population registered to vote varies between areas for equal population**

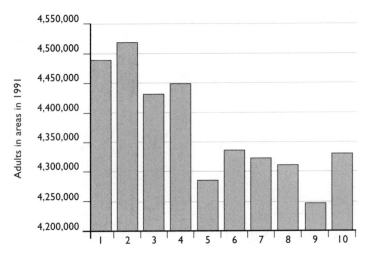

Decile group (of equal numbers of electors by constituency)

Because English and Welsh rates are being used to derive the expected number of deaths in an area, the ratios for Britain are slightly higher than one hundred as they include Scotland where mortality rates are higher than in England and Wales. Figure 9.2 shows the distribution of excess death rates by decile area and demonstrates that there is a near log–linear continuum. Britain is not divided into areas with poor health and areas with good health, but contains a continuum of places which, when graphed, show a neat pecking order in terms of life chances. The people of decile group 1 are slightly out of line – with the jump in mortality from the second to the worst set of areas being greater than that between any other groups. This widening of the gap between the worst areas and the average opened up during the 1980s, and such spatial polarisation in life chances had not been seen before then in Britain (Dorling, 1997).

**Figure 9.2: People's chance of dying below the age of 65**

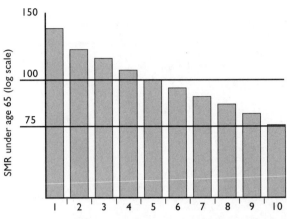

Decile group (of equal numbers of electors by constituency)

The fifth column in Table 9.1 gives the abstention rate (proportion of the registered electorate not casting a valid vote) in the constituencies in each decile group at the 1997 General Election, while the final three columns show the proportion of the electorate who chose to vote for each of the three major parties. In the first seven decile areas, representing 70% of the electors of Britain, the largest proportion voted for New Labour, while in the last three decile groups the Conservatives were most popular. The abstention rate and the Labour vote rose as the mortality rate rose, while the Conservative and Liberal Democrat votes fell. The relationship between the abstention and mortality rates in decile groups is extremely close. For every extra 600 people who died prematurely in a decile area every year between 1981 and 1992, another 1% of the electorate chose not to vote at the General Election of 1997. Because the number of voters is so large and the number of deaths so (relatively) small, this relationship cannot be due to excess mortality rates in an area leading to inflated electoral rolls (although dead people can remain on the electoral roll for many months after they have died). The distribution of support for the three main parties among those who do choose to vote for them is shown in Figure 9.3.

**Figure 9.3: Excess deaths and voting patterns**

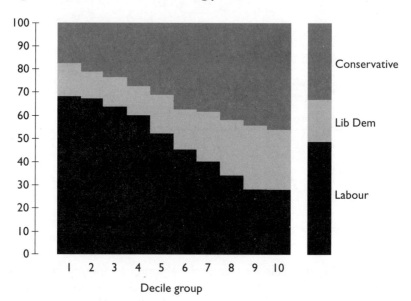

The proportions of the electorate shown in Table 9.1 do not sum to 100% because voting for the minor political parties has not been included on that table. Table 9.2 presents the results for any minor party that gained more than 0.5% of the electorate in any decile group. Note that although Martin Bell (the Independent MP who stood in Tatton, Cheshire) appears in this table, not a single English party to the left of Labour features. Even in the most deprived tenth of constituencies, the Left-wing parties could find no noticeable support. The table shows that inequalities in health work to the detriment of people living in areas where there is support for the Scottish National Party (SNP), and to the benefit of people living in areas where the Referendum Party received its strongest support. The table also shows, in its last column, the proportion of adults in each decile area who were not registered to vote, which is highest in decile group 1. When these adults are added to those who are registered but choose not to vote we see that the most popular 'choice' for adults in the tenth of Britain with the highest premature mortality ratios, chosen by 40%, was not to take part in the political process at all. British democracy is weakest where people's lives are shortest.

*Table 9.2:* **Voting for minor parties and not registering to vote by the 10 groups of parliamentary constituencies**

| Decile group | Scottish Nationalist | Plaid Cymru | Referendum Party | UK Independence | Martin Bell | Adults not registered to vote |
|---|---|---|---|---|---|---|
| 1 | 5% | 0% | 1% | 0% | 0% | 4% |
| 2 | 4% | 0% | 1% | 0% | 0% | 3% |
| 3 | 2% | 0% | 2% | 0% | 0% | 2% |
| 4 | 1% | 1% | 2% | 0% | 0% | 2% |
| 5 | 1% | 1% | 2% | 0% | 0% | 1% |
| 6 | 1% | 1% | 2% | 0% | 0% | 1% |
| 7 | 0% | 1% | 2% | 0% | 0% | 0% |
| 8 | 0% | 0% | 2% | 0% | 1% | 0% |
| 9 | 0% | 0% | 3% | 1% | 0% | 0% |
| 10 | 0% | 0% | 3% | 0% | 0% | 0% |
| Britain | 1% | 0% | 2% | 0% | 0% | 1% |

*Notes:* No other parties registered the votes of more than 0.5% of the electorate in any decile group.

Estimates of the numbers of adults not registered assumes zero net migration between 1991 and 1997 and that the Census count of non-Commonwealth and Irish born adults approximates nationalities.

## New Labour has a monopoly on premature mortality

If instead of looking at votes we look at seats, and the Party elected, we see a very different picture. Despite a minority of adults voting for New Labour in the constituencies with the highest mortality rates (and less than two fifths of those in that group who did vote, voting for that Party – see Table 9.1), they won 67 of the 70 seats. Table 9.3 shows how many seats each Party won in each decile group of constituencies. Labour has a majority of the seats in the 70% of the population with the highest premature mortality rates and the Conservatives have a majority in the remaining 30%. The Liberal Democrats had their greatest success at the interface of these two groups (winning 12 of the 63 constituencies in decile group 7) reflecting their political position between the main two Parties. Figure 9.4 shows the dominance of New Labour more clearly.

*Figure 9.4:* **The Labour Party and decile group voting**

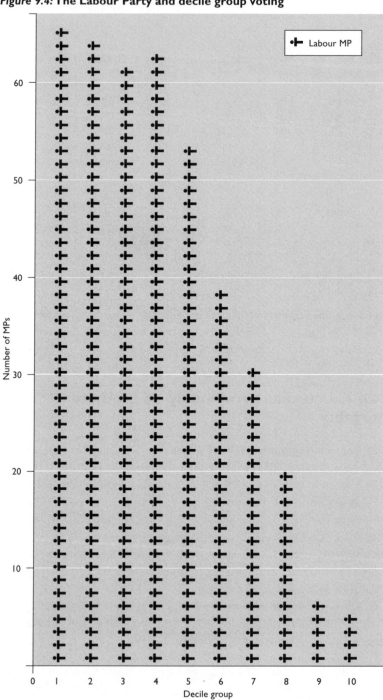

*Table 9.3:* **Seats won in 1997 by the 10 groups of parliamentary constituencies containing equal electoral seats**

| Decile group | Total seats | Labour Party | Conservative Party | Liberal Democrats | Nationalist parties | Others |
|---|---|---|---|---|---|---|
| 1 | 70 | 67 | 0 | 3 | 0 | 0 |
| 2 | 68 | 65 | 1 | 1 | 0 | 1 (Speaker) |
| 3 | 66 | 62 | 0 | 1 | 3 | 0 |
| 4 | 66 | 64 | 1 | 0 | 1 | 0 |
| 5 | 64 | 54 | 2 | 5 | 3 | 0 |
| 6 | 63 | 40 | 16 | 5 | 2 | 0 |
| 7 | 63 | 31 | 19 | 12 | 1 | 0 |
| 8 | 60 | 21 | 30 | 8 | 0 | 1 (Mr Bell) |
| 9 | 60 | 8 | 46 | 6 | 0 | 0 |
| 10 | 61 | 6 | 50 | 5 | 0 | 0 |
| Britain | 641 | 418 | 165 | 46 | 10 | 2 |

*Notes:* There are more seats in decile group 1 because these seats have few electors than average (but more adults).

The Conservative constituency in decile 2 is Cities of London & Westminster (Peter Brooke MP, SMR 175).

Labour MPs in the most healthy constituencies include Stephen Twigg (Southgate).

Politically, the people living in the half of Britain with higher than average premature mortality ratios are represented almost exclusively by one political party: New Labour. Since the Labour Party has always represented poorer people and poorer people are more likely to die prematurely from the effects of poverty, this relationship is not surprising. However, it is interesting to see that the population of the tenth of the country with the highest premature mortality ratios (and, when we look at other measures, the highest levels of poverty overall) is represented by the highest number of Cabinet Ministers and Parliamentary Secretaries of all the groups being analysed here.

Table 9.4 shows which MPs represent the 70 constituencies making up decile group 1. They include, among many others, powerful members of the incoming Labour Cabinet, Donald Dewar (Secretary of State for Scotland), Clare Short (Secretary of State for International Development), Frank Dobson (Secretary of State for Health), George Robertson (Defence), Harriet Harman (Social Security), Alistair Darling (Treasury), Jack Straw (Home Office) and Chris Smith (National Heritage). These are the people who ran the new government ministries, who sat in Cabinet and who were empowered to make the decisions which could either harm or help people's lives. New Labour had a monopoly of the population with premature mortality and Labour ministers represented an even more marginal set of constituents than did their parliamentary party members. In general, the higher the number of premature deaths, the safer the seat and the more senior the Labour politician elected.

The mortality figures for the constituencies of every member of the incoming 1997 Cabinet and Shadow Cabinet are shown in Table 9.5. These include the rank of their constituency in terms of the premature mortality rate of their constituents, the proportion of premature deaths that could be avoided if mortality ratios were equalised, and how many excess deaths a year this proportion represents. Every Cabinet Minister who has a constituency represents people in areas of above average premature mortality. Every day between 1981 and 1992, an extra three people died below the age of 65 in the Cabinet's constituencies than in the country as a whole. Put another way there were 10,000 additional premature deaths in the 1980s decade in the Cabinet's 20 constituencies alone. The Prime Minister Tony Blair's constituents experience 47 more deaths below the age of 65 per year than do the voters of an average constituency (although the premature death rate in his constituency is average for a member of the Cabinet).

The incoming Conservative Shadow Cabinet represents a set of seats which could not be more different to those of the Cabinet. All Shadow Ministers represent constituents living in areas of low premature mortality. This is not true of all Conservative MPs, but Shadow Ministers tend to be the more focused of their colleagues and to secure safe Conservative seats where premature mortality rates are lowest. Labour Ministers represent some of the safest New Labour seats in the country which hence have some of the highest mortality rates. In essence, people who are well-off tend to vote Conservative and tend also to live longer because of their material advantages. Successful politicians in Britain manage to secure the safer seats and hence the widest inequalities in life chances can be seen between the people who live in the constituencies of the Cabinet and those of the Shadow Cabinet.

**Table 9.4: Constituencies which make up decile 1**

| Rank | Rate People/year >100 | Constituency | MP | Party | Title |
|---|---|---|---|---|---|
| 1 | 95% | 151 | Glasgow Shettleston | Mr David MARSHALL | Labour | |
| 2 | 83% | 151 | Glasgow Springburn | Mr Michael MARTIN | Labour | |
| 3 | 74% | 136 | Glasgow Maryhill | Mrs Maria FYFE | Labour | |
| 4 | 64% | 157 | Manchester Central | Mr Tony LLOYD | Labour | Minister of State |
| 5 | 62% | 120 | Glasgow Pollok | Mr Ian DAVIDSON | Labour | |
| 6 | 62% | 142 | Liverpool Riverside | Mrs Louise ELLMAN | Labour | |
| 7 | 60% | 114 | Glasgow Baillieston | Mr Jimmy WRAY | Labour | |
| 8 | 55% | 104 | Glasgow Anniesland | The Rt Hon Donald DEWAR | Labour | Secretary of State for Scotland |
| 9 | 54% | 114 | Salford | Ms Hazel BLEARS | Labour | |
| 10 | 52% | 80 | Glasgow Govan | Mr Mohammed SARWAR | Labour | |
| 11 | 52% | 70 | Glasgow Kelvin | Mr George GALLOWAY | Labour | |
| 12 | 51% | 108 | Tyne Bridge | Mr David CLELLAND | Labour | Assistant Whip |
| 13 | 48% | 80 | Greenock & Inverclyde | Dr Norman GODMAN | Labour | |
| 14 | 46% | 106 | Birmingham Ladywood | Ms Clare SHORT | Labour | Secretary of State for International Development |
| 15 | 45% | 99 | Manchester Blackley | Mr Graham STRINGER | Labour | |
| 16 | 44% | 99 | Vauxhall | Ms Kate HOEY | Labour | |
| 17 | 44% | 96 | Leeds Central | Mr Derek FATCHETT | Labour | Minister of State |
| 18 | 43% | 75 | Hamilton North & Bellshill | Dr John REID | Labour | Minister of State for the Armed Forces |
| 19 | 41% | 100 | Middlesbrough | Mr Stuart BELL | Labour | |
| 20 | 40% | 79 | Birkenhead | Mr Frank FIELD | Labour | Minister of State for Social Security and Welfare Reform |

**Table 9.4: continued**

| Rank | Rate >100 | People/ year | Constituency | MP | Party | Title |
|---|---|---|---|---|---|---|
| 21 | 40% | 63 | Paisley North | Ms Irene ADAMS | Labour | |
| 22 | 40% | 71 | Airdrie & Shotts | Mrs Helen LIDDELL | Labour | Economic Secretary |
| 23 | 39% | 57 | Manchester Gorton | The Rt Hon Gerald KAUFMAN | Labour | |
| 24 | 39% | 80 | Poplar & Canning Town | Mr Jim FITZPATRICK | Labour | |
| 25 | 38% | 70 | Holborn & St Pancras | Mr Frank DOBSON | Labour | Secretary of State for Health |
| 26 | 38% | 70 | Paisley South | Mr Gordon McMASTER | Labour | |
| 27 | 38% | 56 | Cunninghame South | Mr Brian DONOHOE | Labour | |
| 28 | 35% | 56 | Motherwell & Wishaw | Mr Frank ROY | Labour | |
| 29 | 35% | 53 | Hamilton South | Mr George ROBERTSON | Labour | Secretary of State for Defence |
| 30 | 34% | 71 | Stoke Central | Mr Mark FISHER | Labour | Parliamentary Under-Secretary for the Arts |
| 31 | 34% | 54 | Glasgow Rutherglen | Mr Tom McAVOY | Labour | Comptroller to Her Majesty's Household |
| 32 | 34% | 73 | Bradford West | Mr Marsha SINGH | Labour | |
| 33 | 33% | 59 | Camberwell & Peckham | Ms Harriet HARMAN | Labour | Secretary of State for Social Security |
| 34 | 33% | 73 | Bethnal Green & Bow | Ms Oona KING | Labour | |
| 35 | 33% | 53 | Glasgow Cathcart | Mr John MAXTON | Labour | |
| 36 | 32% | 65 | Bootle | Mr Joe BENTON | Labour | |
| 37 | 32% | 65 | Bolton South East | Dr Brian IDDON | Labour | |
| 38 | 32% | 62 | Southwark North & Bermondsey | Mr Simon HUGHES | Liberal Democrat | |

**Table 9.4: continued**

| Rank | Rate >100 | People/year | Constituency | MP | Party | Title |
|---|---|---|---|---|---|---|
| 39 | 31% | 63 | Hackney South & Shoreditch | Mr Brian SEDGEMORE | Labour | |
| 40 | 31% | 51 | Coatbridge & Chryston | Mr Tom CLARKE | Labour | Minister for Film and Tourism |
| 41 | 31% | 61 | Edinburgh North & Leith | Mr Malcolm CHISHOLM | Labour | |
| 42 | 31% | 68 | Birmingham Sparkbrook & Small Heath | Mr Roger GODSIFF | Labour | |
| 43 | 31% | 68 | Liverpool Walton | Mr Peter KILFOYLE | Labour | Parliamentary Under-Secretary |
| 44 | 30% | 70 | Preston | Mrs Audrey WISE | Labour | |
| 45 | 28% | 65 | Liverpool West Derby | Mr Robert WAREING | Labour | |
| 46 | 28% | 64 | Blackburn | Mr Jack STRAW | Labour | Secretary of State for the Home Department |
| 47 | 28% | 57 | Newcastle East & Wallsend | Mr Nick BROWN | Labour | Parliamentary Secretary to the Treasury and Chief Whip |
| 48 | 28% | 42 | Edinburgh Central | Mr Alistair DARLING | Labour | Chief Secretary to the Treasury |
| 49 | 27% | 51 | Kilmarnock & Loudoun | Mr Desmond BROWN | Labour | |
| 50 | 27% | 53 | Nottingham East | Mr John HEPPELL | Labour | |
| 51 | 27% | 59 | Sheffield Central | Mr Richard CABORN | Labour | Minister for Regions, Regeneration and Planning |
| 52 | 27% | 56 | Bradford North | Mr Terry ROONEY | Labour | |
| 53 | 26% | 49 | Merthyr Tydfil & Rhymney | Mr Ted ROWLANDS | Labour | |
| 54 | 26% | 55 | Rochdale | Ms Lorna FITZSIMMONS | Labour | |

**Table 9.4:** continued

| Rank | Rate >100 | People/ year | Constituency | MP | Party | Title |
|---|---|---|---|---|---|---|
| 55 | 26% | 53 | Sunderland North | Mr Bill ETHERINGTON | Labour | |
| 56 | 26% | 58 | Hartlepool | Mr Peter MANDELSON | Labour | Minister without Portfolio |
| 57 | 26% | 46 | Dundee West | Mr Ernie ROSS | Labour | |
| 58 | 26% | 56 | St Helens South | Mr Gerry BERMINGHAM | Labour | |
| 59 | 26% | 42 | Ross, Skye & Inverness West | Mr Charles KENNEDY | Liberal Democrat | |
| 60 | 26% | 55 | Burnley | Mr Peter PIKE | Labour | |
| 61 | 26% | 41 | Aberdeen Central | Mr Frank DORAN | Labour | |
| 62 | 26% | 49 | Islington South & Finsbury | Mr Chris SMITH | Labour | Secretary of State for National Heritage |
| 63 | 26% | 18 | Western Isles | Mr Calum MacDONALD | Labour | |
| 64 | 25% | 57 | Hammersmith & Fulham | Mr Iain COLEMAN | Labour | |
| 65 | 25% | 63 | Blackpool South | Mr Gordon MARSDEN | Labour | |
| 66 | 25% | 42 | Falkirk West | Mr Dennis CANAVAN | Labour | |
| 67 | 25% | 63 | Birmingham Erdington | Mr Robin CORBETT | Labour | |
| 68 | 25% | 32 | Caithness, Sutherland & Easter Ross | Mr Robert MacLENNAN | Liberal Democrat | |
| 69 | 25% | 50 | Stoke North | Mrs Joan WALLEY | Labour | |
| 70 | 24% | 40 | Clydebank & Milngavie | Mr Tony WORTHINGTON | Labour | Parliamentary Under-Secretary for Education, Training, and Employment, Health and Community Relations |

**Table 9.5: Ministers' and Shadow Ministers' mortality league tables (1997)**

*Deaths below the age of 65 between 1981 and 1992*

Ministers

| Name | Title | Rank of 641 | % excess mortality year | Number of excess deaths per mortality year | Constituency |
|---|---|---|---|---|---|
| The Rt Hon Donald DEWAR | Secretary of State for Scotland | 8 | 55% | 104 | Glasgow Anniesland |
| Ms Clare SHORT | Secretary of State for International Development | 14 | 46% | 106 | Birmingham Ladywood |
| Mr Frank DOBSON | Secretary of State for Health | 26 | 38% | 70 | Holborn & St Pancras |
| Mr George ROBERTSON | Secretary of State for Defence | 28 | 35% | 53 | Hamilton South |
| Ms Harriet HARMAN | Secretary of State for Social Security | 33 | 33% | 59 | Camberwell & Peckham |
| Mr Alistair DARLING | Chief Secretary to the Treasury | 46 | 28% | 42 | Edinburgh Central |
| Mr Jack STRAW | Secretary of State for the Home Department | 48 | 28% | 64 | Blackburn |
| Mr Chris SMITH | Secretary of State for National Heritage | 61 | 26% | 49 | Islington South & Finsbury |
| Dr David CLARK | Chancellor of the Duchy of Lancaster | 71 | 24% | 52 | South Shields |
| Dr Gavin STRANG | Minister of Transport | 70 | 24% | 42 | Edinburgh East & Musselburgh |
| Mr David BLUNKETT | Secretary of State for Education and Employment | 85 | 23% | 47 | Sheffield Brightside |
| The Rt Hon Tony BLAIR | Prime Minister | 95 | 22% | 47 | Sedgefield |
| The Rt Hon Gordon BROWN | Chancellor | 106 | 21% | 36 | Dunfermline East |
| The Rt Hon Robin COOK | Foreign Secretary | 128 | 18% | 27 | Livingston |
| Mrs Ann TAYLOR | Leader of the House | 129 | 18% | 28 | Dewsbury |
| Dr Mo MOWLAM | Secretary of State for Northern Ireland | 139 | 17% | 40 | Redcar |
| The Rt Hon Jack CUNNINGHAM | Minster for Agriculture, Fisheries and Food | 155 | 15% | 26 | Copeland |

**Table 9.5: continued**

*Deaths below the age of 65 between 1981 and 1992*

| | Title | Rank of 641 | % excess mortality | Number of excess deaths per year | |
|---|---|---|---|---|---|
| The Rt Hon John PRESCOTT | Deputy Prime Minister | 156 | 15% | 38 | Hull East |
| The Rt Hon Margaret BECKETT | Secretary of State for Trade and Industry | 184 | 13% | 30 | Derby South |
| Mr Ron DAVIES | Secretary of State for Wales | 216 | 9% | 18 | Caerphilly |
| *Shadow Ministers* | | | | | |
| Mr Michael JACK | Shadow Secretary of State for Agriculture, Fisheries and Food | 345 | -2% | -4 | Fylde |
| The Rt Hon Alistair GOODLAD | Shadow Secretary of State for International Development | 366 | -4% | -8 | Eddisbury |
| The Rt Hon Michael HOWARD | Shadow Foreign Secretary | 379 | -5% | -10 | Folkestone & Hythe |
| The Rt Hon Sir Nicholas LYELL | Shadow Attorney General | 439 | -9% | -17 | North East Bedfordshire |
| The Rt Hon Mrs Gillian SHEPHARD | Shadow Leader of the House | 429 | -9% | -21 | South West Norfolk |
| The Rt Hon William HAGUE | Leader of the Opposition | 431 | -9% | -18 | Richmond |
| The Rt Hon Dr Brian MAWHINNEY | Shadow Home Secretary | 449 | -10% | -19 | North West Cambridgeshire |
| The Rt Hon Michael ANCRAM | Constitutional Affairs | 472 | -12% | -26 | Devizes |
| Mr John MAPLES | Shadow Secretary of State for Health | 521 | -15% | -35 | Stratford-on-Avon |
| Mr Andrew MacKAY | Shadow Secretary of State for Northern Ireland | 544 | -17% | -35 | Bracknell |
| The Rt Hon Sir George YOUNG | Shadow Secretary of State for Defence | 543 | -17% | -36 | North West Hampshire |
| The Rt Hon Peter LILLEY | Shadow Chancellor | 577 | -20% | -41 | Hitchin & Harpenden |

**Table 9.5:** continued

*Deaths below the age of 65 between 1981 and 1992*

| | Title | Rank of 641 | % excess mortality year | Number of excess deaths per | |
|---|---|---|---|---|---|
| Mr Iain DUNCAN-SMITH | Shadow Secretary of State for Social Security | 600 | -22% | -43 | Chingford & Woodford Green |
| The Rt Hon Stephen DORRELL | Shadow Secretary of State for Education and Employment | 610 | -23% | -49 | Charnwood |
| The Rt Hon Sir Norman FOWLER | Shadow Secretary of State for the Environment | 617 | -24% | -53 | Sutton Coldfield |
| The Rt Hon John REDWOOD | Shadow Secretary of State for Trade and Industry | 638 | -26% | -45 | Wokingham |
| The Rt Hon Francis MAUDE | Shadow Secretary of State for Culture, Media and Sport | 636 | -26% | -48 | Horsham |

## Changes in the Cabinet 1997 to 1999

Table 9.5 refers to the Cabinet and Shadow Cabinet that were in place immediately after the General Election of 1997. Table 9.6 updates these lists for the Cabinet and Shadow Cabinet in place in February 1999. There have been a few changes to the Labour Cabinet. Alistair Darling, Ann Taylor, Jack Cunningham and Margaret Beckett have changed posts since 1997 but remain in the Cabinet. Four ministers have left the Cabinet and four junior ministers have been promoted. Most notably, Peter Mandelson has entered and left the Cabinet. But as he was neither a minister in May 1997, nor in February 1999, his comings and goings do not effect the overall picture (at the time of editing this chapter he had just returned to Cabinet again as Secretary of State for Northern Ireland). These changes have led to government ministers representing people who are slightly better off in terms of mortality, with, in total, 952 of their constituents dying prematurely per year between 1981 and 1992. This amounts to on average just more than one less premature death per minister per year, but is due entirely to reshuffling rather than to any improvement in inequalities.

On the Conservative side of the house the reshuffling of the Shadow Cabinet has been too complex to describe briefly. Only Michael Howard, Nicholas Lyell, William Hague and Andrew MacKay remain at their original posts, and who knows for how long? The net effect of all these changes to the Shadow Cabinet has been to increase the number of avoided premature deaths to 604, so making inequalities in mortality even less of an issue for the Conservatives. However, note that the recasting of Peter Lilley as Deputy Leader has increased the size of the Shadow Cabinet by one.

**Table 9.6: Ministers' and Shadow Ministers' mortality league tables (1999)**

*Deaths below the age of 65 between 1981 and 1992*

*Ministers*

| | Title | Rank of 641 | % excess mortality year | Number of excess deaths per year | |
|---|---|---|---|---|---|
| The Rt Hon Donald DEWAR | Secretary of State for Scotland | 8 | 55 | 104 | Glasgow Anniesland |
| Ms Clare SHORT | Secretary of State for International Development | 14 | 46 | 106 | Birmingham Ladywood |
| Mr Frank DOBSON | Secretary of State for Health | 26 | 38 | 70 | Holborn & St Pancras |
| Mr George ROBERTSON | Secretary of State for Defence | 28 | 35 | 53 | Hamilton South |
| Mr Alistair DARLING | Secretary of State for Social Security | 46 | 28 | 42 | Edinburgh Central |
| Mr Nick BROWN | now Minister for Agriculture, Fisheries and Food | 47 | 28 | 57 | Newcastle East & Wallsend |
| Mr Jack STRAW | Secretary of State for the Home Department | 48 | 28 | 64 | Blackburn |
| Mr Chris SMITH | Secretary of State for Culture, Media and Sport | 61 | 26 | 49 | Islington South & Finsbury |
| Mr David BLUNKETT | Secretary of State for Education and Employment | 85 | 23 | 47 | Sheffield Brightside |
| The Rt Hon Tony BLAIR | Prime Minister | 95 | 22 | 47 | Sedgefield |
| The Rt Hon Gordon BROWN | Chancellor | 106 | 21 | 36 | Dunfermline East |
| Mr Stephen BYERS | now Secretary of State for Trade and Industry | 127 | 18 | 37 | North Tyneside |
| The Rt Hon Robin COOK | Foreign Secretary | 128 | 18 | 27 | Livingston |
| Mrs Ann TAYLOR | now Chief Whip | 129 | 18 | 28 | Dewsbury |
| Dr Mo MOWLAM | Secretary of State for Northern Ireland | 139 | 17 | 40 | Redcar |
| The Rt Hon Jack CUNNINGHAM | now Minister for the Cabinet Office | 155 | 15 | 26 | Copeland |
| The Rt Hon John PRESCOTT | Deputy Prime Minister | 156 | 15 | 38 | Hull East |
| Mr Alan MILBURN | now Chief Secretary to the Treasury | 177 | 13 | 27 | Darlington |
| The Rt Hon Margaret BECKETT | now Leader of the House | 184 | 13 | 30 | Derby South |
| Mr Alun MICHAEL | now Secretary of State for Wales | 191 | 12 | 24 | Cardiff South & Penarth |

**Table 9.6: continued**

*Deaths below the age of 65 between 1981 and 1992*

| | Title | Rank of 641 | % excess mortality year | Number of excess deaths per year | |
|---|---|---|---|---|---|
| Ms Harriet HARMAN | was Secretary of State for Social Security | 33 | 33 | 59 | Camberwell & Peckham |
| Mr Peter MANDELSON | was Minister without Portfolio and then Secretary of State for Trade and Industry | 55 | 26 | 58 | Hartlepool |
| Dr Gavin STRANG | was Minister of Transport | 70 | 24 | 42 | Edinburgh East & Musselburgh |
| Dr David CLARK | was Chancellor of the Duchy of Lancaster | 71 | 24 | 52 | South Shields |
| Mr Ron DAVIES | was Secretary of State for Wales | 216 | 9 | 18 | Caerphilly |
| *Shadow Ministers* | | | | | |
| The Rt Hon Michael HOWARD | still Shadow Foreign Secretary | 379 | -5 | -10 | Folkestone & Hythe |
| Mr David WILLETTS | now Shadow Secretary of State for Education and Employment | 415 | -8 | -17 | Havant |
| The Rt Hon Mrs Gillian SHEPHARD | now Shadow Secretary of State for the Environment | 429 | -9 | -21 | South West Norfolk |
| The Rt Hon William HAGUE | still Leader of the Opposition | 431 | -9 | -18 | Richmond |
| The Rt Hon Sir Nicholas LYELL | still Shadow Attorney General | 439 | -9 | -17 | North East Bedfordshire |
| The Rt Hon Ann WIDDECOMBE | new Shadow Secretary of State for Health | 500 | -13 | -28 | Maidstone & the Weald |
| Mr Peter AINSWORTH | now Shadow Secretary of State for Culture, Media and Sport | 508 | -14 | -33 | East Surrey |
| Mr John MAPLES | now Shadow Secretary of State for Defence | 521 | -15 | -35 | Stratford-on-Avon |

**Table 9.6: continued**

Deaths below the age of 65 between 1981 and 1992

|  | Title | Rank of 641 | % excess mortality year | Number of excess deaths per year |  |
|---|---|---|---|---|---|
| The Rt Hon Sir George YOUNG | now Shadow Leader of the House | 543 | -17 | -36 | North West Hampshire |
| Mr Andrew MacKAY | still Shadow Secretary of State for Northern Ireland | 544 | -17 | -35 | Bracknell |
| The Rt Hon Peter LILLEY | now Deputy Leader of the Opposition | 577 | -20 | -41 | Hitchin & Harpenden |
| Mr Tim YEO | now Shadow Secretary of State for Agriculture, Fisheries and Food | 584 | -20 | -38 | South Suffolk |
| Mr Gary STREETER | now Shadow Secretary of State for International Development and Overseas Pensions | 585 | -20 | -37 | South West Devon |
| Mr Iain DUNCAN-SMITH | still Shadow Secretary of State for Social Security | 600 | -22 | -43 | Chingford & Woodford Green |
| Dr Liam FOX | now Shadow Minister for Constitutional Affairs | 615 | -24 | -49 | Woodspring |
| The Rt Hon Sir Norman FOWLER | now Shadow Home Secretary | 617 | -24 | -53 | Sutton Coldfield |
| Rt Hon Francis MAUDE | now Shadow Chancellor | 636 | -26 | -48 | Horsham |
| The Rt Hon John REDWOOD | still Shadow Secretary of State for Trade and Industry | 638 | -26 | -45 | Wokingham |
| Mr Michael JACK | was Shadow Secretary of State for Agriculture, Fisheries and Food | 345 | -2 | -4 | Fylde |
| The Rt Hon Alistair GOODLAD | was Shadow Secretary of State for International Development | 366 | -4 | -8 | Eddisbury |

**Table 9.6:** continued

*Deaths below the age of 65 between 1981 and 1992*

| Title | Rank of 641 | % excess mortality year | Number of excess deaths per | |
|---|---|---|---|---|
| The Rt Hon Dr Brian MAWHINNEY  was Shadow Home Secretary | 449 | -10 | -19 | North West Cambridgeshire |
| The Rt Hon Michael ANCRAM  was Shadow Minister for Constitutional Affairs | 472 | -12 | -26 | Devizes |
| The Rt Hon Stephen DORRELL  was Shadow Secretary of State for Education and | 610 | -23 | -49 | Charnwood Employment |

Note: since May 1997 four ministers have left the Cabinet as well as Peter Mandelson who came late and went early (these are listed below). Four junior ministers were promoted to the Cabinet and are included above: Nick Brown, Stephen Byers, Alun Michael and Alan Milburn.

# Changes in mortality 1981 to 1995

It would be wrong to assume that Cabinet reshuffles have actually resulted in the constituents of the New Labour Cabinet being slightly better off in terms of indicators of their health because the geography of health changes, just as the geography of Cabinet Ministers' constituents change. We will not have figures on mortality for 1999 until about 2001, but what we can do is look at the most recent data we do have (for 1991–95) by the current Cabinet and this is shown in Table 9.7.

Because inequalities in mortality continued to rise into the 1990s these most recent figures for the most recent Cabinet produce the most extreme picture of variation across the country. The biggest relative increases in mortality ratios have been in the constituencies of the Secretary of State for Scotland (Donald Dewar), the Secretary of State for Health (Frank Dobson) and the Deputy Prime Minister (John Prescott). By 1995 more than 1,000 extra people per year were dying early in the Cabinet's constituencies, or almost two extra a week for each Cabinet minister (compared to the average for England and Wales).

The changes were less conspicuous for the Shadow Cabinet, although the largest relative falls in mortality were for the constituents of three new Shadow Cabinet Ministers: the Shadow Minister for Constitutional Affairs (Liam Fox), the Shadow Secretary of State for Agriculture, Fisheries and Food (Tim Yeo) and the Shadow Leader of the House (George Young – who was Secretary of State for Defence). The premature mortality position of the constituents of the New Labour Cabinet has deteriorated over time, while the advantage of the Shadow Cabinet's constituents has been maintained. Britain has become even more unequal in terms of the life chances of its people and some of the worst aspects of this rising inequality are reflected by contrasting the day-to-day experiences of the constituents of the people who are, nominally, in charge of the country or in opposition to the government.

**Table 9.7: Ministers' and Shadow ministers' mortality league tables (1999)**

*Deaths below the age of 65 between 1991 and 1995*

| | Title | Rank of 641 | % excess mortality year | Number of excess deaths per year | |
|---|---|---|---|---|---|
| **Ministers** | | | | | |
| The Rt Hon Donald DEWAR | Secretary of State for Scotland | 5 | 81 | 192 | Glasgow Anniesland |
| Mr Frank DOBSON | Secretary of State for Health | 21 | 50 | 119 | Holborn & St Pancras |
| Ms Clare SHORT | Secretary of State for International Development | 22 | 48 | 133 | Birmingham Ladywood |
| Mr George ROBERTSON | Secretary of State for Defence | 34 | 42 | 78 | Hamilton South |
| Mr Alistair DARLING | Secretary of State for Social Security | 43 | 37 | 63 | Edinburgh Central |
| Mr Nick BROWN | now Minister for Agriculture, Fisheries and Food | 56 | 31 | 64 | Newcastle East & Wallsend |
| Mr Jack STRAW | Secretary of State for the Home Department | 59 | 30 | 72 | Blackburn |
| Mr Chris SMITH | Secretary of State for Culture, Media and Sport | 64 | 28 | 56 | Islington South & Finsbury |
| The Rt Hon John PRESCOTT | Deputy Prime Minister | 82 | 25 | 61 | Hull East |
| Mr David BLUNKETT | Secretary of State for Education and Employment | 86 | 24 | 49 | Sheffield Brightside |
| Mr Alun MICHAEL | now Secretary of State for Wales | 120 | 19 | 39 | Cardiff South & Penarth |
| Dr Mo MOWLAM | Secretary of State for Northern Ireland | 124 | 19 | 44 | Redcar |
| Mr Alan MILBURN | now Chief Secretary to the Treasury | 127 | 18 | 37 | Darlington |
| Mr Stephen BYERS | now Secretary of State for Trade and Industry | 141 | 17 | 33 | North Tyneside |
| The Rt Hon Tony BLAIR | Prime Minister | 156 | 16 | 32 | Sedgefield |
| The Rt Hon Gordon BROWN | Chancellor | 163 | 14 | 25 | Dunfermline East |
| The Rt Hon Robin COOK | Foreign Secretary | 166 | 14 | 24 | Livingston |
| The Rt Hon Jack CUNNINGHAM | now Minister for the Cabinet Office | 192 | 11 | 18 | Copeland |
| The Rt Hon Margaret BECKETT | now Leader of the House | 196 | 11 | 23 | Derby South |
| Mrs Ann TAYLOR | now Chief Whip | 233 | 5 | 8 | Dewsbury |

**Table 9.7: continued**

*Deaths below the age of 65 between 1991 and 1995*

| Title | Rank of 641 | % excess mortality year | Number of excess deaths per year | |
|---|---|---|---|---|
| **Shadow Ministers** | | | | |
| Dr Liam FOX — now Shadow Minister for Constitutional Affairs | 640 | -35 | -44 | Woodspring |
| Mr Tim YEO — now Shadow Secretary of State for Agriculture, Fisheries and Food | 633 | -31 | -37 | South Suffolk |
| The Rt Hon Sir George YOUNG — now Shadow Leader of the House | 618 | -27 | -40 | North West Hampshire |
| The Rt Hon William HAGUE — still Leader of the Opposition | 511 | -18 | -27 | Richmond |
| The Rt Hon John REDWOOD — still Shadow Secretary of State for Trade and Industry | 641 | -35 | -42 | Wokingham |
| Mr Andrew MacKAY — still Shadow Secretary of State for Northern Ireland | 584 | -24 | -37 | Bracknell |
| The Rt Hon Ann WIDDECOMBE — new Shadow Secretary of State for Health | 538 | -20 | -31 | Maidstone & the Weald |
| Mr Peter AINSWORTH — now Shadow Secretary of State for Culutre, Media and Sport | 540 | -20 | -33 | East Surrey |
| Mr John MAPLES — now Shadow Secretary of State for Defence | 533 | -20 | -35 | Stratford-on-Avon |
| The Rt Hon Sir Nicholas LYELL — still Shadow Attorney General | 458 | -13 | -20 | North East Bedfordshire |
| The Rt Hon Mrs Gillian SHEPHARD — now Shadow Secretary of State for the Environment | 453 | -13 | -24 | South West Norfolk |
| Mr Gary STREETER — now Shadow Secretary of State for International Development and Overseas Pensions | 582 | -24 | -32 | South West Devon |
| The Rt Hon Peter LILLEY — now Deputy Leader of the Opposition | 574 | -23 | -32 | Hitchin & Harpenden |
| The Rt Hon Michael HOWARD — still Shadow Foreign Secretary | 398 | -8 | -13 | Folkestone & Hythe |
| The Rt Hon Sir Norman FOWLER — now Shadow Home Secretary | 607 | -26 | -37 | Sutton Coldfield |
| Rt Hon Francis MAUDE — now Shadow Chancellor | 609 | -26 | -33 | Horsham |
| Mr Iain DUNCAN-SMITH — still Shadow Secretary of State for Social Security | 549 | -21 | -27 | Chingford & Woodford Green |
| Mr David WILLETTS — now Shadow Secretary of State for Education and Employment | 325 | -2 | -4 | Havant |

## The 1997 General Election was not won by New Labour, but lost by the Conservatives

The medical–political geography of Britain described above may not be too surprising to many readers, although the degree of polarisation between those living in areas of poor and good health may be larger than expected. What may be more interesting is to look at how the Labour Party won the last general election with such a huge landslide, in terms of the premature mortality rates of its constituents. Table 9.7 presents the swings in aggregate votes for the main parties between 1992 and 1997 and the changes in abstentions and in the electorate, in terms of the premature mortality ratios experienced in the preceding 12 years (1981-92). To be able to conduct this analysis, the results of the 1992 General Election had to be reassigned to 1997 constituencies (see also Pattie et al, 1996, 1997; Johnston et al, 1997; Dorling et al, 1998).

The general election of 1997 was not won by New Labour but was lost by the Conservatives. Nationally, New Labour increased their vote (as a share of the electorate) by only 4%, while the Conservative vote fell by 11%. However, Labour was very careful to ensure that it won votes in the right places, whereas the Conservatives lost them most where they needed them most. It appears likely that most former Conservative voters who chose not to vote for that Party abstained and so the national abstention rate rose by 6% of the electorate between 1992 and 1997. The Liberal Democrats lost 2% of its support while other parties (mainly the Referendum Party, who won votes from the Conservatives) gained 2%.

From Table 9.8 it is possible to see how parts of the country with different excess mortality rates changed their votes. The rise in abstentions was quite uniform across the decile groups. It is likely that this was the result of abstentions rising in poor areas due to dissatisfaction with the political process and in rich areas due to voters who were dissatisfied with the Conservatives but could not bring themselves to vote for any other Party. The Labour Party's swing was strongest where it needed the votes most, in decile 6 areas, where many votes were required to win what were thought to be safe Conservative seats. Its vote swing was weakest in the areas where it already held most of the seats, in the decile 1 group of constituencies, with the poorest health. These were also the areas where the Conservatives lost fewest votes. The poor (in terms of health among other measures) did not swing to Labour half (or even a quarter as much) as the richer voters did in 1997. Column seven shows how the electorates of the constituencies in each group changed over the five years. The areas with the highest premature mortality ratios lost the most registered voters, while the number of potential voters increased in the areas now largely represented by Conservative MPs. It is difficult to disentangle the factors behind this shift in the registered population. A combination of natural change (births less deaths), migration effects and changes in the propensity of adults to register to vote will all have contributed.

*Table 9.8:* **Change in voting between 1992-97 in the 10 groups of parliamentary constituencies containing equal electorates**

| Decile group | Absten- tions | Labour Party | Conservative Party | Liberal Democrats | Nationalist Parties | Other parties | Change in electorate |
|---|---|---|---|---|---|---|---|
| 1 | 6% | 1% | -7% | -2% | 0% | 2% | -2% |
| 2 | 7% | 3% | -9% | -2% | 0% | 2% | -2% |
| 3 | 7% | 3% | -11% | -1% | 0% | 2% | -2% |
| 4 | 7% | 4% | -10% | -2% | 0% | 2% | -1% |
| 5 | 6% | 5% | -11% | -2% | 0% | 2% | 0% |
| 6 | 6% | 7% | -12% | -3% | 0% | 2% | 1% |
| 7 | 6% | 6% | -12% | -3% | 0% | 2% | 1% |
| 8 | 6% | 6% | -13% | -2% | 0% | 3% | 2% |
| 9 | 6% | 6% | -13% | -2% | 0% | 3% | 3% |
| 10 | 5% | 6% | -13% | -1% | 0% | 3% | 2% |
| Britain | 6% | 4% | -11% | -2% | 0% | 2% | 0% |

*Notes:* For Britain as a whole the first six columns sum to 0% and show the changing proportion of the electorate voting for each party.

The final column shows the change in the electorate as a proportion of the 1992 electorate and hence represents a combination of the effects of net migration and voter registration and non-registration in each decile group.

## Conclusions

The relationship between voting, premature mortality and political representation in Britain is remarkably close. The recent polarisation in mortality rates by area and the swings in the marginals seats at the last general election made that relationship even clearer than before. The poorer half of Britain votes for the Labour Party and dies earlier. The poorest tenth of Britain dies earliest and now supports some of the most powerful politicians in this country through their votes. Are the politicians likely to try to reduce this level of inequality in life chances? The 1979-97 Conservative governments had little direct incentive or experience to attempt this. Their constituents were unlikely to present stories about their lives that made the reality of health polarisation evident and this was most true of the constituents of that Party's leaders. Conservative MPs were probably unaware of the differences in health to be found across Britain, and if they were aware they probably blamed this on the behaviour of people they were unlikely to have ever met and whose political support they never relied on.

The story with New Labour should be different. It is difficult to believe that MPs, some of whom have represented their constituencies for many years, are not aware that their constituents tend to live very much poorer lives than themselves and certainly have much higher chances of dying young than the MPs themselves. Many MPs do not live in their constituency, of course, and some may not care at all about their constituents, other than requiring their votes every five years. If they do know their constituents well they may still not be aware that in other parts of the country life chances are so much better. However, to date the Labour government has not committed itself to any actions that are likely to narrow the gap in life chances between their constituents and the rest of British society. It has made an enormous number of token gestures and many, many speeches, but none of these can have an effect of any relevance. For instance, take the Health Action Zones initiative. Even if their introduction reduced mortality to the average for Britain in the proposed areas, the areas are too small to have any significant effect on the national pattern of inequality (see Chapter Seven). The Green Paper's targets for health do not focus on inequality – indeed these new targets could all be met without any reduction in the level of inequality in health in Britain. *The Independent Inquiry into Inequalities in Health* (Acheson, 1998) has brought little that is new to the debate and has not presented what was known before with any degree of force. New Labour may care, but so far it does not appear to care enough to act decisively.

At the root of inequalities in health are inequalities in wealth, poverty, income and opportunity. This has been known for long enough. Unfortunately, those without wealth, with low incomes and little opportunity are unlikely to punish their political representatives if the latter do not improve their life chances. Those who are poor and Left-leaning have no Party to vote for now that Labour has moved to the centre. They are a captive set of Labour supporters and can hence be ignored. Instead it is, as Figure 9.4 shows, the middle fifth of the country in terms of health (and by inference wealth) that determines which Party is in power. The constituencies in decile groups 5 and 6 are the most marginal politically and have SMRs that are close to the national average.

Since the Second World War, the rich have always elected Conservative MPs while the poor have always elected Labour MPs. The Liberals have confused this pattern only slightly. The last election did not alter that pattern, but it did, through the rhetoric of its campaign, and the subsequent actions of its victors, show that the real concern of the Party of the poorest had shifted to the centre, to the average, to the voters who live in areas where the chances of dying young are already close to the national norm. In terms of winning elections in Britain, inequality is not an issue for the voters who matter most. They are, on average, neither rich nor poor, healthy nor unhealthy. To them, initiating untargeted action, such as 'reducing waiting lists' nationally, to raise the general level of any service or condition is most likely to be beneficial. Squeezing 'fat cats' and 'scroungers' simultaneously will be most popular. The policy makers of the present government appear to agree. Their actions suggest that they believe that Ms/Mr Average is not interested in inequality and Ms/Mr Average matters most. It is rare to be average, in that most people in Britain aren't, or don't live in 'average areas'. Thus policy to suit the average is policy for the few rather than the many.

## References

Acheson, D. (Chair) (1998) *Independent Inquiry into Inequalities in Health Report*, London: The Stationery Office.

Davey Smith, G. and Dorling, D. (1996) 'I'm all right John: voting patterns and mortality in England and Wales, 1981-92', *BMJ*, vol 313, pp 1573-7.

Davey Smith, G. and Dorling D. (1997) 'Association between voting and mortality remains', Refereed letter, *BMJ*, vol 315, pp 430-1.

Davey Smith, G., Morris, J.N. and Shaw, M. (1998) 'The Independent Inquiry into Inequalities in Health', *BMJ*, vol 317, pp 1465-6.

Dobson, F. (1998) 'Government committed to greatest ever reduction in health inequalities', DoH Press Release 98/0547, 26 November.

DoH (Department of Health) (1998) *Our healthier nation*, London: The Stationery Office.

Dorling, D. (1997) *Death in Britain: How local mortality rates have changed: 1950s-1990s*, York: Joseph Rowntree Foundation.

Dorling, D. (1998) 'Whose voters suffer if inequalities in health remain?', *Journal of Contemporary Health*, vol 7, pp 50-4.

Dorling, D., Rallings, C. and Thrasher, M. (1998) 'The epidemiology of the Lib Dem vote', *Political Geography*, vol 17, no 1, pp 45-80.

Gordon, D. and Forrest, R. (1995) *People and places 2: Social and economic distinctions in England*, Bristol: SAUS Publications.

Johnston, R., Pattie, C., Dorling, D., Rossiter, D., Tunstall, H. and MacAllister, I. (1997) 'Spatial variations in voter choice: modelling tactical voting at the 1997 general election in Great Britain', *Geographical and Environmental Modelling*, vol 1, no 2.

Pattie, C., Dorling, D., Johnston, R. and Rossiter, D. (1996) 'Electoral registration, population mobility and the democratic franchise: the geography of postal voters, overseas voters and missing voters in Great Britain', *International Journal of Population Geography*, vol 2, pp 239-59.

Pattie, C., Johnston, R., Dorling, D., Rossiter, D., Tunstall, H. and MacAllister, I. (1997) 'New Labour, new geography? The electoral geography of the 1997 British General Election', *Area*, vol 29, no 3, pp 253-9.

# TEN

# Ending world poverty
# in the 21st century

*Peter Townsend*

At the end of the 1990s the reports from different international agencies on the progress made in reducing poverty seem to blow hot and cold – and provoke public bewilderment. On the one hand, there are claims of unprecedented success for human development. During the last 30 years life expectancy has grown in all regions of the world and in some poor regions has grown spectacularly. Rates of infant mortality and of underweight children aged below five have declined. More people in most countries have gained access to safe drinking water. Levels of adult literacy and school enrolment have improved – although the rates are still relatively low in many of the poorest countries. With marked fluctuations there has been economic growth in the last three decades in poor as well as rich countries – and *average* living standards have improved (UNDP, 1997, 1998, 1999; World Bank, 1999a; DfID, 1997).

On the other hand, the incomes of the richest 20% grew faster than those of the poorest 20% of the world's population between 1960 and the 1990s, the comparative increase being in the ratio 30:1 in 1960 and 74:1 in 1994 (UNDP, 1997, p 9). Inequality widened *within* many countries as well as between groups of rich and groups of poor countries. Population numbers living on less than $1 per person per day remained stubbornly high in many developing countries. "Nearly 1.3 billion people, about one-quarter of the world's population, live on the equivalent of about $1 a day or less at 1985 international prices, or roughly the equivalent of $1.50 a day at 1997 prices in the US." Nearly or more than half the populations of 16 countries, including India, Kenya, Guatemala, Nepal, Zambia, Ethiopia, Uganda, Rwanda, Zimbabwe and Nicaragua, live at this low level. Over a fifth of the population of China live on below $1 a day and as many as 58% below $2 a day (World Bank, 1999a, pp 196-7). Altogether "nearly 3 billion people, roughly half of the world's population, subsist on the scarcely more generous figure of $3 a day at 1997 US prices" (World Bank, 1999a, p 117; see also DfID, 1997, pp 9-11). The poorest 20% had only 2.3% of global income in 1960 but this had more than halved to 1.1% in 1994 (UNDP, 1997, p 9). Even the percentage of the population living on less than $1 per person a day in the least developed countries barely declined at all, and the numbers increased (UNDP, 1997, p 33).

There are other grounds for taking a critical view. The statistics allowing conclusions to be drawn from development trends have become difficult to compile in many places. Some countries are unstable; others have civil war or are torn by ethnic divisions following war. A large number of countries are not represented in reviews of world development by means of statistical indicators or can be represented only by snap-shots rather than long-lasting trends. Some published indicators, especially those relating to the 'transitional' economies, or in those relating to industrial countries about the ratio between the richest and poorest 20%, are years out of date. When unmeasured disasters are related to the measured growth of inequality it becomes less easy to approve long-established development strategies. In the words of one leading social scientist, the structural concentration of affluence and poverty is "creating a deeply divided and increasingly violent social world" (Massey, 1996, p 395).

## Doubts about social progress

There are other reasons for raising doubts about social progress in tackling world poverty. These go to the heart of observation and analysis. Measurement of elements of the problem of poverty, and of the effects of specific policies on trends in poverty, is neither as reliable nor as exact as it should be. There is a technical or scientific problem, but also a political problem, that demands to be solved. Both measurement and analysis are being politicised to an extent that is becoming unacceptable. For example, when there are competing measures of poverty, with political interests mobilised behind each of them, there is a temptation to leave the meaning of poverty ambiguous, or so arbitrarily and crudely defined as to be less than useful. Again, if poverty is not monitored exactly and changes in specific policies are not related to trends in poverty, it becomes difficult to establish which changes are, and are not, successful in reducing poverty. Ideologically preferred policies, some of which need to be axed, are not placed under sufficient scrutiny.

These are not minor issues. It seems to be generally admitted that development strategies have not worked as well as they were intended to work since the 1960s. Once there has been rapid technical progress in compiling and monitoring statistical data, we should be able, through good operational measurement, to identify the elements of those strategies and policies that need to be replaced.

The development agencies have found it difficult to defend the declared policies of economic growth and of liberalisation, including cuts in state expenditure and privatisation of public institutions and services, applied since 1960. It was Robert Macnamara who confirmed these strategies when, as President of the World Bank, he stated in 1960 that year that poverty would be its top priority. In the late 1990s James Wolfensohn, the current President of the World Bank, has consistently called attention to the defeat of poverty as the Bank's aim. At the same time the United Nations Development Programme (UNDP) and the International Monetary Fund (IMF) have vied with the Bank to take the lead role in describing the problem in relation to new events.

By restating poverty as the top priority in 1980, and even more emphatically in 1990 and subsequently in many different reports, the Bank indirectly implies it has failed in nearly 40 years to make much, or any, headway in achieving its principal aim of radically reducing poverty. Accordingly, might a change of plan be called for? There has been no recognisable change of direction, and there seems to have been no substantial effort to report the swelling tide of criticism from non-governmental organisations (NGOs), scientific observers and representatives of poor countries. The plan was simply re-asserted more strongly, although there were changes in the titles and handling of different programmes. In 1996 and again in 1997 the World Bank reiterated its three principal anti-poverty strategies: broad-based economic growth; developing human capital; and social safety nets for vulnerable groups (World Bank, 1996, 1997). These strategies have been reflected in successive programmes in different parts of the world, and criticisms, for example, of the 'structural adjustment' and 'safety-net' programmes of recent years, supported by both the World Bank (1996, 1997) and the IMF (see, for example, Chu and Gupta, 1998, and their list of 26 IMF papers on 'safety-net' programmes, pp 259-60) have become widespread. For example, a study sponsored by the United Nations University concluded that these programmes had made people in the poorest countries more vulnerable to hunger and food and other services less affordable (DeRose et al, 1998, pp 182-3).

It is hard to keep up with the flow of published reports. In the 1990s investigations of the persistence and even growth of poverty have proliferated. One major illustration is the mounting stream of World

Bank reports. By 1999 the Bank had published more than 400 technical papers, more than 400 discussion papers, nearly 150 Living Standards Measurement Study (LSMS) working papers, probably more than 200 country studies and many other reports and papers to do with macro-economic, environmental, urban management, education and sustainable development issues – many addressing poverty in different forms.

## Myths and realities

Myths about poverty continue to be treated seriously, even after being dismissed by expert witnesses. One is that poverty does not really exist in the industrial or 'advanced' countries (see Chapter One). Another is that even if poverty exists it is of a more tolerable type than the variety experienced in poor countries: 'absolute' poverty does not exist. These are familiar myths which, as in the case of the one peddled by John Moore, the then Secretary of State for Social Security (Moore, 1989), have been addressed critically by social scientists. A third myth that is also now prevalent is the idea that social exclusion is a more fundamental, but also more manageable, problem than poverty.

These myths obstruct agreement about social development and illustrate the need to arrive at scientific consensus in the treatment of poverty, and in its international, and not just European or American, treatment. The key question is whether poverty really matters *only* in the Third World. There are different answers. One is that there has to be rigorously collected comparative evidence to decide the matter one way or the other: after all, there are endless problems of 'degree' even if the basic contention is accepted. The second is that in every society need is socially constructed and certain needs in rich countries, such as access to transport, are a creation of an urbanised, industrial society for which resources have to be found by individual members of the population. Those resources may not be available to some people if they are already struggling to pay for other basic needs. Such a 'need' for cash resources may apply much less strongly to the majority of the population of poor countries – where homes, and the labour market, are not distanced from each other. A third answer to the question involves the shift from country-specific or regional poverty to global poverty. The differences between rich and poor are becoming more extreme everywhere, at the same time as goods and certain services are becoming available cross-nationally. This is a form of international 'standardisation'. By international standards there are likely to be many more poor people in some countries than in others for many years ahead.

## An international breakthrough: two Copenhagen measures

How could the connected problems of meaning, measurement, cause and policy, in eradicating poverty, be resolved? There was a breakthrough at the World Summit on Social Development in Copenhagen in March 1995. As many as 117 Heads of State signed up to a declaration and action programme which included providing a two-level definition of poverty as well as agreement to prepare and monitor annual surveys of poverty. The definition is important because it is necessary to the organisation and ordering of a mass of information about the phenomenon. It also shows where poverty is most severe or extensive, and enables better judgements to be made about causes and priorities so that action can be better planned and taken.

The summit was held because many governments were becoming concerned about the lack of progress in resolving the problems of the Third World and especially their indebtedness, which made government-specific solutions less plausible. Governments were also conscious that the gap in living standards between rich and poor countries, despite the work of the international financial agencies, was growing. There were also other, associated, problems of large-scale unemployment and social disintegration which were clamouring for equally urgent attention.

Like reports in the late 1990s from the international agencies (see in particular UNDP, 1997, 1999; World Bank, 1996, 1997, 1999a, 1999b) the 1995 World Summit report (UN, 1995) repeatedly emphasised that the gap between rich and poor within both developed and developing societies was widening, just as the gap between developed and developing societies was also widening. Calling world attention to this dual structural phenomenon is perhaps the most notable achievement of the Summit – whatever might be said in criticism of the attempts in the report to please different governments and to satisfy their conflicting objectives.

The intention was to try to promote sustained economic growth within the context of sustainable development and by:

> ... formulating or strengthening, preferably by 1996, and implementing national poverty eradication plans to address the structural causes of poverty, encompassing action on the local, national, sub-regional, and international levels. These plans should establish, within each

national context, strategies and affordable, time-bound, goals and targets for the substantial reduction of overall poverty and the eradication of absolute poverty.... Each country should develop a precise definition and assessment of absolute poverty. (UN, 1995, pp 60-1)

In 1996 and 1997 the follow-up after the Copenhagen agreement was disappointing (UN, 1995 and 1999; and see the commentary in Townsend, 1996a). There were a few government reports on poverty alleviation (for example, Irish Government, 1996). The Royal Danish Ministry of Foreign Affairs (through its Ministry for Development Cooperation) initiated the Copenhagen Seminars for Social Progress in which each year experts from across the world have participated (see, for example, Royal Danish Ministry of Foreign Affairs, 1996). But it was only when it was decided to hold a 'Copenhagen Plus 5' conference in Geneva in June 2000 (UN, 1999) that work in some countries began to gather speed. The British government announced in January 1999 the preparation of a poverty audit, for publication late in that year (see Chapter One).

## 'Absolute' and 'overall' poverty

The two-level definition of poverty is the first designed to bridge first and third worlds and to afford a basis for cross-national measurement. Absolute poverty is defined as:

> ... a condition characterised by severe deprivation of basic human needs, including food, safe drinking water, sanitation facilities, health, shelter, education and information. It depends not only on income but also on access to services. (UN, 1995, p 57)

Overall poverty takes various forms, including:

> ... lack of income and productive resources to ensure sustainable livelihoods; hunger and malnutrition; ill health; limited or lack of access to education and other basic services; increased morbidity and mortality from illness; homelessness and inadequate housing; unsafe environments and social discrimination and exclusion. It is also characterised by lack of participation in decision-making and in civil, social and cultural life. It occurs in all countries: as mass poverty in many developing countries, pockets of poverty amid wealth

in developed countries, loss of livelihoods as a result of economic recession, sudden poverty as a result of disaster or conflict, the poverty of low-wage workers, and the utter destitution of people who fall outside family support systems, social institutions and safety nets. (UN, 1995, p 57)

Along with every other government signing the Copenhagen agreement the British government is expected to prepare a national poverty eradication plan on this basis.

## Need for a scientific consensus

Despite a flood of published reports on poverty little progress has been made in developing internationally acceptable standards of definition and measurement. Many of the best known European studies are little known in the US, for example, and rarely quoted by the international agencies in their work. Despite the obvious need for local or national adjustment of indicators, to suit cultural and labour market variations, support for core definitions and measures is badly needed. This was the prime objective of a European initiative – now signed by more than 100 leading European social scientists. The scientists call for the Copenhagen definitions of poverty to be adopted in cross-European studies (Townsend et al, 1997; Townsend, 2000: forthcoming). A series of international conferences sponsored by the Economic and Social Research Council (ESRC) have been designed to back this initiative and from them a series of books illustrating the best European research on poverty will be produced (Townsend and Gordon, 2000: forthcoming).

## Social perceptions of poverty

The development of the two-level Copenhagen definition can either be 'subjective' or 'objective'. One method of approach is to build on social perceptions. In 1997 a joint study between MORI and the Bristol Statistical Monitoring Unit invited a random sample of the population to give the weekly sum of income which would enable a household of their type to escape first absolute, and then overall, poverty (Townsend et al, 1997). The figures of income required were on average a lot higher than levels of Income Support. As many as 20% of the national sample said they had less income than the amounts said to be necessary for a household of their composition to surmount absolute poverty.

The results were surprising. However, in relation to other information about the household they were plausible. This methodology resembles that developed many years ago in the Gallup poll in the US and is to be repeated in the new Poverty and Social Exclusion Survey of Britain financed by the Joseph Rowntree Foundation (Bradshaw et al, 1998).

## Collaboration

The different international agencies have distinct styles and subject matter when reporting poverty but, with relatively minor variations, observe a standard ideology. They invite comparison and analysis, not only for what they say, but why truths and falsehoods are so highly coloured, and for what they do not say. Someone, somewhere, should issue a mercilessly critical audit of what these agencies produce.

In raising the level – and perhaps the temperature – of statistical discussion of world poverty, there are major contributions to be made. Something has to be done to relate sample and area information of a representative type to the superficial and often unreliable accounts derived from indices compiled from national censuses. Something has to be done to expose the slender justification for the World Bank's dollar-a-day measure of poverty for Africa, two dollars a day for Latin America and four dollars a day for the so-called transitional economies (see, for example, Townsend, 1997, and Clarke, 1998). The UNDP has added to the irony by taking the US measure of $14.4 a day to apply it to the industrialised countries (UNDP, 1997, pp 13, 32-3).

## Dual style of the approach to the statistics of poverty

Progress has to be made on poverty relating to concepts, operational definition and measurement, explanation and policy packages. More than ever before, statisticians have to become good generalists and internationalists as well as specialists. It is like wearing two hats, one in conformity with the limited role which is assigned in an organisation, but the other to pursue alternative presentations, deeper meanings, explanations and modes of analysis inspired by the subject matter and which truly establish the context in which far better specialised work can be produced.

It is now appropriate to discuss policies – not just the orthodox contemporary policies, some would call them 'appeasement' or even 'counterfeit' policies, of the neo-liberals in the IMF or Organisation for

Economic Co-operation and Development (OECD), but the alternative policies to which any comprehensive analysis of world problems points.

There must be international and national policies which make a positive contribution. Across the world, structural changes in taxation and benefits need to be embarked on to give gains to the population. There is wide consensus about green policies which, far from leading to unacceptably high costs, reduce inequalities and improve the quality and standard of life and produce jobs (see, for example, the fascinating debate on the appropriate measure of international GDP initiated by the New Economics Foundation and others). Again, the Welfare to Work debate in the UK is only half a debate. It is more about opportunity to work instead of the amount of work and the type of jobs which need to be created. Some issues are politically contentious and some are not. Millions of jobs could be created in Europe. We need to move back to planning full employment. It was not simply a good historical objective but is a good contemporary one. The growth of the economy should move in a more labour intensive and socially desirable way. Too few latch on to the implications of current trends towards privatisation where power and control is being transferred uncritically and without forethought into the private sector.

## The European Social Policy Forum

An example of what issues are at stake in employment policy relates to the European Social Policy Forum, held in June 1998. The objective of the Forum was to build on the particular strengths of European society and to develop a new strategy to maximise productive and satisfying work at European, national and local levels. Part of this assignment was for the European Community and member states to inspire effective and responsible forms of market competitiveness, reduce unemployment, materially recognise unpaid work and service, promote full employment, appraise and redefine the desirable balance between private and public sectors of the economy, and between private and public services, and put in place new systems of welfare to strengthen incentives to work, encourage individual savings behaviour and enhance individual well-being (see the EC introductory paper [Townsend, 1998] issued to those attending the Forum on 'The future world of work').

A new pact or contract of social employment might be formulated and implemented as a result of the Forum. It would draw on the Copenhagen agreement for social development, signed by 117 Heads of State, including those of Europe (UN, 1995). A list of recommendations to create jobs, support self-help schemes and small businesses, strengthen both public and private employment services, enhance the quality of work and achieve "a broader recognition and understanding of work and emp loyment" (p 5), including "unremunerated work", could be drawn up in each country.

The 'threat' of globalisation to the future of work and employment must not be overemphasised. However, the full employment goal must be related to realistic analysis of trends in officially defined but also alternatively measured, unemployment. Official unemployment in the OECD and EC countries in the 1990s is approximately double what it was in the 1960s. In the EC it was 3.7% in 1975, 9.9% in 1985 and 10.8% in 1995 (EC, 1996, p 40). The rate is expected to grow rather than to fall.

## Investment in jobs

Investment in jobs must have higher priority. Research on environmental protection and resource conservation measures, for example, suggests that, far from leading to unacceptably high costs, redundancies, job losses and firms being driven out of business, there are realistic opportunities for increasing job numbers and enhancing industrial competitiveness and efficiency. It is estimated that half a million jobs directly and another six million indirectly, could be created in Europe. Five areas are listed: waste reduction and the re-use and recycling of materials; renewable energy sources; energy conservation and efficient use; organic farming; and public transport. The 1997 Kyoto Conference revealed the strength of opposition on the part of some leading multinationals. However, there is evidence in the 1990s of the growing influence of environmentalism in some corporations.

This will bring a new need for skills and training. At least six sectors where training should be expanded have been identified: industrial pollution control; environmental control in agriculture; environmental management control in the public sector; water management; solid waste management; and amenity development.

There have been strong efforts to include the valuation of unpaid work in national economic statistics. The need to measure and value this work was first publicised as a common concern for both developed and developing countries at the first International Women's Conference in Mexico City in 1975. In measuring unpaid work, some organisations see it as an example of the important task of correcting GNP as the best measure either of real economic growth or sustainable development (INSTRAW, 1995).

## Reorganising the public and private sectors

At the 1995 Copenhagen World Summit attention was drawn sharply to the need to establish "an economically and socially responsible private sector" and to "rehabilitate the state, the public service and the political process" (UN, 1995).

In 1996, privatisation produced US$88 billion worldwide. This represented an increase of 21% since 1995 and 37% since 1994, when the figure was $64 billion (Privatisation International, 1997). During two months of 1996, for example, $28 billion was raised by nine governments, in seven cases exceeding $1 billion. Europe's biggest ever privatisation is included (the share issue of $13.3 billion Deutsche Telekom). Several European countries are planning sales of considerable value – Italy $20 billion, France $11 billion, Spain $8.6 billion and Germany $5 billion. In Eastern Europe and Russia, there are proposals to sell national gas, oil, copper and pharmaceutical companies and, in the case of Hungary, the state-owned former foreign trade bank.

### Transnational power

The process of the growth of wealth and inequality through privatisation is one engineered by market mergers and the accelerating growth of transnational corporations. As noted above, inequality between rich and poor countries, but also *within* most countries, whether rich or poor, has been growing. One primary cause has been the depression of low wages and loss of employment – through deregulation, cuts in public expenditure and in personal income taxation, privatisation and the extension of world trade. The various World Bank and IMF policies around the world of structural adjustment, liberalisation and sustainable development are interconnected. Three hundred transnational corporations now account for 25% of the world's assets. The annual value of the sales of each of the six largest transnational corporations, varying between $111 and $126 billion, are now exceeded by the GDPs of only 21 nation states. As many as 37 corporations have larger annual sales than the annual GDP of Ireland (Donald, 1997, p 7). As a result the ranked social inequality within countries is gradually being converted into the ranked social inequality shared by all countries.

After 1979, the Labour Party began to review previous policies on public ownership. Its opposition to privatisation became low key and new proposals for public ownership were no longer put forward. The costs were believed to be huge. Instead, doubts about the government's procedures, costs and subsidies in handling privatisation were raised. The problem became one of managing privatisation to get the right results and no longer one of creating enough State-run industries or services to serve particular public interests and simultaneously provide models for the activities of private sector companies. Perhaps there was insufficient analysis of the outcomes of privatisation in the 1980s and 1990s for producers and consumers or the public at large. Independent work has now shown that national assets have been grossly undervalued at the point of sale; incentives for intending shareholders and managerial staff and executive officers have been indecently excessive, and some regulatory regimes have been so weak as to invite complaints of market-compliance.

The structural argument for privatisation in general seems to have been accepted by default. Certainly the concept and the programme has not attracted the searching scrutiny given endlessly over the years to 'redistribution', that is, the large number of research reports and books dealing with the benefits and tax systems, the rights of workers, citizens and consumers and equal opportunities by gender, race, age and disability. The intriguing fact is that, even on its own terms, privatisation in the UK cannot be shown to have been an unqualified success. One of the most sophisticated research studies is by David Parker and Stephen Martin (1995). They measured total factor productivity in the four year periods before and after privatisation, taking into account the periods before privatisation but after the schemes were announced and during recessions. A total of 11 enterprises were examined: British Airways, British Airports Authority, Britoil, British Gas, British Steel, British Aerospace, Jaguar, Rolls-Royce, National Freight, Associated British Ports and British Telecom. Annual rates of productivity grew faster after privatisation for five of these 11 enterprises but declined for the other six (see also Parker and Martin, 1997).

Nor can privatisation be shown to have led to increased economic growth. In the 18 years before the 1979 Election, the growth rate, on average, was marginally greater than it has been since. The government had unprecedented opportunities to invest and grow and serve. Few are aware of the scale of receipts from privatisation and North Sea Oil. If they are averaged over the period 1980-97, the proceeds from privatisation have amounted to £13 million a day and from North Sea Oil, £22 million a day.

'Efficiency' measurements of some orthodox kind can be undertaken best for manufacturing enterprises but they do not take account of wider economic factors such as security in the workforce, quality incentives, training inputs and long-term stability versus short-term upheaval, or vice versa. Nor do they take account of loss of employee rights, reduced pay and conditions, effects on health and vulnerability to redundancy.

The above discussion has been an attempt to indicate the transformation in 'structural' thinking about work and employment that is needed if the right balance is to be struck in the economy between the public and the private sectors. The problem looms larger when we consider public social services, such as residential homes, community care, health and education and the privatisation that has occurred and is proposed. The reorganisation of productive, and satisfying, social and individual activity is both feasible and desirable.

## International action

Globalisation and the expansion of free trade, financial markets and large companies have necessary consequences for many organisations at regional, national and local levels. For example, the consolidation of the single market and of European Monetary Union (EMU) are intended to sharpen competitiveness, increase productivity and bring about greater efficiency, usually interpreted as the downsizing of workforces. That will prompt change in the role of the EC, the unions, and also employers' organisations. The prospect of smaller and more productive workforces in some industries and services, leading to reduced employment, can be offset by a new version of the European employment and social model. Should steps be taken to develop any of the following strategies, or alternatives?

- A job replacement and creation strategy in both private and public sectors, and also action programmes devised by local authorities, employers and independent organisations to tap new markets.
- A work expansion strategy for small businesses to be developed by employers and major employer organisations, in partnership with governments; and unremunerated work to be given greater recognition through systems of tax and benefit credits and in other ways.
- A basic income strategy to bring together a minimum wage and a minimum level of benefit in a coordinated form. This would build on the gradual introduction of an international measure of poverty

so that regional and eventually worldwide minimal income rights might be established.

- An NGO strategy to promote volunteer public service and environmental conservation and improvement activities for three population categories: people unable to work for physical or mental reasons; people of economically active age who are performing valued unpaid services for children, disabled and elderly people; people of economically active age who are able and willing to work and entitled to some form of benefit. New partnerships in promoting 'social employment' are envisaged – examples being public/private sector, central/local, NGOs/trades unions/companies.
- An integrated strategy for and about transnational corporations, and their democratic place in the global economy.
- A strategy to boost the representativeness, accountability and independence of the international agencies. The OECD, for example, has acknowledged that there is a greater need for international cooperation and coordination, among other things, in employment policy "to deepen study of the relations between globalisation and employment, particularly regarding restructuring of firms and shifts in their location and associated impacts on employment and human resources" (OECD, 1996, p 63). The agency has issued *Guidelines for multinational enterprises* and these could lead to the preparation of regular reports on developments in employment (OECD, 1994). The problem is that the agency has also been responsible for preparing the Multilateral Agreement on Investment (MAI) – said to be in the interests of the already-rich rather than poorer countries.

Even when set out summarily such a programme implies organisational innovation. An example is 'Europeanisation' of collaborative work between trade unions and governments. This is already a key feature of the European employment and social model. Thus, in describing labour relations in Germany:

> ... many things now taken for granted are social rights that were fought for and won with much struggle by the trade unions: freedom of association, the right to strike and to bargain collectively, industrial health and safety standards, industrial law, universal suffrage, co-determination and worker participation in the workplace and the company and representation on public bodies responsible for everything from social insurance to radio.... Worker councils and co-determination at local levels have been decisive in guaranteeing

social progress, even in times of slow growth. The model was based
on negotiation and compromise, and the alternative model on
'exclusion and polarisation'. (Schneider, 1991; Block, 1995; as
summarised in UNDP, 1997, p 98)

Events have demonstrated that success 100 years ago was not final.
Globalisation and liberalisation have reopened the problem.

At the international level the challenge is to find some means of
arbitrating between transnational corporations and nation states.
Corporation power is a feature of globalisation (see, for example, Korten,
1996). An illustration of the problems for governments, and especially
for the poorest, of corporate influence in formulating international
policies is the Multilateral Agreement on Investment (MAI, 1998),
produced by the 29 richest countries of the world under the guidance
of the OECD. The agreement draws on the earlier work of GATT
(General Agreement on Tariffs and Trade) and the WTO (Warsaw Treaty
Organisation). It grants new powers to transnational corporations which
will affect large areas of the future world of work, with governments
playing a smaller role than in the past. The corporations have many
employees. Their employment policies also influence the policies of
within-border companies and of the agencies and departments of
government. The intention of the MAI is to increase economic growth.
Governments will not be able to place restrictions on inward investment
which might damage competition, without being liable to be sued for
compensation.

According to a network of 600 NGOs from 67 countries this will
nullify attempts by governments to protect their environments. Demands
for clean technology to cut carbon dioxide emissions would be outlawed;
protection of genetic resources and bio-diversity could not be given;
attempts to preserve fish stocks would be stopped. The effects on the
poorest countries are likely to be large, and will, they believe, affect
their likelihood of obtaining overseas aid.

At the start of the new millennium a note of intellectual alarm is
being struck about the consequences of 'destructive' globalisation for
governance and social stability. In the early 1990s privatisation was still
being treated as the necessary and inevitable strategy for the world, and
nation states, to follow. The impetus of that orthodoxy was to dismantle
even good public services in the so-called 'transitional' economies of
Eastern Europe and the republics making up the territories of the former
Soviet Union, replace some public services in Western industrialised
countries and at the same time transform remaining parts of the public

sector with a new 'entrepreneurial spirit', scrapping bureaucratic controls deriving from the 1930s and even the 19th century, and substituting "more decentralised, more entrepreneurial, more responsive organisations designed for the rapidly changing, information-rich world of the 1990s" (Osborne and Gaebler, 1992).

That dominant mood is now giving way to second thoughts and a more serious discussion of alternatives. Economic and political success no longer beckons as convincingly to governments as seemed to be the case at the height of the influential years of the Thatcher–Reagan axis and the collapse of the Soviet Union. Examples are not difficult to find. Some commentators are conscious of a new battle between governments and the marketplace. In pointing to the recent supremacy of privatisation, they go on to trace subsequent reactions in favour of more state regulation (see, for example, Yergin and Stanislaw, 1998). Others linger over the claims for latter-day capitalism – which seem to them more difficult to substantiate (for example, Gray, 1998). Or they return to the successful days of Keynesianism to show that there are convincing alternatives (for example, Palley, 1998).

However, the increasing power of transnational corporations and the connected trend of widening inequality, or polarisation, in the great majority of countries is not, in these texts, adequately addressed. Academic analysts *are* beginning to address the problem (for recent examples see Hoogvelt, 1997; Deacon et al, 1997; Hirst and Thompson, 1995). The international agencies are not doing the same. With some partial exceptions (for example, UNCTAD, 1995), they are not concerned to trace the rapid growth in powers of the transnational corporations, explain in detail their employment and social policies, specify their legal responsibilities, their exact relationships with affiliates, the earnings from top to bottom of their employees, and the redistributive effects in different countries of their commercial policies. Reports that are being issued comply with current controls and ideological influences instead of questioning them (Guerlain, 1997; World Bank, 1999b). The authors are averse from tracing and explaining historical and especially structural developments. Neither are they concerned to review the respective cases for public and private sector control or ownership in different areas of society and the economy.

Many examples could be drawn from international agency reports. One involves the UN agreement at the 1995 World Summit in Copenhagen. In reconciling the diverse views of the 117 governments that were represented, the final report contained constructive agreements about future action leading to desirable social development. One concerned the application of definitions of 'absolute' and 'overall' poverty in the measurement in each country of poverty and the preparation of national anti-poverty plans. It is noteworthy, if not surprising, that agencies such as World Bank and the IMF have made no attempt to pick up and pursue this agreement. The World Bank continues its irrational treatment of 'poverty'. What is more difficult to condone is the indifference to constructive follow-up action shown by other agencies, for example UNDP (even in fulfilling its own professed cause). In its 1997 annual report, specifically addressed to a review of world poverty, UNDP failed to pursue the 1995 agreement, failed to discuss the place of transnational corporations in the deepening structural hierarchy of State and corporate power and wealth, and therefore failed to penetrate the growing world problem with any feasible strategy.

There is a problem in coordinating and democratising the international agencies to bring about genuine social development. This deserves to be given public attention. The problem is certainly as considerable as that of democratising the UN itself.

The problem of control of transnational corporations is now the crucial political factor in global developments. There is rising concern about the abuse of market power (for example, DTI, 1992). The international agencies have not responded. The problems of over-hasty privatisation, unaccountable corporations and companies, a greatly weakened public sector, and a lack of balance between private or individual interests and public or collective interests have not yet been given serious attention. The international financial agencies have got little further than issuing exhortations to companies for responsible behaviour (see for example, OECD, 1994). The social problems of poverty and social polarisation cannot, in logic, be ameliorated if markets as they expand continue to enable big corporations to grow uncontrollably, restrict competition, transfer prices and taxes as they please to enhance profitability, acquire the assets of impoverished countries and localities, reduce labour and public sector costs, and have privileged access to governments, professions and the law.

At the start of the 20th century national social policies had to be invented and set in place across the world to meet the growing problems posed by industrialisation. At the start of the new century international social policies are desperately needed to counter the problems posed by globalisation.

## References

Block, T. (1995) 'Human development and economic growth in Germany', Background paper for *Human Development Report, 1996*.

Bradshaw, J., Gordon, D., Levitas, R., Pantazis, C., Payne, S. and Townsend, P. (1998) *Perceptions of poverty and social exclusion 1998*, Bristol: Townsend Centre for International Poverty Research, University of Bristol.

Chu, K.-Y. and Gupta, S. (1998) *Social safety nets: Issues and recent experiences*, Washington, DC: IMF.

Clarke, S. (1998) *Poverty in transition: A report prepared for the Department for International Development*, Warwick: University of Warwick.

Deacon, B. with Hulse, M. and Stubbs, P. (1997) *Global social policy: International organisations and the future of welfare*, London: Sage Publications.

DeRose, L., Messer, E. and Millman, S. (1998) *Who's hungry? And how do we know? Food shortage, poverty and deprivation*, Tokyo, New York, NY, and Paris: United Nations University Press.

DfID (Department for International Development) (1997) *Eliminating world poverty: A challenge for the 21st century*, White Paper on International Development, Cm 3789, London: The Stationery Office.

Donald, A. (1997) 'Developing international law', *Global Security*, Spring.

DTI (Department of Trade and Industry) (1992) *Abuse of market power: A consultative document on possible legislative options*, Cm 2100, London: HMSO.

EC (European Commission) (1996) *Employment in Europe 1996*, Luxembourg: Office for Official Publications of the European Communities.

Gray, J. (1998) *False dawn: The delusions of global capitalism*, London: Granta Books.

Guerlain, P. (1997) *The privatisation challenge: A strategic, legal, and institutional analysis of international experience*, Washington, DC: World Bank.

Hirst, P. and Thompson, G. (1995) *Globalization in question*, Cambridge: Polity Press.

Hoogvelt, A. (1997) *Globalisation and the postcolonial world: The new political economy of development*, Basingstoke: Macmillan.

INSTRAW (1995) *Measurement and valuation of unpaid contribution: Accounting through time and output*, Santo Domingo, Dominican Republic: INSTRAW.

Korten, D.C. (1996) *When corporations rule the world*, London: Earthscan.

Massey, D.S. (1996) 'The age of extremes: concentrated affluence and poverty in the twenty-first century', *Demography*, vol 33, no 4, pp 395-412.

Moore, J. (1989) *The end of the line for poverty*, London: Conservative Political Centre.

OECD (Organisation for Economic Co-operation and Development) (1994) *The OECD guidelines for multinational enterprises*, Paris: OECD.

OECD (1996) *Globalisation of industry: Overview and sector reports*, Paris: OECD.

Osborne, D. and Gaebler, T. (1992) *Reinventing government: How the entrepreneurial spirit is transforming the public sector – from school house, to statehouse, City Hall to the Pentagon*, New York, NY: Addison-Wesley.

Palley, T. (1998) *Plenty of nothing: The downsizing of the American dream and the case for structural Keynesianism*, Princeton, NJ: Princeton University Press.

Parker, D. and Martin, S. (1995) 'The impact of UK privatisation on labour and total factor productivity', *Scottish Journal of Political Economy*, vol 42, no 2, pp 201-20.

Parker, D. and Martin, S. (1997) *The impact of privatisation*, London: Routledge.

Privatisation International (1997) *The Privatisation Yearbook, 1997*.

Royal Danish Ministry of Foreign Affairs (1996) 'Conditions for social progress: a world economy for the benefit of all', Copenhagen Seminar for Social Progress, Copenhagen, Ministry of Foreign Affairs.

Schneider, M. (1991) *A brief history of the German trade unions*, Bonn: Verlag J.H.W. Dietz Nachf.

Townsend, P. (1996a) 'Will the rich countries pay more attention to problems in their own backyards?', *International Social Development Review*, vol 1, no 1, New York, NY: United Nations Department of Public Information.

Townsend, P. (1996b) *A poor future: Can we counter growing poverty in Britain and across the world?*, London, Lemos and Crane.

Townsend, P. (1997) 'The poverty line: methodology and international comparisons', in D. Gordon and C. Pantazis (eds) *Breadline Britain in the 1990s*, Aldershot: Ashgate.

Townsend, P. (1998) *The future world of work*, European Social Policy Forum 98, Brussels: European Commission DG V.

Townsend, P. (2000: forthcoming) 'Post-war poverty research', in J. Bradshaw and R. Sainsbury (eds) *Centenary celebration to mark the centenary of Seebohm Rowntree's first study of poverty in York, 18-20 March 1998*.

Townsend, P. and Gordon, D. (2000: forthcoming) *European poverty research*, London: Macmillan.

Townsend, P., Gordon, D., Bradshaw, J. and Gosschalk, B. (1997) *Absolute and overall poverty in Britain in 1997: What the population themselves say*, Bristol: Bristol Statistical Monitoring Unit, University of Bristol.

UN (United Nations) (1995) *The World Summit for Social Development: The Copenhagen Declaration and Programme of Action*, New York, NY: UN.

UN (1999) *Further initiatives for the implementation of the outcome of the World Summit for Social Development*, Report of the Secretary General, Preparatory Committee for the Special Session of the General Assembly in June 2000, New York, NY: UN.

UNCTAD (United Nations Committee on Trade and Development) (1995) *Comparative experiences with privatisation: Policy insights and lessons learned*, New York and Geneva.

UNDP (United Nations Development Project) (1997) *Human Development Report 1997*, New York, NY, and Oxford: Oxford University Press.

UNDP (1998) *Human Development Report 1998*, New York, NY, and Oxford: Oxford University Press.

UNDP (1999) *Human Development Report 1999*, New York, NY, and Oxford: Oxford University Press.

World Bank (1996) *Poverty reduction and the World Bank: Progress and challenges in the 1990s*, Washington, DC: World Bank.

World Bank (1997) *Poverty reduction and the World Bank: Progress in fiscal 1996 and 1997*, Washington, DC: World Bank.

World Bank (1999a) *The World Development Report 1998/99: Knowledge for development*, Washington, DC: World Bank.

World Bank (1999b) *Global economic prospects for the developing countries: 1998/99 beyond financial crisis*, Washington, DC: World Bank.

Yergin, D. and Stanislaw, J. (1998) *The commanding heights: The battle between government and the marketplace that is remaking the modern world*, New York, NY: Simon and Schuster.